PRAISE FOR SUSTAINABLE CULTURAL TOURISM

This definitive handbook to sustainable cultural tourism reflects 25 years of experience, covering the process and nuances required to establish successful projects in collaboration with traditional, rural, and indigenous people. It should be required reading for anyone involved in cultural tourism or tourism development interested in learning how to work within cultural frameworks.
—**Brian T. Mullis, Founder and President
Sustainable Travel International**

Susan Guyette has written a comprehensive and indispensable guide for planning a sustainable cultural tourism enterprise. Study this text before you begin your cultural tourism endeavors. Unlike many books, the author covers cultural entrepreneurs in several areas. Her Native American roots make the book sensitive to traditional cultures.
—**Tom Aageson, Executive Director
Global Center for Cultural Entrepreneurship**

Sustainable Cultural Tourism does what so many other books in the field fail to do: it gives practical, step-by-step guidance for rural and Indigenous communities, putting control of tourism planning in the hands of local people, where it belongs. This handbook enables development of culturally responsible tourism experiences that will benefit both communities and visitors alike.
—**Jonathan B. Tourtellot, Geotourism Editor
National Geographic Traveler; Portal Editor,
www.DestinationCenter.org**

Dr. Guyette has created an exceptional text that offers highly useful guidance for developing the right kind of cultural tourism. The book is loaded with knowledge and wisdom gained from her extensive studies and experience. Her approach to planning builds on a foundation of core values so necessary for authentic cultural experiences.
—**Ben Sherman, Founder
World Indigenous Tourism Alliance**

Indigenous and rural communities will benefit from the perspective that Susan Guyette conveys in her unique guide to sustainable cultural tourism. It is a reflection of her deliberate interactions with, and understanding of, Native American and other Indigenous communities where core values are the backdrop for any entrepreneurial effort. Susan's unique background and experience make *Sustainable Cultural Tourism* a distinctive and exceptional guide for cultural entrepreneurs in Indigenous and rural communities.

—**Ron Solimon**
Director of the Center for Lifelong Education at the Institute of American Indian Arts in Santa Fe, New Mexico

This guide on integrating authentic cultural experiences into sustainable tourism celebrates cultural diversity and cultural traditions of hospitality. It offers strategies for cultural retention at a time when many traditions and languages are becoming extinct. I highly recommend *Sustainable Cultural Tourism* for all who are interested in preserving Indigenous or rural cultures and ecosystems, as well as sharing their wisdom and value through tourism.

—**Beth Beloff, Principal**
Beth Beloff & Associates: Inciting Sustainability

Creating sustainable cultural tourism has become an essential consideration for Indigenous community planners and for many national governments around the world as they explore ways to improve the economic conditions of their Indigenous populations. In this regard, Susan Guyette has produced one of the most comprehensive guides for the development and implementation of programs and initiatives in sustainable cultural tourism that I have read. It forms a firm foundation for educational curricula in schools and colleges. Susan's work takes the concept and practice of sustainable cultural tourism to a deeper level of meaning and practice. I recommend this guide as required reading for students, faculty and administrators working in the field of cultural tourism.

—**Gregory Cajete Ph.D.**
Director of Native American Studies at the University of New Mexico, author of *Native Science* and *A People's Ecology*

A career of direct experience assisting tribal and non-tribal communities develop sustainable tourism practices is reflected in this guide to small-scale sustainable tourism development. I hope everyone interested in tourism will read and use this book.

—**Jana Prewitt, tourism consultant**
co-author *Lewis and Clark for Dummies*

Sustainable Cultural Tourism

Small-Scale Solutions

Susan M. Guyette, Ph.D.

VOLUME 1

Resilient Communities Series

SUSTAINABLE CULTURAL TOURISM

is an innovative guide for both communities and sustainable development assistance providers. This book's content presents:

- A step-by-step process for cultural tourism planning and sustainable community development,
- A methodology for planning cultural tourism from within cultures,
- A framework for integrating culture into each step of the process,
- An emphasis on the regional approach and collaborative actions,
- Methods for both community and visitor surveys,
- Strategies for cultural retention and teaching programs,
- Guidelines for culturally-based entrepreneurial programs and small enterprise development,
- A process for developing a cultural center,
- Techniques for writing a business plan and starting a culturally-based tour enterprise, and
- A framework for assessing sustainability.

Sharing wisdom and building strengths globally
through the spoken and written word.

Sustainable Cultural Tourism

Small-Scale Solutions

Susan M. Guyette, Ph.D.

Santa Fe, New Mexico

© Copyright 2013 Susan M. Guyette. All rights reserved.

No part of this publication may be reproduced, stored in a retrieval system or transmitted in any form or by any means electronic, mechanical, photocopying, recording or otherwise without the prior written permission of the author.
www.susanguyette.com

Printing by Createspace
Distributor: www.amazon.com
Ebook availability: January 2014
  ISBN: 978-0-9858788-0-1

Publisher's Cataloging-in-Publication Data
Guyette, Susan.

    Sustainable cultural tourism: small-scale solutions / Susan Marie Guyette.
    377 pages cm. – (Resilient communities series)

    ISBN: 978-0-9858788-0-1 (pbk.)
    Includes bibliographical references.

    1. Sustainable tourism. 2. Tourism—Planning. 3. Tourism—Social aspects. 4. Cultural landscapes. 4. Entrepreneurs. 5. Business. 6. Indigenous methodology. I. Guyette, Susan Marie. II. Title.

G156.5.H47 G89 2013   OCLC 2013904221
371.102'01—dc23

Cover: Palace of the Governors, Santa Fe, New Mexico (USA)
Cover photo: Seth Roffman
Layout: Ann Lowe
Preliminary Layout: Robby Bates
Cover: Bad Dog Design
Logo: BLUUhouse
Editor: Susan Waterman

To David

TABLE OF CONTENTS

Preface   i

Introduction   1
   Conscious Travel   2
   A New Paradigm for Cultural Tourism   3
   Planning from Within   4
   Sustainability and Culture   6

1. Understanding Tourism   9
   The Tourism Industry   10
   The Visitor   12
   The Community   13
   Tourism Options   14
   Culture and Sustainability   16
   Value-Based Planning   18
   Form, Scale, and Timing   21
   Culturally-Based Livelihood   24
   Bridging Cultures   25
   Cultural Bias in the Tourism Industry   27
   Resolving Mixed Feelings about Tourism   29
   The Starting Point   31
   Small-Economy Emphasis   32
   Tourism Success Factors   33
   Community-Based Solution:
      Sustainable Travel International   34

2. Winning With a Regional Approach   37
   The Regional Tourism Concept   39
   The Tourism System   42
   Coordination of Tourism Sectors   45
   The Tourism Partner   47
   The Power of Linking   53
   Developing a Vacation Concept   54
   Tourism and Economic Development   57

Increasing Economic Multipliers	60
Organizing for Effective Tourism	62
Community-Based Solution:	
Makah Nation	63

3. Beginning the Planning Process — 67

Planning as a Process	69
Assessing Community Views and Concerns	72
Listening and Talking Circles	73
Intergenerational Involvement	78
From Meeting to Ongoing Participation	79
Outline for a Tourism Plan	80
Exploring Key Issues	81
Analyzing the Tourism Service System	82
The SCOT Analysis	88
Conducting the Skills Inventory	90
Developing a Tourism Vision	91
Achieving Balance	93
A Community Approach	95
Community-Based Solution:	
Ganados del Valle, Los Ojos	97

4. Community and Visitor Surveys — 101

Qualitative and Quantitative Approaches	102
Conducting the Community Survey	104
The Visitor Survey	108
Training in Survey Procedures	118
The Importance of Interpretation	121
Sharing Survey Results	125
Strategies for Inclusion on Larger Surveys	126
From Survey to Action	128
Community-Based Solution: Zuni Tribe	129

5. Analyzing the Market — 131

About Market Research	132
Market Data Sources	136
Assessing a Range of Tourism Markets	138
Interpretation of Market Data	139

The Marketing Section of the Tourism Plan	140
Designing the Tourism Draw	142
The Unifying Concept or Brand	146
Diversifying Ways of Marketing	151
Distribution	155
The Tourism Website	155
The Marketing Budget	159
Sustainability	160
Community-Based Solution: International Folk Art Market	162

6. Completing the Tourism Plan — 165

Addressing Key Issues	166
Developing Policy and Etiquette	168
Setting Goals	171
Using the Market Analysis	175
Designing Projects	176
Addressing Safety Issues	180
Timelines	181
Budgets and Funding	187
The Draft Plan	191
Bringing Plan Findings to the Community	191
Community-Based Solution: Eight Northern Indian Pueblos, USA	193

7. Interpretive Centers, Cultural Centers, and Museums — 195

Meeting Cultural Needs	197
Living Museums	200
Steps for Moving Forward	205
A Place for Visitor Education	206
Communicating Culture	207
Artists and Entrepreneurs	212
Creating a Database for Cultural Arts	214
The Virtual Museum	216
Encouraging Support of Local Initiatives	219
Moving Forward with an Eye to the Past	221

    Community-Based Solution:
        Sister Indigenous Cultural Centers   222

8. Creating Jobs   225
    Employment and Cultural Survival   226
    Expanding Jobs   227
    Quality of Employment   228
    The Skills Database   230
    Product Development   231
    Training Programs   236
    Authenticity Issues   240
    Customer Service   246
    Pricing   247
    Vending   248
    The Mini-Business Plan   248
    Key Reasons for Entrepreneurial Success   254
    Key Reasons for Entrepreneurial Failure   255
    An Inclusive Process   256
    Community-Based Solution:
        The Huichol Center for Cultural Survival   257

9. The Tourism Enterprise   259
    Culture and Business Style   261
    Focusing the Business Concept   265
    The Tourism-Related Business Plan:
        Native Tour Example   266
    Starting a Tour Enterprise   284
    From Plan to Action   287
    Community-Based Solution:
        Sky City Tours, Acoma Pueblo   289

10. Increasing Sustainability   291
    Sustainability Factors   292
    The Managed Tourism Program   297
    Improving Customer Service   301
    Feedback from the Community   304
    Evaluating Visitor Satisfaction   305
    Sustainable Evaluation Criteria   310

When Tourism Results Are Not Optimal		313
Redirection and Sustainability		314
Sustaining the Culturally Meaningful		316
Community-Based Solution:		
Cape Fox Tours, Saxman Nation		317
Conclusion: Cultural Resilience		319
Sustainability in Nature		320
Sustaining Tradition		322
Notes		327
Selected Bibliography		333
Appendix A	Tourism and Sustainability Organizations Online	339
Appendix B	Tourism Trade Shows	347
Appendix C	Basic Tourism Concepts	349
Index		353
Acknowledgments		357
About the Author		359

PREFACE

Small-scale tourism offers an opportunity to increase human well-being through entrepreneurial livelihood, retention of cultural diversity, and the protection of ecosystems. A value-based framework for sustainable development, applicable across cultures, is the key to increasing access for all. Each year, my planning experience with peoples from diverse cultures teaches me deeper meanings to the topic of tourism.

Caring for people is at the heart of hospitality. The journey is the central theme of this practical text—how small-scale, rural, and culturally distinct communities interact with visitors, enhance their experience, and send them along the next step of the regional trip. Urban areas link to these communities and urban hosts will find these methods useful as well.

This planning and development guide is written for ethnically unique groups, rural communities, students, local governments, planners, architects, and technical assistance providers who have a concern for creating equity in tourism. Sources explaining planning methods for small-scale, community-sustained tourism are rare, since the texts available for tourism planning and development tend to be focused on the urban and mass tourism setting.

I became a tourism planner twenty-five years ago as a means of generating support for tribal cultural centers, museums, and cultural artists. Direct benefits to cultural learning are possible when tourism is planned carefully and shares within the intentions of communities. Finding the good, sustainable fit between local offerings and visitor interests, while maintaining a level of comfort with tourism as an industry, is possible.

There is an urgent need for a new cultural tourism paradigm to address the special concerns of a cultural-value and place-based approach, applicable for all cultures. Sharing these methods is of utmost importance at this time, to protect our mother, Earth.

INTRODUCTION

The concept of the journey is central to true hospitality. Diverse cultures hold unique ways of caring for visitors. And contemporary communities can benefit by learning from them.

My understanding of the journey deepened on a business trip to a remotely located American Indian tribe on the Olympic Peninsula in Washington State (USA). After a discussion with the Tribal Council on the perceived potentials for cultural tourism and an amicable visit, the Tribal Chairman handed me two bags filled with his personally smoked salmon, prepared in the traditional way. "This is for the next leg of your trip," he explained.

As I drove to visit the next tribe on my trip, the smell of smoked salmon filled the car with an intense aroma. While this extraordinary aroma increased, so did my appreciation for Native hospitality. The caring concern toward me as a visitor extended through my entire trip, not just during the time spent with the community.

At that moment a cultural difference, a fundamental concept about Native tourism renewed in my mind. In the Native concept, hospitality involves caring about the visitor's entire journey, connecting the trip on the way to the visit and the return—not just the exchange of service and money at the destination. This caring turned what might have been a routine business meeting into an experience of true Native hospitality.

Focusing on a journey concept encourages communities of diverse cultures to recall their traditional ways of welcoming and extending hospitality. Richness is brought to cultural tourism when planning is value based and authentic experiences are refined through community participation. This book emphasizes ways of integrating cultural concerns into each of the tourism planning and sustainable development steps.

CONSCIOUS TRAVEL

Entering an age of increasingly diminished resources, many travelers are rethinking their journeys. For some travelers, pure leisure or pleasure and recreation no longer justify the energy consumption of a long trip. These visitors want more—a purposeful or educational travel experience. Increasingly, travelers are becoming "seekers," a unique type of visitor, prevalent as an adaptation to living on a changing planet comes to the forefront. Visitors are searching for the experiential. A glimpse into a way of life different from the day-to-day life of the visitor is an exciting and renewing break from the routine of jobs and everyday life.

Feeling the warmth around a fire inside a wigwam on a cold day offers a new concept of shelter. Or, sharing the traditional practice of throwing clamshells on a path—feeling the crushing under one's feet as the path of broken shells is created with each footstep—raises a feeling of intrigue. Cultural experiences bring forth unique perceptions to the visitor.

The conscious traveler:

- Wants to learn from other cultures and is respectful of local ecosystems;[1]
- Desires to contribute to a local economy without imposing one's values;
- Seeks the experiential, to get involved in ways determined by the host community, usually over a continued period of time;
- Intends to do no ecosystem harm, and frequently contributes to conservation efforts; and
- Appreciates the authenticity of the experience.

Tourism worldwide is in a state of great change, yet the exact direction of that change is unknown. Predictions at the national level indicate that U.S. visitors will seek vacation experiences closer to home. International visitors are coming in increased numbers. Voluntourism is on the rise. And studies on heritage tourists indicate a search for authentic experiences.

Tourism trends indicate that a positive approach—seeking the opportunity to capture the interest of tourists who do visit, attracting those from nearby states, and creating a draw from international visitors—carries a likelihood of success. Increasing business offerings for cultural art items, tours, and demonstrations can result in heightened capacity for visitor education and a mutually beneficial cultural tourism experience.

A proactive community attracts and educates the conscious traveler by developing enterprises and programs that speak to the importance of local values, teaching traditions, preserving ecosystems important for cultural practices, and buying from locally owned businesses. Effective visitor education presents history, the importance of the visitor's contribution to support traditional lifestyles, arts and agricultural products—as well as specific information on events, markets, and entrepreneurial businesses.

> *An approach concentrating on fewer visitors and offering a cohesive, awareness-enhancing, yet restful vacation experience, is likely to succeed.*

A NEW PARADIGM FOR CULTURAL TOURISM

Cultural tourism offers the opportunity for an exchange of information on lifeways, customs, beliefs, values, language, views of the environment, and other cultural resources.[2] This exchange contributes to the conscious traveler as well as to the community. The challenge in planning for cultural tourism is to ensure that an exchange takes place as equitably as possible, in a manner seen as appropriate by members of the host community. Payment is usually part of the exchange.

The sustainable, small-scale tourism paradigm presented in this book is essential for realizing minimal negative impacts and maximized positive benefits for the socio-cultural, economic, and ecological environments. Effective planning and management are key to these outcomes.[3]

A new paradigm for cultural tourism, as defined from within a community is:

- Value-based and reinforcing of cultural values;
- Derived from an understanding of traditional internal processes for planning;

- Based on concepts of small-scale economy and linked tourism networks;
- Supportive of entrepreneurs, who provide the majority of services in tourism;
- Focused on the authentic experience, as defined by rural communities;
- Correcting of cultural and historical misinterpretations;
- Interpreting from within the community;
- Inclusive of all groups within the community; and
- Incorporating sustainable options in terms of culture, economics, and nature.

Participation by the local community is recognized as basic to managing sustainable tourism, as well as long-term viability of tourism.[4] Planning cultural tourism with an understanding of the cultural perspectives and methods from within the culture involved is at the core of this new paradigm.

PLANNING FROM WITHIN

Whether planning from within one's own culture, or assisting a community to plan from within, the methods in this book address working beyond the profit motive as a primary reason to engage in tourism. Dan Shilling, in *Civic Tourism*,[5] calls for a responsible tourism ethic, one that produces social, cultural, environmental and economic regeneration. "What do we want to sustain and for whom?" is a critical question brought forward. Only by listening to identify cultural needs and solutions from within a community, will this question be addressed.

Lessons from Indigenous methodology, applicable to other cultures, are used throughout this book to illustrate the importance of listening and understanding culture as a foundation for sustainable tourism practices. Central to Indigenous methodology are ways of working with local cultural values and local ecosystems.

Cultural strength and renewal come from within a community, and foster authentic learning experiences for travelers. By developing skills and resources, smaller and larger communities both gain by working together for win/win regional scenarios. Benefits increase to both smaller and larger enterprises, by creating linked, powerful tourism networks.

> *The new cultural tourism will not be a tourism of culture on display, but rather a meaningful connection between cultures.*

Equity in Tourism

One of the basic tourism-related questions of our time concerns equity. Can small and culturally diverse communities benefit from tourism? There is an aspect of the tourism industry unsettling to rural and small communities: large corporations usually garner the greatest profits and the higher paying jobs. The pursuit of a commodified tourism product in the search for increased efficiency and global profits produces negative impacts.[6] A shift to sustainable development must recognize this core aspect of colonialism.

The conventional paradigm in tourism is focused on large numbers of visitors through mass tourism, profits, and broad marketing approaches. Tourism entities and organizations tend to function primarily as marketing programs, based on assumptions of growth as the goal. Biases inherent in industry concepts and "best practices" frequently do not take into account cultural considerations and differences. In other words, what works best for one culture may not for another.

In contrast, a small-scale paradigm responds to the opportunity presented by the conscious traveler—encouraging reciprocity and equity. This text presents an alternative, value-based planning method to foster small-scale tourism.

Redirection in the tourism industry is needed to overcome biases and to work cooperatively with communities for planning culturally supportive development, appropriate scales of development, and ways of gaining access to resources. Additionally, redirected methods lead to engaging visitor experiences.

In several communities where I have worked, tour companies from outside the region or country realize the financial benefits rather than the local community. Current industry practices emphasizing growth through an increase in visitors do not necessarily translate to increased local benefits, either culturally or economically. In contrast, the authentic, small-scale experience is precious not only to the visitor, but to the host community as well.

Small-scale tourism offers a community the opportunity to tell a valuable story to the public, educating with messages significant to the community. These messages are relevant to the survival of the community in terms of garnering assistance for protection of land and livelihood. There is potential for ethnically distinct communities, small farmers, and ranchers to retain traditional lifestyles tied to the land through a new form of educational cultural tourism—as defined appropriately from within the community.

SUSTAINABILITY AND CULTURE

Rather than seeing culture as solely one of the three "triple bottom line" variables of sustainability—culture, economy, and ecology—culture is regarded in this book as central to all sustainability. Cultural values are at the core of everyday actions.

By looking closely at current conditions and the rapid rate of global change, certain trends become clear. Smaller-scale approaches tend to be more flexible, amenable to change, and are more likely to be sustainable. And culturally-rooted enterprises tend to endure over generations. Striving for enough—rather than more—conserves resources in times of scarcity.

Sustainable cultural tourism fosters respect for the privacy necessary to practice and perpetuate traditions. The community goal of sustaining culture as a basis for adapting to change does not necessarily imply achieving equilibrium in one point of time or steady growth—as the concept of sustainability sometimes implies. Sustainable cultural tourism contributes to the renewal of local traditions over time, as they evolve.

These are some of the basic factors characterizing both rural and traditional sustainable cultural tourism.

- Economic gain is not always a primary motivator, although important for providing basic needs and sustaining the traditional community.
- Preservation of traditional lifeways and the environment may be essential concerns and take precedence over potential economic gain.

- Consensus plays a central role in the planning process of rural and tribal communities, compared to "majority" voting on projects as an urban process.
- Creating the maximum number of jobs to sustain the community and preventing out-migration may be a higher priority than high profit. "There should be a place for everyone" is a commonly expressed intention in traditional communities.
- Rural and tribal families tend to depend upon multiple income streams or ways of securing income; tourism may become only one piece in the total income of a family.
- Rural and tribal communities tend to develop at a slower pace than urban communities; phased projects and smaller-scale, linked projects are more likely to reach implementation.
- Urban economic networks practice cooperation and collaboration for business development and referral; in contrast, rural and tribal communities tend to work in isolation and often need to develop supportive tourism networks.

This book illustrates a step-by-step method for tourism planning and sustainable development. Chapter 1 presents an overview of sectors in the tourism industry, explaining basic tourism concepts, and pointing out cultural bias in tourism terminology. The importance of regionalism and partnerships in effective tourism linkages is the focus of Chapter 2.

A cultural value-based planning method for tourism is described in Chapters 3 through 6. In Chapter 3, an innovative methodology for working within a cultural framework, while balancing qualitative methods with quantitative considerations, is explained. A foundation for community-based participation is also presented in Chapter 3, followed by techniques for conducting both community assessments and visitor surveys in Chapter 4. Methods for assessing the market and developing strategies to effectively tap the potential market are covered in Chapter 5.

In Chapter 6, steps for completing a tourism plan are explained: defining key issues, developing tourism policy, forming tourism goals and objectives, designing projects, developing timelines, projecting budgets, and identifying funding for projects. Chapters 7 through 9 focus on sustainable development steps and employment creation. Cultural centers or museums serving both visitor education and a community's internal cultural teaching needs are detailed in Chapter 7. Culturally-based job creation at the entrepreneurial level is detailed in Chapter 8, and Chapter 9 focuses on small business development, with details and examples for creating a business plan.

Evaluating success by the criteria of sustainability and redirecting as necessary are explained in Chapter 10. The importance of retaining culture through culturally-based livelihood is related to resilience, or the ability to adapt to change, in the Conclusion.

A new paradigm—focused on small-scale enterprise and the conscious traveler, offering interactive educational experiences while caring for the environment and inspiring cultural learning—is tourism within reach. Communities large and small, rural and urban, benefit from this approach. Both are able to learn from each other, as well as link together to form a more powerful tourism network.

This book offers the basic skills for tourism planning, marketing, and management, using community-determined directions and pace to take the mystery and frustration out of tourism development. Tourism planning is a pathway for retaining that uniqueness while bringing about culturally relevant opportunities and solutions. For communities large and small, value-based planning for sustainability and resilience underlies the future of cultural tourism.

1

UNDERSTANDING TOURISM

*Tourism seen from multiple cultural
perspectives enriches participation for all.*

Tourism works on the basis of cooperation. By definition, a tour is a number of stops comprising a trip itinerary. Travelers look for a series of inviting stops and need to know how to link them together. Since visitors generally do not travel 500, 1,000 or 3,000 miles to visit one business—interesting activities, comfortable lodging, and fascinating dining experiences create a vacation concept. The concept of the journey is the central, and frequently overlooked, principle to remember when communities begin tourism development. The industry, the visitor, and the community are all essential to the journey.

Targets in tourism development are stated by governmental agencies in terms of dollar amounts brought into a country, state or region. Tax dollars recorded are used as a base, to measure the size of the industry. Employment, measured by numbers of full-time jobs, is counted for hotels, restaurants and other basic services (such as transportation and primary businesses accommodating visitors). Yet, these quantitative measures do not accurately reflect the total tourism benefit of widespread entrepreneurial activity.

To work within the community context effectively, distinguishing between an industry focus and a community focus is the starting place.

Framework for Integrating Culture

- Identify cultural values relating to tourism.
- Recognize similarities and differences between communities in the region, then link.
- Look closely at the local tourism industry to identify cultural bias and educate partners.
- Understand connections in the local economy and ways of incorporating economic forms already working.
- Recognize economic scales that work well now.
- Determine readiness and timing for tourism.

THE TOURISM INDUSTRY

As an industry, tourism is comprised of several sectors. Global, national, regional, statewide, and local tourism organizations assess the market through visitor surveys and market analyses, then promote tourism based on visitor interest and local offerings. These organizations include Chambers of Commerce, Convention and Visitor Bureaus, welcome centers, business assistance centers, and economic development corporations, as well as organizations dedicated specifically to tourism outcomes.

Services of tourism organizations include: visitor surveys, market analyses, insurance, training, promotional opportunities (visitor guides, vacation planners), introduction in visitor guide articles, calendar listings, internet media, and the basic function of referrals.

Tourism organizations interface with the hospitality industry and providers comprised of travel agents, tour companies, transportation providers, advertising companies, lodging, food service, attractions, as well as other amenities and activities. Coordinating with the hospitality industry and related businesses creates inclusion in a tourism network, essential for referrals. (Organizations providing resources for sustainable and green tourism are listed in Appendix A and links to tourism trade shows are included in Appendix B).

Governmental agencies also participate, offering promotion (websites, visitor guides, brochures), data collection, conferences, and sometimes training. These agencies include departments of tourism, commerce, and economic development. Arts commissions and local organizations sponsor artist tours, art shows, and festivals. Tourism organizations sponsor FAM, or familiarization tours, taking representatives from the hospitality industry to view different attractions and amenities in a region. Such a tour may be likened to connecting the dots on a journey. Which amenities are chosen relates highly to future itinerary building; therefore, community and small-scale enterprise connections to these entities better ensure future inclusion.

Tourism is largely an entrepreneurial industry. Eighty percent of USA tourism is handled by small business, including guides, food preparers, artists, bed and breakfasts, storytellers, and vendors. Yet, the 80% earn a small percentage of the total tourism profits. Who benefits? Corporations garner the larger share, through lodging and food service in multiple locations, promoted with large advertising budgets.

Communities then shoulder the burden of infrastructure and privacy costs. Diversifying tourism options creates the attractive vacation concept while generating a maximum range of jobs. Not becoming dependent upon one activity increases sustainability and reduces environmental impacts.

Entrepreneurs supply 80% of tourism services, indicating a need for support in training, capital, and promotion.

At the crux of achieving a greater economic impact in tourism is looking at small-scale approaches, with the capability of greatly extending tourism's employment benefits. Specifically, the paradigm shift to be reached through cultural tourism involves looking beyond tax dollars generated by mainstream businesses to total desired employment impacts, as well as improvement of quality-of-life through small-scale or micro-enterprises.

Through close participation in the tourism industry, culturally identified communities can encourage survey questions specific to their cultures, and as a result benefit from data relevant for community-based tourism planning—gaining access to resources and marketing opportunity. Continued participation is essential for continued referrals.

This chapter suggests a diversified approach to employment, for different scales of enterprises offer variety, flexibility, and opportunity to local entrepreneurs. Currently in the United States, international tourism is the fastest growing tourism market segment. Cultural tourism is a good match to the growing interests of the international tourism market segment.

THE VISITOR

"What do we call them?" is a basic question relating to visitor ease. Some locales choose the word "visitor" as a more welcoming phrase than "tourist." Others call those who come "guests," with the receiving culture a "host"[1] or receiving community. The term "tourist" may seem less personal and more business oriented. Yet communities may have their own concepts and terms for visitors, embedded in their protocols for receiving visitors. When a community makes a collaborative decision on "what to call them," there is consistency in the local tourism network. This increases the comfort level of the visitor.

> *Results from national tourism surveys show primary visitor interests as shopping, local cultures, recreation, and scenic beauty.*

Rather than existing in a vacuum, successful tourism is highly dependent on those linkages constituting an entire trip for the traveler. When a visitor plans a vacation, a one-week or two-week trip is generally considered. "Where will we stay?", "Where will we eat?", and "What will we do?" are the main questions for comfort and an appealing vacation. Even the question "Where will we go to the restroom?" becomes essential, especially for families with children or for seniors. These questions may seem simple, yet are fundamental to tourism development. When urban people travel, they want to escape from job and urban lifestyle stress, and statistics show they love to shop. The successful link between industry, the visitor, and a community depends upon gaining an understanding of visitor interests, potential regional offerings, assessment of visitor satisfaction, maintenance of environmental integrity, and local benefits.

THE COMMUNITY

Communities provide the majority of tourism activities. Fundamental to community participation is the recognition of two views of culture. Culture with a capital "C" connotes museums, music events, fine art, and is otherwise referred to as "high" culture, whereas the customs, lifeways, and cultural arts or crafts are referred to as "everyday" culture with a small "c." Smaller, traditional communities are aware of the need for a paradigm shift to everyday culture.

In the following chapters, other factors relevant to a cultural tourism paradigm shift are defined, to create powerful links beyond the urban for a strong cultural tourism network. To the extent that a community participates, provides services complementary to the network, and stays in communication with tourism partners—then referrals are the likely outcome.

Tourism benefits most often accrue to those who initiate the tourism activities. Thus it is essential for those communities whose culture attracts tourists to be integrally involved in deciding who should be encouraged to visit, what the appropriate scale and focus of tourist activities should be, where tourists should be encouraged and allowed to go, when interactions with tourists will best mesh with the rhythms of the local culture, and why tourism is (or is not) good to encourage. Consideration of these factors will attract the conscious traveler.

Communities also need a voice in how many tourists are desirable, and how to structure businesses developed to tap into the tourism opportunity (such as individually owned, or owned by the community). Ideally, communities would be able to control all of these factors. In the real world, one or more factors may be difficult or impossible for the community to manage. Planning is a basic step for determining the best possible scenario.

Integral to this book is the theme of cultural choices and the power of bringing about alternatives through continuous community discussion. The idea of planning a future in times of rapid change may seem futile, yet planning for different economic scenarios is productive. Keeping informed of market trends, product trends, and local offerings is the key to tapping opportunities for earned livelihood. To some communities, the idea of determining a future is not culturally or spiritually acceptable. Being aware of a culture's views on determining a future, or seeing alternatives for the future, is essential for working with another culture.

Frequently I hear community members from culturally distinct settings return from conferences and trainings on economic development or tourism, despairing over what they don't have in terms of larger-scale enterprises. "We don't have anything here," is the lamenting refrain. When the unseen richness of their scenic beauty, cultural stories, nutritious and interesting foods, knowledge of basic skills relating to the earth, and the examples they portray of cohesive, family-centered communities are discussed—opportunities for small-scale tourism become apparent.

Planning from within a community may occur with local guidance, or with the addition of a planning or tourism specialist from outside the community—and most productively with both. Good listening skills and community-directed decision making are essential with either scenario. Inclusion of a person experienced in tourism is valuable for understanding the tourism industry, linking to industry resources, project planning, designing promotion, and identifying funding available for tourism. Being proactive as a community while working with the tourism industry involves recognizing differences in approaches toward tourism, and choosing a path productive for the community.

Yet the challenge is to not alter this richness of local cultures. When looking at alternatives under the new tourism paradigm, planning explores and utilizes traditional knowledge. The good match between cultural values, local resources, and interests of visitors requires a thoughtful process. Tourism perceived on a community's own terms is easier to develop sustainably and manage well.

TOURISM OPTIONS

To think through tourism options, a community needs to be aware of the different types of tourism. One type may be appropriate for one community, while another is not a good fit. For example, some American Indian tribes do not want the intrusion of cultural tourism, yet are willing to develop recreational enterprises. Other American Indian tribes want only a few limited intrusions on their land, yet are willing to interpret history or sell cultural arts. Developing tourism away from the community location is yet another possibility. Tourism today offers a broad range of educational, leisure, and recreational options.

While there is importance in educating the public about history, there is also an urgent need to support the continuation of living cultures. Tourism may encourage both, for there is often a need to reinterpret history from multiple viewpoints.

Cultural tourism frequently interfaces with other types of tourism, such as:

- Adventure tourism (outdoor experiences);
- Agritourism (agriculture);
- Avitourism (birding);
- Creative tourism (arts and hands-on demonstrations);
- Culinary tourism (local flavors);
- Ecotourism (nature-based experiences);
- Green tourism (environmentally responsible travel);
- Heritage tourism (focus on history);
- Leisure tourism;
- Ranching tourism;
- Sports tourism; and
- Voluntourism (for environmental restoration or well-being of communities).

Cultural tourism is perceived as the learning experience about living cultures, whereas heritage tourism is seen as interpretation of the past.

Geotourism refers to an overlap between cultural and nature-based tourism, as tourism that sustains or enhances the geographical character of a place—its environment, culture, aesthetics, heritage, and the well-being of its residents.[2] Fostering place-based tourism is valuable for increasing market potential for the quality, authentic visitation experience.

Attracting a focused market creates a community's unique niche and supports smaller-scale approaches. Enterprises that incorporate local values in the developmental process are easier to accomplish in the smaller-scale. Green, environmental concerns are better addressed on this scale as well. Assessments are valuable for determining the most suitable type of tourism for a given community.

CULTURE AND SUSTAINABILITY

To be sustainable, actions are guided by cultural values central to one's belief system. Conscious visitors are aware of both their own values and those of the community visited. Where does responsibility lie for respectful tourism? The host community must educate the visitor and the visitor must also enter a community with openness and awareness.

Designing tourism in a way that creates a satisfying vacation, yet is harmonious with the host community's values, involves thorough planning. Understanding the complexities of cultural systems is central to a process-oriented approach. And, communicating intangible aspects of culture—those not readily visible or material—is basic for integrating values into the design of amenities and services.

Development actions supporting more than one cultural subsystem—such as kinship, religion, the political system, the educational system, the economic system, and the ecosystem—are culturally appropriate and will have long-term impacts. When a single development action positively affects more than one of those systems, it becomes more reinforced or culturally meaningful and will have a long-term and widespread impact within the community.[3]

In a value-based planning process, development actions that support more than one cultural subsystem must be initiated to attain sustainability. The following chart illustrates these relationships. This systems view of culture is not intended to be used for a dissection of available data, but rather as a guide to seeing connections and interrelationships.

Artistic—Visitors are fascinated by authentic cultural art and learning the meaning or interpretation of art, in relation to culture. The arts are a significant source of cultural pride. Yet, the downside of cultural arts being altered in form due to market pressures or copied by visitors should be considered.

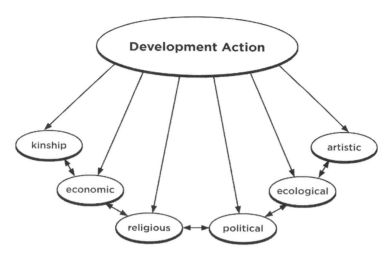

Chart 1.1 CULTURE AND SUSTAINABILITY

(Source: Planning for Balanced Development by Susan Guyette).

Ecological—Land is highly significant in terms of sense of place, history, sacred places, traditional foods, art-making materials, and medicinal plants. Issues around land must be identified and negative impacts prevented to address community concerns.

Political—Involving community leadership in the planning process is valuable to ensure implementation, access to resources, and redirection when necessary. Governance—or planning, developing, monitoring and redirection—is different from government.

Religious—Cultural privacy is often needed for ceremonial practice. Tourism planning must consider locations where access should be restricted. Increased attention on traditional activities by youth may occur, as a result of outside interest and respect for local culture.

Economic—In traditional economies, families tend to rely upon several "income streams," or sources of income which combine to provide enough support. Combining "income streams" to include traditional activity reinforces traditional values. Small-scale tourism may become one of the income streams, with others providing continuity through the low tourism season.

Kinship—Extended family cooperation strengthens small-scale tourism development by increasing family owned and operated businesses, and keeping family interaction more intact than other forms of employment.

Sustainable development proactively addresses multiple issues in a community. By identifying the sustainable aspects of development, a careful planning process takes into consideration the provision of basic needs, land protection needs, and conservation needs, as well as new development ideas.

VALUE-BASED PLANNING

Small-scale, culturally-based development affords traditional peoples the opportunity to work locally or near to their homes, and the opportunity to participate in cultural activities. When new initiatives are based upon local values, cultural expression provides satisfaction to both the community and visitors. As communities incorporate traditional forms into small-scale enterprises, management capability develops appropriately and environmental impacts tend to be reduced.

Locally controlled development based on local strengths, both cultural and economic, comprises the greatest potential for long-term stability and a track record of job creation. Sustainable development impetus from within communities frequently comes from a desire to care for the community and to provide a means of livelihood.

Examples from methods based in traditional and Indigenous cultures are used throughout this book to illustrate ways of working with cross-cultural differences. The term *traditional* is used within the context of the time-honored practice of lifeways expressed through cultural systems, usually learned in the family setting. These practices foster successful stewardship of the surrounding ecosystem while caring for our mother, Earth.

Traditional communities pass down values, beliefs, and information from generation to generation, sometimes for thousands of years. Being group-oriented, and sometimes communal, these communities tend to be less individualistic and less oriented toward a change concept of "progress" as a future orientation.

"Indigenous" can have several meanings, ranging from local, to a specific geographic area, and to Native peoples. Indigenous in this book is intended to refer to Native Americans, First Nations, and other Native peoples worldwide. They are also considered to be traditional if practicing their native cultures.

While the approaches presented in this text were developed over my twenty-five years of tourism planning and development with

Native American, Hispanic, and rural communities in the United States, the methods also work well internationally according to those using my prior books. A connection to sense of place, living by values enduring over generations, living in a cultural-caring harmony as stewards of the land, and living a closely knit community lifestyle—all characterize rural, traditional, and Indigenous communities. There is much to be learned about sustainability, for any culture, from Indigenous, ethnically rooted, and rural communities.

> **Traditional Values Relating to Tourism**
> - Generosity
> - Extended Family Support
> - Community
> - Cooperation
> - Cultural Learning

Integrating Values

By identifying cultural values to frame tourism and key participants to include in planning, a solid foundation is formed for moving forward with tourism development. A unique character of many traditional cultures—not revealing all cultural details—should be respected and preserved. In the long term, value-based tourism development increases cultural pride and expresses cultural values. Maintaining balance and sustainability are also aligning outcomes.

Tourism within the multi-cultural context may emphasize a range of value-based behaviors:

- Hospitality—greeting guests, welcoming;
- Individual privacy;
- Sense of place;
- Sense of identity;
- Participation and belonging;
- Continuity;
- Consensus;
- Generosity;

- Extended family cooperation;
- Religious privacy;
- Certain aspects of culture not shared or sold (e.g., language, some varieties of seeds, weaving techniques);
- Awareness of culturally defined roles and responsibilities for men and women;
- Quality or pride in work;
- Cooperation between enterprises rather than competition;
- Creativity;
- Uniqueness—reinforcing culture;
- Humor, and preservation and protection of tradition and culture (historical).

These qualities set a solid cultural foundation for planning discussions. The chapters ahead include planning processes and an example community-based solution is given at the end of each.

PLANNING PROCESS:
Values From Within

A group facilitator asks the questions, allowing time for participants to reflect. Then, a group discussion is encouraged.

- *What are the cultural values important to the community?*
- *How are values communicated through visitor education and storytelling?*
- *Which values will become the foundation for small-scale enterprises?*
- *What existing cultural links form the basis of a small-scale network?*
- *How is the expression of cultural values strengthened and supported by sharing culture?*
- *How will an exchange concept be developed?*

There may be more than one set of values within a community due to varying levels of acculturation or a mixture of cultural groups within a community. Inclusion of different points of view lends strength to the tourism planning process. Chart 1.2 on the next page illustrates an integrated approach in a Native Hawaiian example.

Integrating cultural values into the entrepreneurial development process supports cultural continuance. When generosity is a central community value, an uncomfortable cultural pull may result from tourism. The community will have difficulty charging for hospitality, yet the alternative is the community incurring high levels of costs and impacts, both culturally and environmentally. An equitable scenario must then be defined to ensure the comfort of both visitors and community. A shift from seeing a tourism outcome as a shopping experience, to a satisfying and informative visitor experience, gains recognition for cultural heritage.

FORM, SCALE, AND TIMING

Three variables—form, scale, and timing—are factors to guide a sustainable approach. When seen within the context of local values, community uniqueness becomes apparent.

Form

For tourism with a good cultural fit, new initiatives may be introduced while retaining *forms* of a rural or culturally traditional economy. For example, in many rural or reservation areas, small-scale cottage industries develop spontaneously by extended family units. Strengths of this business form are cooperation within the family, small-scale management, and flexibility of hours to allow for participation in traditional activities.

Barter is an example of a traditional economic form that increases resources for improved economic quality. Perception of economic success is gauged by quality-in-life rather than by absolute dollar amounts, the criterion generally used by funders of economic development projects. Success defined on a community's own terms incorporates existing characteristics of form.

Chart 1.2

NATIVE HAWAIIAN VALUES IN RELATION TO ENTERPRISE DEVELOPMENT

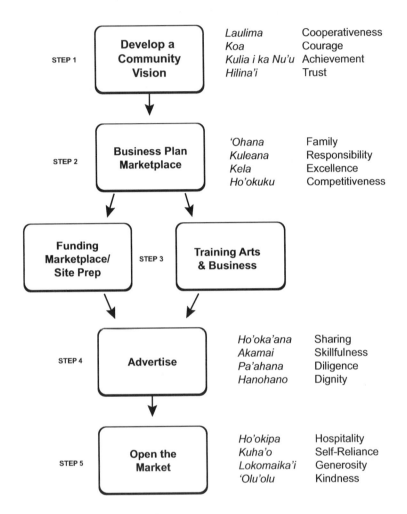

Other examples of form are:

- Enterprises based on traditional activities;
- Enterprises reflecting cultural values;
- Activities that are culturally unique and appropriate;
- Seasonally appropriate cultural practices, such as celebrations;
- Enterprises reflecting conservation of natural resources;

- Family cooperation in making cultural items and cottage industry; and
- Cooperatives.

Scale

Appropriate *scale* increases the potential for success. Scale may be defined in relation to available capital, management expertise and lowered environmental impacts. For example, a series of small businesses networked together forms a larger-scale attraction. A series of small bed and breakfasts may be an appropriate scale, rather than a large motel or hotel for a community. Numerous, smaller businesses provide employment to local people, and require less complicated management skills.

Rapid and large development is a growth-oriented urban model, not based upon capacity-building. A central concept in my earlier planning texts is the option of two different ways to develop a large result. One is to plan larger-scale, secure financing, and import management staff experienced with larger-scale enterprises. The alternative is to plan smaller-scale enterprises and to link them together for a week-long vacation experience. Deciding on a local direction or "theme" for tourism, training local people in management, and linking together for promotional efforts, create a larger concept from a network of locally managed, smaller enterprises.

Slower, gradual and linked development leads to a larger and more powerful outcome in terms of a solid community foundation. Examples include:

- Extended family or other local organizations recognized;
- Smaller, locally owned enterprises begin to link;
- Growth capability incorporated as management capability increases;
- Infrastructure capability expanding without impacting resources for community;
- Limiting numbers of visitors prevents impacts on local ecosystems;
- Cultural practice not impacted negatively; and
- Seasonal flexibility accommodated.

Timing

The last variable, *timing* relates to building community capacity. When development is phased in stages—occurring when communities are receptive, infrastructure is in place, and capital is generated—readiness is better perceived. For example, some tourism-related businesses may start small and expand over time, as management capability is developed. These businesses are stronger and show a lower incidence of failure over the long term. Factors important to timing include:

- Assessing readiness;
- Developing gradually over time;
- Increasing internal capacity to manage;
- Promoting according to capacity to manage; and
- Assessing sustainable measures of progress and redirecting as necessary.

CULTURALLY-BASED LIVELIHOOD

Because cultural enterprises are value based, they often develop with traditional economic forms. For example, these enterprises usually develop with low capital investment, plus are family owned and operated. Frequently, cultural enterprises incorporate traditional economic forms such as barter for materials or labor, and operate through extended family collaboration.

Cultural enterprises involving the arts, tours, storytelling, and small-scale lodging,[4] require support specific to the community. The critical variables for a culturally-based enterprise business model include identification of product, pricing, promotion, location, production, and financing. Integrating cultural concerns tailors the approach through local participation.

Community members who work away from their community or village are not always available when traditional activities occur. Traditional activities tend to not follow a schedule compatible with work hours, with practices late into the night or on work days. A gap in cultural practice is then created. When employees cannot participate culturally due to work schedules, constant exposure to a different set of values brings about change, whether conscious or not conscious. Desire to avoid such changes may influence tourism decisions, or the forms of business adopted in a value-based approach.

> *When community members must leave a traditional, rural lifestyle to commute and work in an urban setting, cultural loss occurs.*

While there are downsides to local tourism or having visitors come to a community, there are alternatives such as taking handmade, cultural items to the city to sell in markets. Weighing the possible gains from tourism versus potential negative impacts is useful in decision making. When thorough, the planning process produces assessments and options for discussions, useful for defining choices and directions.

Each chapter in this book illustrates how cultural values are integrated into specific stages of the tourism planning process. Value-based economy emphasizes support for the community as a whole and encourages community members to flourish in their skills and jobs. Value-based economic development may expand the community's developmental progress through a model for economic, social and cultural retention linked to the natural environment. Reinforcing local culture increases sustainability, encouraging economies based on generations of experience.

BRIDGING CULTURES

Every planning effort working with diverse cultures must consider internal concerns, strengths, and solutions. Bridging cultures is a two-way process between the planning professional and the internal community, or between the community and visitors.

Tourism is frequently designed as a "show" or a staged production, pitched to the visiting culture. This form of tourism is sometimes seen as disrespectful to authentic traditions. Instead, the communication of place and people is possible when people tell their own stories. Yet the issue of demonstration is complex. When certain traditions are deemed private and internal to the community only, a demonstration with limited content is one means of interfacing with the outside world while maintaining cultural privacy.

Respect in cultural tourism development is fundamental to success. In traditional cultures, respect is a central value. Therefore, for sustainable development to proceed in a participatory way that creates equity in economic systems, respect must always be a guiding principle. Local, cultural forms and ways of doing business have evolved because they work well with cultural values. Therefore, respecting these local forms is central to cultural retention and sustainability.

Decisions from within a community, communicated well to the industry, foster favorable outcomes for culturally sensitive—or what is known as "respectful visitation" in traditional communities. Examples of "disrespectful" behavior are peering into the windows of local households, wearing skimpy clothing, asking intrusive questions, intruding into sacred places, scattering trash, or taking photographs where prohibited. Careful planning and visitor education improve the process of communicating respectful behaviors.

With rising public fears about safety in travel, particularly since the events of 9/11/2001 in the United States, those rural areas with scenic beauty, fascinating cultures, or just the peaceful respite from urban stress, are sought by many travelers. Yet, care must be taken to not impact these treasured places in a negative way. Planning from within a culture and seeing internal connections forwards the central considerations for those working in tourism. Once local connections are understood, negative impacts are better anticipated and prevented.

Such an approach is useful for any community, since few in contemporary times are totally homogeneous. Taking the time and care to explore community strengths, needs, and gaps in capacity is invaluable for guiding a community towards both a good cultural and capacity fit. Value-based approaches are adaptable from culture to culture and tend to encourage the revitalization of cultural practice.

The Amish, a traditional rural community located in Pennsylvania (USA) are known for their concerns about tourism. "Tourism in general, symbolizes worldly pleasure in the Amish mind. Tourists waste time, seek entertainment, and waste money—all of which contradict basic Amish virtues," describes Donald Kraybill.[5] This belief, combined with the Amish aversion to views of controlling the future, intrusion to cultural practice, and the impact of outside value influences, reflects potential disconnects between tourism and Amish culture. Solutions have been found by selling products and arts away from Amish communities, online, and in restricted locations. The Amish stance toward tourism is a good example of community engagement and defining a community's own directions for tourism from within.

Unless cultural boundaries are understood, traditional communities will be impacted negatively by the intrusion of visitors. Respecting community perspectives is the starting place for bridging cultural gaps and creating an understanding of the true issues and solutions. When a framework for analyzing tourism systems and hospitality is introduced from outside a culture, the internal strengths of existing cultural systems tend to be missed. To bridge the cultural gap, training in local communities must also educate the receiving community on the values of their visitors.

CULTURAL BIAS IN THE TOURISM INDUSTRY

Cultural bias skews development, particularly when resource providers rely upon a set of jargon constructed by one cultural interpretation. There exists a substantial amount of cultural bias, unknowingly, in the tourism industry. Often seen as an "extractive industry," dollars produced and numbers of visitors are the primary measure of success used by the industry. Taking the time to identify cultural values is useful for determining the broad meaning of tourism to a community—beyond jobs. For example, cultural bias is commonly embedded in the following terms:

- ***Product*** as a term is viewed by traditional communities as objectifying culture, not appreciating fully the cultural significance of activities.

- ***Best practices*** imply one way of conducting business as better than others. Cultural diversity and the strengths of different ways of interacting should be taken into account when a community designs an appropriate set of tourism practices. "Best" needs to be defined from within a community, based on cultural values and long-term sustainability considerations.

- The concept of ***tourism product*** is generally viewed in the industry as a packaged tour, limiting the concept and opportunity.

- The term ***asset*** commodifies cultural activities, places, and arts.

These are viewed as sacred in numerous traditional cultures, and the implication that culture can be sold is a sensitive topic.

- Communities may perceive a cultural jar over the term *attractions*, generally developed as staged activities to "watch," rather than a part of daily lifeways. Practicing culture is not a performance for sale or to be applauded, even with appreciation.
- *"Culture is not for sale."* Cultural boundaries on activity content must be defined internally by the community By providing alternative visitor education activities, a community has the freedom to close off private community areas while still allowing some visitation.
- *Cultural arts* tend to not be viewed as "objects" by the traditional community and may have sacred significance. Internal community discussion on which arts and songs are appropriate to share with the public, and which should be kept private, helps maintain consistency in tourism policy as well as positive internal cohesion.
- The term *host* may be jarring when tourism is viewed as an expression of friendship.
- Division between the concepts of host and guest implies *services for sale* or entertainment. Communities living a traditional lifestyle tend to perceive tourism as "sharing" and frequently have difficulty charging for what is given. An exchange view implies an even interaction and fair compensation in relation to community values.
- *ROI*, or return on investment, implies measurement of tourism income gained. Yet, cultural loss is immeasurable in dollars. Cultural retention is also beyond measurement.
- *Profit*, when seen purely in financial terms, ignores the richness of cultural retention or community survival. Tourism investments encouraging learning may earn less income, yet encourage the richness of cultural learning.
- The term *cultural properties* implies ownership. Places of cultural, community, and historic significance need to be protected, yet be accessible for traditional uses. Communal use rather than ownership—in the sense of belonging to an individual in the Western worldview—applies in many traditional communities.

Explaining the appropriate use of these terms helps avoid communication of cultural bias. The tourism industry tends to be fond of jargon. This affinity often becomes a barrier for communities in the initial stages of planning for tourism. Refer to Appendix C to become familiar with basic tourism terms.

By understanding tourism terminology and potential industry biases, smaller communities are able to communicate for better linked tourism efforts. They may bridge cultural gaps by communicating their own terms and perceptions of bias. Itineraries, training, broader impact marketing, and referrals are primary benefits of linking. As cultures connect and communicate about differences and similarities in tourism goals, then a common direction for moving forward together is possible.

RESOLVING MIXED FEELINGS ABOUT TOURISM

Communities in conflict around tourism practices are not appealing to visitors. The majority of travelers to rural regions come from stressful urban life. A compelling need for a peaceful place to regenerate, whether rural or urban, is commonly the driving force behind vacation expenditures. Visitors need to feel welcome and they need information on where to obtain the basic services for their stay.

Several strategies are useful for resolving those internal love/hate feelings toward tourism.

- Focus on equity and the distribution of benefits.
- Diversify economies by creating export markets through cultural tourism and education.
- Reduce the numbers of tourists coming into an area.

Small-scale, low-impact, local-profit tourism is often the ideal outcome. Take the best approaches available from planning, tourism, anthropology, and folklore—the methods with the best cultural fit—and encourage integrated, cross-disciplinary approaches. Technical assistance providers need to be educated by communities on the sensitive issues of the particular culture.

Inclusive Processes

A thorough planning process identifies the elements needed for a mutually beneficial visitation experience. By collaborating with the community for direction and data collection, either internal or hired planners build alliances and create a foundation for proceeding with tourism. By valuing the ideas of both those optimistic and those pessimistic about tourism, planning may facilitate a win/win situation. The effective tourism plan bridges the gap between these two groups and develops an approach for moving ahead.

A community will improve its own satisfaction with tourism if an equal opportunity exists to tap into the benefits of the intrusion. Beyond the planning stage is the need for increasing community capability and capacity. Training in business development, customer service, and evaluation of effectiveness must be provided, if small-scale enterprises are to flourish.

I encounter resistance to tourism so strong in some rural communities that tourism is best referred to as the "T" word. This situation exists where frustrated community members have not seen the direct benefits from visitation or do not experience equity through entrepreneurial potential. Tourism may be the primary industry and the financial benefits are desired, yet there has not been a process to reduce unwanted negative impacts.

Sometimes individuals are unwilling to hear the word "tourism" in communities where the entire economy is based on tourism. Planning can bring a community together by initiating discussions on sensitive topics. Tourism solutions, discovered by a group process, move a community forward. Delivering smaller results along the way keeps the community moving together.

Another benefit of planning is gaining access to resources. The plan is valuable for demonstrating to potential resource providers and funders a cohesive effort and the larger development picture. In the view of resource providers, understanding how the short-term fits into the longer view is essential for funding a single project. Those linkages both internal and external to the community, important to long-term continuation, must be identified.

THE STARTING POINT

The new paradigm in cultural tourism is characterized by a different, decolonized, concept of development. A distinction when considering traditional economies concerns enculturation—or the process of learning one's culture at an early age—and acculturation, or the learning of the values and customs of another culture.

> *Sustainability can occur only when the practice of trading off one set of values for another ceases and instead tourism and cultural heritage management interests work toward the achievement of common goals.*[6]

This statement by Bob McKercher and Hilary du Cros is particularly true in traditional communities—frequently small and tightly interwoven through kinship—with economic forms practiced for the past several generations. Cultural change tends to occur slowly in these traditions. The impacts of tourism become particularly disruptive for traditional communities, unless values are integrated as the foundation of initiatives and acculturation is reduced.

In terms of worldview, the time is now to step back from the standard definitions of development and look at a concept of sustainable development that retains values, continues traditions, maintains harmony, conserves resources, and creates equity. When meaning is perceived from only one cultural perspective, significant differences are not realized. Looking for and recognizing multiple perspectives, are the underlying factors in gaining cultural understanding.

Technical assistance efforts from outside the community tend to fall apart when initial discussions are laden with tourism terminology carrying cultural bias. Failure to listen to what communities are discussing *within* is another point of breakdown. A concept so expertly developed by Linda Tuhiwai Smith[7] in relation to Indigenous methodology, is the importance of decolonizing methodologies or developing approaches that work with culture, rather than being superimposed. Certain initial conversations may need to occur in private to protect internal information.

Asking simply what a community wants is another approach rarely leading to community-based involvement, for without seeing other small-scale models from communities with a similar value system, the options and benefits of engaging may not be perceived. Training, successful examples, and connections to other communities must occur before the question of local needs will be answered within the culture's own terms.

In relation to sustainability—rather than starting with the environmental, economic, and socio-cultural impacts of tourism—the nurturing starting place seeks to understand how cultural, economic, and political processes operate through tourism.[8] Only then are the dynamics of tourism understood.

SMALL-ECONOMY EMPHASIS

Mainstream, mass tourism typically targets large numbers of tourists, and large volume is where mainstream tourism methods run amuck in small communities. Alternatives to mass tourism are pivotal to explore. Strains on infrastructure, impacts on cultural privacy, environmental impacts, and a lack of resources to learn tourism management skills—all are barriers to tourism development with a good cultural or scale "fit."

To avoid cultural bias, it is crucial that a primarily economic-motivated growth model is not superimposed upon traditional cultures. As Bill McKibben points to in *Deep Economy*,[9] the standard measurements of economic success based upon growth criteria have led to global depletion of resources and profit by a small elite.

Frequently in development assistance, the underlying assumption made by those assisting is that superimposing another set of values will "help the community to progress" or improve. Connotations of "improvement" tend to assume superiority of a cash economy, natural resource exploitation, and a benefit to acculturation. In reality, methods with a poor cultural fit, particularly when introduced rapidly, cause acculturative stress. Under such stress a community and individuals are less resilient and less able to adapt to changing conditions.

This progress-based notion of development implies a consumptive model of the universe, rather than a sustainable development view of maintaining traditions in harmony with nature and our mother, Earth. A different starting place occurs when planning comes from within a traditional community, one without assumptions of growth and a primary profit motive. "Will there be tourism?", "What are the alternatives?", "What has developed spontaneously in the local economy?" and "What is needed to nurture these forms of earned livelihood, barter, and subsistence activities?"—all are essential questions.

Notions of the superiority of "progress" are now melting away as the failures of unwise ecological decisions become apparent globally, and progress in light of natural resource depletion is being questioned. A shift in the meaning of "development" needs to occur. As Shawn Wilson explains,[10] the concept of indigeneity emphasizes a responsibility to ensure respectful and reciprocal relationships, as well as creativity. Many traditional communities are now viewing progress as "regaining the old ways." Traditional communities are becoming recognized and respected globally as the keepers of knowledge for living harmoniously in nature.

Looking at contemporary communities in economic crisis, the pitfalls of large scale are evident. Lack of flexibility puts larger-scale development at the mercy of economic fluctuations, and subject to collapse when market potential and access to capital decreases. In contrast, small-scale and culturally-based livelihood builds upon local strengths.

TOURISM SUCCESS FACTORS

Addressing the needed shift from external to internal community practices, this book serves as a community-based guide for planning and developing sustainable cultural tourism. In summary, common success factors in this new paradigm for small-scale sustainable tourism include:

- Working with the community for internal alignment by anticipating possible positive gains as well as negative impacts, and identifying strategies to avoid negative impacts;
- Assessing visitor preferences with visitor surveys, comment cards, and personal feedback, thus improving services;
- Developing a concept to unify an experience;
- Developing a clear, long-term plan and phased projects, to match community capacity;

- Linking to statewide and national efforts, and working regionally;
- Securing resources by communicating projects, needs, and sustainable evaluation criteria;
- Providing basic amenities, such as restrooms, water, food, and lodging, to increase length-of-stay;
- Developing on several scales—entrepreneurial, small scale business, as well as larger scale—and linking all enterprises;
- Educating visitors on interpretations of history, respectful etiquette, and cultural stories;
- Promoting tourism, including individual entrepreneurs;
- Protecting local ecosystems, sacred sites, and cultural privacy; and
- Managing tourists to create a flow, contain them, educate, and create a mutually satisfying visitation.

How to make the bridge from details to the creative concept without getting lost? The skill in planning for cultural tourism lies in "bringing the community along" in the process, allowing cultural creativity to come forth and shape the experience. Experiential concepts then emerge.

COMMUNITY-BASED SOLUTION

Sustainable Travel International

A thought leader in sustainable tourism development since 2002, the organization Sustainable Travel International (STI) provides global leadership in travel and tourism, The organization assists destinations and businesses of all sizes to develop innovative solutions that protect the environment, adapt to climate change, preserve cultural heritage, and generate economic benefits across the tourism value chain.

Sustainable Travel International provides education and training programs to tourism businesses, government agencies, and non-profits. Innovative assessment and planning tools identify the key players in the value chain, fundamental to reducing the carbon footprint and protecting both cultural and economic assets. In 2013, over 1 billion people will travel internationally and this number is growing at 4% per year. Much of this travel will occur in the most fragile ecosystems and communities remaining on the planet. Preserving a sense of place is truly becoming a competitive advantage.

STI offers support to small and medium-sized businesses through access to self-assessment tools, a carbon calculator, a globally recognized certification program called STEP (Sustainable Tourism Education Program) and participation in an eco-directory called the *Responsible Travel Report* which serves as a blog and online newsletter.

Additionally, STI manages a number of Traveler's Philanthropy and carbon offset funds, attracting financial and in-kind support for sustainable development oriented projects that help the environment and local people, and support community self-reliance. (www.sustainabletravelinternational.org)

FURTHER READING

Richards, Greg, editor. *Cultural Tourism: Global and Local Perspectives.* New York: Routledge, 2007.

> Although cultural tourism now appeals to a mass market and is one means of finding external sources of income to support cultural facilities, globalization also has deep consequences. Issues are discussed in relation to global examples.

Shilling, Dan. *Civic Tourism.* Prescott, AZ: Sharlot Hall Museum Press, 2007.

> Civic tourism reframes tourism's purpose from an end to a means, and from a market-driven growth tool to a tool that helps preserve place, while revitalizing the local economy. The book presents strategies to rethink economics, connect the public, and invest in story.

Smith, Melanie. *Issues in Cultural Tourism Studies.* London, UK: Routledge, 2009.

> This text explores pertinent issues in heritage, arts, festivals, indigenous, ethnic and experiential tourism in both urban and rural environments—to include policy and politics; impact management and sustainable development; interpretation and representation; marketing and branding; regeneration and planning.

Weaver, David. *Sustainable Tourism.* Burlington, MA: Elsevier. 2006.

> Specific measurement criteria are given for the World Tourism Organization's core indicators of sustainable tourism. Suggested "alternative tourism products" present options for communities that are compatible with cultural and environmental sustainability, compared to mass tourism. A network of global organizations supporting sustainable tourism development is well explained.

2

WINNING WITH A REGIONAL APPROACH

Linking between rural and urban areas increases the tourism potential of both.

Regionalism sets the context for effective tourism. Since visitors tend to spend several days and look for a variety of engaging activities and amenities, a connecting perspective is essential. Providing information—before arriving, during the visit, and after leaving—on how local resources are linked for the vacation experience, contributes to the comfort level of the visitor.

A region can be defined in different ways. Sometimes the term "region" is used to define a geographical grouping within a country, such as the Northeast or the Southwest. Another meaning of "region" is a part of a state, district or a province—emphasizing rural and urban communities—as well as ways of linking these areas together. When tourism entities define regions for a state, these delineations may not follow cultural, geographic, or activity similarities among communities. Rethinking primary alliances, yet working with the industry's regional identification, will maximize options for tourism success.

A win/win urban and rural tourism network succeeds by raising overall visitor spending in a region. In a true partnership, both rural and urban communities realize a gain. Additionally, linked networks of small-scale businesses have the strongest resilience or adaptability in changing economic times.

> **Framework for Integrating Culture**
>
> - Identify communities with similarities, both cultural and geographic, to form a region.
> - Identify business niches compatible with cultural values.
> - Establish linkages with the tourism industry and communicate cultural values, unique situations, activities, and services.
> - See the ways in which tourism can impart cultural understanding to potential partners.
> - Create links between communities and form interesting itineraries, with interpretation.

By linking local offerings, the *tourism draw* is enhanced through additional opportunities for itineraries. Managing tourism according to sustainable criteria becomes easier when tourism seasons are extended with a range of activities and visitation numbers are more evenly distributed.

Community readiness for entry into tourism is critical to consider. A sudden tourism draw can be too much, too soon. For this reason, tourism planning at both the regional and community levels is important to determine community capacity and to identify steps for capacity-building.

Some communities do not want greater numbers of tourists—but rather additional expenditures from existing visitation. Increasing the number of visitors according to a growth model does not always correlate with more income directly for the host community. Guiding fewer visitors into a quality, small-scale, locally owned experience brings the benefit to a region comprised of smaller communities.

Rather than readily adopting an industry perspective toward increased numbers of visitors, thinking through community intentions for tourism will produce the best cultural fit. Conducting assessments and developing a regional profile are starting points for becoming specific with marketing. Then, unique collaborations create a powerful tourism draw, as they form inviting vacation concepts.

The term "destination" is broadly defined as an area attracting non-local visitors. In rural areas, I repeatedly hear the term "destination" being used to describe a project idea. Originally defined as a region or a specific community, the term is now used to define a "destination resort," with the goal of keeping tourist spending within the resort's boundaries, including food service and boutique shops. Developers focused on larger-scale profits and negligent of ecological concerns tend to embrace this concept. The profits then accrue to the large corporation that operates the resort.

When this type of larger-scale development occurs, less income is gained in the local economy. For this reason, rural and culturally diverse communities benefit from tourism by pooling resources and developing regional entrepreneurial activity. Participation of organizations and cultural groups at the town, tribal, city, regional, statewide, national and international levels is valuable for both linking and promotional opportunities. Referrals are gained from such connections.

THE REGIONAL TOURISM CONCEPT

When regional linkages constitute a journey and are seen as collaboration, a powerful tourism network is formed. A region is one context within which individual businesses may thrive. Unifying for planning purposes assists communities to develop complementary services.

Competition and Cooperation

Businesses in urban areas tend to understand the value of local ***cooperation*** in achieving effective ***competition*** with other urban settings. Rural areas often conceptualize differently, seeing each business in competition. To see beyond what may at first glance seem like a contradiction involves a shift in the way business is viewed. Yes, businesses compete against each other. Yet, cooperating to form a network of exciting businesses creates a tourism draw.

Attracting visitors who are supportive of local businesses always requires a team effort. Urban communities use this concept well, creating referral networks to retain visitors in their area. Urban areas are adept at distributing a broad range of information on activities and amenities, linking their offerings. This principle of cooperation realizes the value of choice, since visitors have a broad range of interests. Rather than seeing each business in competition with each other, urban businesses realize the importance of providing enough variety and price ranges to hold visitors for extra days. These are valuable lessons in tourism for rural communities.

Extending *length-of-stay* is a focal concept in tourism, since visitors staying longer tend to spend more money in a local economy. When the stay is not only longer, but also engaging, these visitors will recommend the trip to their friends and relatives. Word-of-mouth is the most effective and the least expensive way to market in the tourism industry.

> **Visitors rarely travel to see one business; rather, they visit an interesting region.**

Knowing how to be connected to people—or to be in relationship—is a strength of Indigenous peoples and rural communities still connected to the land. The greater level of cooperation heightens the bottom line in tourism expenditures, due to a satisfying visitation experience. As a win/win situation is created for visitors, communities, and businesses, a larger tourism benefit accrues to all. "Larger" is defined in terms of numbers of visitors, jobs created, income, or extended cultural understanding. Explaining the cooperative principle of tourism as a community benefit is likely to foster a referral network.

Learners and seekers like to visit a cluster of museum or educational activities and observe demonstrators in context. This trend holds promise for cultural entrepreneurs. Shoppers like to compare prices as well as quality, and are more likely to buy when a wider range of options is readily available.

Visitation increases whether a community sponsors an outdoor market with entrepreneurial booths or a larger, physical building supporting space for entrepreneurs. Some communities successfully convert older grocery store buildings or an outgrown school into a marketplace with entrepreneurial booths. Shared marketing, management, and space costs are benefits accruing from collaboration.

Given a set of choices, visitors also stay longer and tend to purchase more with additional options. The informed visitor—one with an understanding of history, cultural etiquette, authenticity of cultural arts, and local ecological concerns—is easier to guide, whether informally or on a guided tour.

Success through collaboration is an underlying principle of the urban regional shopping center. This business factor is essential for small communities to understand, in relation to clusters of small-scale enterprises. Several stores selling the same type of inventory invite comparison, favored by shoppers. For example, a region emphasizing artists focuses a market draw from that particular market segment. Since tourism works on the basis of cooperation and collaboration rather than competition, referrals to other businesses in the region create ease in visitation.

The Regional Draw

Solutions for creating a regional draw are basic. Increasing visitor length-of-stay requires access to lodging and food service. When lodging is not available in rural areas, the link to urban services becomes an essential part of a complete tourism system. Urban and rural resources become complementary, valuable for keeping visitors within a region.

> *Cultural tourists consider lodging and local foods as part of the learning experience.*

Where are the largest economic benefits? The providers of lodging and food service garner the larger share of tourism dollars. For this reason, moving toward the development of small-scale or appropriate-scale lodging and food service keeps the income from tourism local. Some traditional communities have made the decision to keep lodging separate from their communities, to minimize cultural privacy impacts. Trade-offs concern economic gain versus maximum cultural privacy. Carefully considered, the solution determines the balance between the two, fitting the comfort level of the community.

One means of extending the length of stay is to provide locally unique lodging and food service. Visitors need to have food service available when hungry. Otherwise they leave a community by midday and spend elsewhere on shopping and activities where food service is located—commonly where they lodge. Do rural communities then lose? A great deal, but not entirely, for services lacking locally but present regionally hold the visitor in the region—offering the potential of a pleasant vacation and a repeat visit.

THE TOURISM SYSTEM

A systems approach to tourism planning considers both demand—in terms of market and characteristics—as well as supply, and the match between the two. Understanding these relationships with cultural sensitivity is at the core of planning locally. When tourism is desired, communities must be careful not to merely respond to an existing market for economic gain, otherwise negative socio-cultural and environmental impacts could be created. Sustainable development creates balances between cultural, economic, and environmental factors based on the strengths of all three in relation to local values, since values underlie motivation and actions.

> *To increase sustainability, the tourism system must be considered within the context of nature.*

Sustainable tourism recognizes interdependence within the tourism system. In this section the tourism system model developed by Clare Gunn[1] is adapted, expanding five functional components—attractions, services, transportation, promotion, and visitor education—to include cultural considerations. Interrelatedness and cooperation between the components of a tourism system are seen as pivotal for success, perceived as the pleasant visitor experience.

Attractions are considered to be local cultural events, significant places, or locations that are planned and managed for visitor activity and enjoyment. These are the energizing elements of a tourism system, and strengthen the tourism draw by being clustered. Events, festivals, and markets are examples of smaller-impact, traditionally based, and lower-cost visitor activities. Including small businesses and entrepreneurs creates the most authentic experience and the broadest earned livelihood benefit. Consistency in attractions and events from year-to-year is significant for interface with the tourism industry.

> *Cultural consideration:* The word "attraction" may create a "cultural jar" implying commodification of traditional activities. Local design of visitor activities, based upon sensitivity to non-exploitation and

communication of visitor etiquette, increases both visitor and local comfort with participation or observation. Demonstrations provide a way of limiting visitor access to privately held information, while imparting valuable basic knowledge about an art, history, or other visitor education topics. Not presenting a stereotyped image of cultures in the past—but rather a continuum from past, present, to future—is a new and informative trend of interest to cultural tourists.

Services are travel-oriented businesses such as accommodations, food service, travel agencies, gas stations, and other businesses serving basic and luxury traveler needs. They generate the greatest amount of jobs, income and tax revenues. Services derive from 1) independent ownership, 2) franchise chains, 3) quasi-governmental operations such as concessions, and 4) a non-profit or a non-governmental organization (NGO). The smaller community tends to benefit primarily from independent ownership and non-profit forms. For example, concessions in parks rarely purchase locally, and franchises generally compete with "Mom and Pop" businesses, leading to local closures. Given these trends, the visitor must be able to find locally owned service businesses easily.

Cultural consideration: *Service ideas defined from local traditions reflect authenticity and local values. Friendly businesses, based upon extended family cooperation and making the effort to sell locally handmade items in addition to services, maximize the number of culturally-based jobs. Referrals from one service-oriented business to another reflect cooperation rather than competition and further overall community goals. Services clustered geographically tend to reduce negative environmental impacts.*

Transportation considered on a regional basis is conventionally defined as the means of getting the visitor to a destination. Air travel, boat, car rental, bus, mini-vans, and pedestrian routes are modal alternatives. Inter-modal connections are increasing every year, as reducing the carbon footprint of tourism comes to the forefront.

Some traditional communities lower ecological and cultural privacy impacts by allowing only mini-van transportation to their lands. Good examples of managed tourism utilizing limited access mini-van transport are two Native communities—Saxman in Alaska, USA (www.cape foxtours.com/saxman.html) and Acoma Pueblo in New Mexico, USA (www.acomaskycity.org).

Effective signage relates to visitor comfort and guiding visitors to locally owned businesses. Preventing the lost visitor from wandering into residential and ecologically fragile areas by guiding them to the appropriate areas is valuable for avoiding negative environmental impacts. Hostile "Keep Out" signs drive visitors away by creating an unfriendly atmosphere. "No visitors beyond this point. Please respect our land and culture" is a possible alternative expression.

> *Cultural consideration: How destinations are considered affects equitable returns to a great extent. Small-scale transport by mini-van reduces environmental impacts compared to large buses. Stops along the way to locally owned businesses create entrepreneurial jobs. Large resorts are fond of providing the transport from the airport, driving through small communities without stops, thereby encouraging all expenditures directly to the resort. Local transport can structure itineraries to include multiple stops.*

Information provides basic guidance to visitors and is different from promotion. A visitor center or an intake point, such as a museum, are focal places for visitor orientation. Information basics for a respectful and safe visit include: weather conditions and needed clothing; etiquette (e.g., customs, taboos, privacy restrictions, areas off limit); local foods; physical demands; maps; itineraries; and health information (e.g., nearest local services, incidences of Giardia or Lyme-bearing ticks, or water dangers).

> *Cultural consideration: Hospitality training blending tourism management practices with local cultural hospitality and values for relating to visitors will produce the unique welcoming. Information then becomes attractive in style as well as content. Specific information on locally made items and foods creates local job creation and support of cultural entrepreneurs. A business directory listing specifics on locally owned businesses and entrepreneurs becomes essential for encouraging expenditures.*

Promotion targets market segments and creates a visitation draw. Both hardcopy (brochures, maps, visitor guides) and internet promotion reach potential travelers as they plan vacations, and for guidance on the needed elements for their trip. Use of social networking (Facebook, LinkedIn, YouTube, Twitter, and those tools yet to come along) is becoming a prevalent and low-cost way to promote. Publicity may be available at no cost (articles in magazines, newspapers, and online sources), whereas advertising, public relations efforts, and incentives (gifts and discounts) require cash outlay.

Targeted promotion expands visitor awareness of offerings, encourages authenticity, and increases the market draw. Avoiding generalized promotion by providing specifics on attractions, events, and basic services benefits the community directly. Locator maps are essential for guiding visitors directly to local businesses.

> *Cultural consideration: If a community decides upon its own historical and cultural interpretation, then cultural understanding is furthered, along with cultural pride. A positive presentation aligns visitors, and if customer service matches the messages put forth in promotion, the majority of visitors will go out of their way to purchase in local businesses and will tend to donate to cultural teaching efforts.*

A fully developed tourism system on the community or regional scale is the key to both visitor and community satisfaction in the tourism equation. A framework for analyzing these components of a tourism system is presented in the next chapter. Addressing these elements minimizes negative impacts and maximizes positive gains, according to definitions from within.

COORDINATION OF TOURISM SECTORS

Tourism is considered to occur in the business sector of the economy. Yet, in rural and tribal locations, other contributors are valuable for technical assistance, training, and securing resources. Creating a strong tourism support network, on regional and community levels, considers potential collaborations between three sectors: government, businesses, and non-profit organizations.

A strong economic system is created when government and private enterprise work together, linking for promotion and stemming expenditure leakages external to the regional economy. Strengthening these businesses by providing referrals, training, and small business services, is the means to growing a strong tourism sector of the local economy.

Tourism Cooperation

Businesses, entrepreneurs, programs, associations, and governmental entities interfacing with tourism in a community are contributors in a small network. An innovative tourism model aimed at increased sustainability and increased benefits to the community is created when a managed tourism program coordinates the interactions of tourism contributors in the community and the region.

Non-profits and locally owned enterprises provide basic services, rather than hiring these from outside of the area. Including several cultural groups in planning and launching a central intake place for tourism creates a hub for visitor education and support services. The diagram below illustrates a few of the possible connections between these three sectors.

Chart 2.1   SUSTAINABLE TOURISM COOPERATION

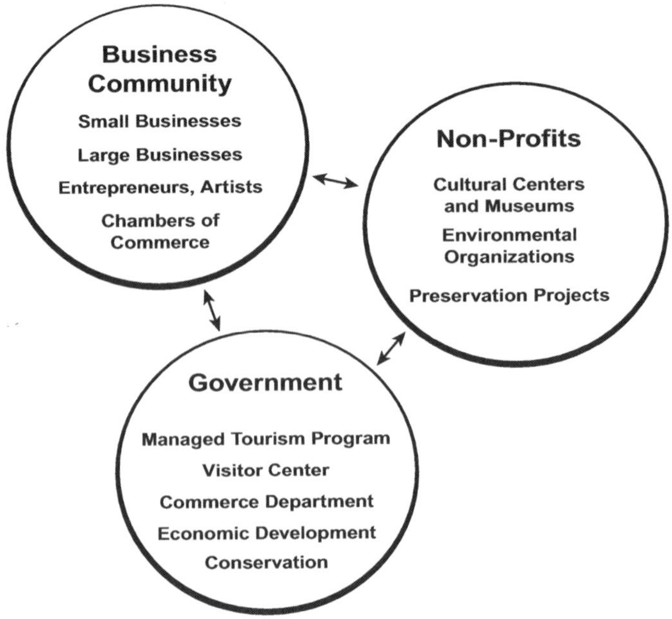

Business Community
- Small Businesses
- Large Businesses
- Entrepreneurs, Artists
- Chambers of Commerce

Non-Profits
- Cultural Centers and Museums
- Environmental Organizations
- Preservation Projects

Government
- Managed Tourism Program
- Visitor Center
- Commerce Department
- Economic Development
- Conservation

Collaborations must go beyond promotion to provide a quality visitation experience while managing the flow of visitors. For example, non-profits and culturally-based programs may produce educational materials for use by tours. Businesses are able to contribute to the production of a visitor guide not only to promote their businesses, but also to educate visitors on culturally respectful behavior. Cultural tourists who seek learning experiences are receptive and appreciative of such efforts.

To work together effectively, these sectors must understand the differences among the perspectives of development, community, and the traveler. Rather than making decisions based on the needs of the tourism industry, communities have the opportunity to choose tourism directions in relation to community needs and visitor preferences.

THE TOURISM PARTNER

"Partnership" is a common term used in tourism. To increase effective regional tourism development, a close examination of how "partnership" is interpreted will be beneficial. Ways of creating truly equitable tourism must be explored. In part, a clearer grasp of partnership requires an understanding of the difference in urban and rural value systems. In other words, what is significant to an urban economy is often different than the way an economy is perceived in a rural area. A partner is a sharer, one who participates in a common effort. Partnership implies cooperation for a two-way exchange or benefit. There is a tendency for rural and/or ethnic groups to attend tourism meetings upon invitation by urban groups, yet not gain the full benefits due to a scarcity of implementation resources in their community.

Rural communities may not have the financial resources to contribute the same amount for membership fees or marketing efforts. A sliding scale for membership fees furthers balanced urban/rural participation. To become a true tourism partner requires communities of different sizes and ethnic diversity to understand the needs and intentions of participation and to talk openly about cultural or economic differences. In this way, understanding and respect increase, in turn increasing an appropriate cultural fit for tourism development within a region. As true collaborations increase, benefits are accrued to all sizes of communities.

PLANNING PROCESS:
Defining Regions and Partners

- *What are the cultural differences and similarities in the region?*
- *Which geographic features or scenic beauty could be highlighted?*
- *Where are ecological protections needed in your region?*
- *Who represents or cares for these natural and cultural resources?*
- *How will reciprocation occur if organizations and keepers of traditions are brought together?*
- *What are the local needs for skills and resources and how does each partner contribute to the other?*

As small-scale, entrepreneurial and locally owned businesses develop, economic leakages to a larger urban economy are reduced—by offering a diversified and linked range of services. When referrals from the urban setting to small communities increase, urban communities benefit from the expanded regional draw of additional visitor activities. Pointing out this benefit in regional tourism meetings reduces the natural tendency to assume a competitive value. Small or culturally distinct communities only become true tourism "partners" if the skills necessary for planning and development are in practice.

A common barrier to reciprocation frequently occurs when only tourism organizations come together. If cultural knowledge keepers are not included in discussions surrounding protections and opportunities, important points are missed. For the exchange to be equitable, the values and special needs of all partners must be addressed, requiring excellent listening skills. The process of gaining rapport does not come overnight. Rather, a discussion process is required to understand each other. Here are a few examples of topics to explore.

Urban tourism or economic entities may offer rural groups the following:

- Training;
- Distribution of promotional materials;

- Models for effective networking and referrals;
- Referrals to rural businesses;
- Museums and cultural centers offering interpretation of regional history;
- Collaborative marketing with widespread distribution;
- Conference locations for training; and
- Lodging opportunities for rural-linked itineraries.

Rural groups can link to urban areas through:
- Scenic beauty areas;
- Historic sites;
- Recreational opportunities;
- Authentic cultural experiences;
- Cultural, historic tours;
- Recreational tours;
- Ethnic foods; and
- Guide services (hunting, fishing, historic).

Urban and rural linkages can form unique vacation themes, such as historical interpretation. Yet, sometimes urban communities desire to network with surrounding rural communities and then encounter difficulties with the process of linking.

For referrals from urban areas to occur effectively, rural communities must first identify their businesses—with detailed information available in a brochure or visitor guide. The principle is basic: visitors must be able to find businesses easily to be a customer. Expenditure levels tend to be planned ahead of the visit, targeting known businesses.

Urgent situations exist, both nationally and internationally, where geographic and/or cultural survival depends upon job creation. For example, tourism projects may result in the jobs created by renovation of historic properties, conservation of fragile ecosystems, and protection of sacred places. Informed partnerships support sustainable benefits.

Decreasing Negative Impacts

The methods presented in this book come from years of experience working with communities feeling overrun by tourism, invaded by tourists, or "victimized" by tourism imposed upon them by large industry forces. These communities are heavily impacted in terms of privacy and resources, yet realize few of the positive benefits of tourism, such as jobs and increased well-being of their people. The central question to keep asking in the planning process is "Who benefits and who pays?" Shifting the benefits to an equitable urban/rural situation involves planning and development to enlarge the regional tourism income "pie" with local businesses benefitting—rather than rural communities competing for a small slice of an existing small income "pie."

There are numerous downsides to tourism that are valuable for a community to consider. Visitor preferences change as new tourism "hot spots" develop. Economic inequities then start to take hold. Movie stars buying homes or ranches in a locale, concerns over urban safety and the desire to escape stress and traffic, are a few of the reasons visitor attention shifts to rural areas.

Rural communities develop well-justified concerns about losing farm lands or escalating house prices, for visitors may be attracted by the prospect of relocating for retirement or a second home as a peaceful retreat. As Deborah McLaren warns in *Rethinking Tourism and Ecotravel*[2]—displacement, environmental degradation, and impacts on cultural values can be large. When tourism develops as a mono-industry without diversification in the local economy and on a large scale, fluctuations in the tourism market may precipitate devastating effects in a local economy.

Yes, there are dangers associated with reliance on larger-scale tourism developed from outside the community. When attractive rural landscapes are consumed for resorts, then environmental impacts, low-paying jobs, and unwanted cultural influences are among the negative consequences. Weighing the potential negative impacts from tourism against other forms of industry and other alternatives for economic activity, well planned and managed tourism tends to provide a positive source of job creation. Add cultural considerations into the process, and a development option with a good "cultural fit" is created. Reducing cultural and environmental impacts is a viable part of the process.

Why doesn't small-scale development happen more often? This is usually a question of resources. Urban areas have technical assistance and funding available through local government. Funding becomes available from local taxes plus the ability to tap federal programs through experienced and highly paid grant writers. Rural areas tend to lack these resources and the skills for funding applications. Creating the win/win regional tourism relationship expands access to available funding as well as business development to fit both rural and urban scales. Linkages between the two improve access to development resources and stabilize regional tourism.

The shift that must occur for traditional communities to benefit in regional tourism is away from the profit motive, and toward the community motive. This does not imply a lack of profits or jobs, only that profit is not the driving factor in tourism at the expense of culture, environment, and community cohesion. Small-scale development carries less financial risk. The lower the capital investment needs—and the stronger reliance on "cultural capital" as knowledge of working within the local ecosystem and with cultural skills—the greater resilience the enterprise is likely to have in economic and seasonal fluctuation. Linking regionally for collaboration strengthens the shift.

There are several ways in which a community benefits from careful planning. When community ambivalence toward tourism is resolved, alignment within the community moves tourism ahead at a pace matched to the community. Customer service is then likely to improve in a style consistent with traditional hospitality.

Creating a common vision in the tourism planning process keeps a group cohesive, and sustains momentum beyond the planning stage. Targeting specific types of visitors, determining the number of tourists appropriate for a community's capacity, delivering a quality experience, and capturing more of their dollars spent—form the basis for being proactive in tourism. The strategy of attracting fewer visitors and designing activities for the visitors' experience tends to lower negative impacts. Smaller-scale tourism carries the advantage of easier management. And repeat business translates to fewer dollars needed for marketing and better-informed guests, through the process of continued visitor education.

Feedback to Communities

Creating a feedback loop from the planning process back to the region's communities stimulates ongoing community involvement in enterprise development. New ideas and instilling incentives for training and entrepreneurial contributions are benefits of community involvement. Both regional meetings and a series of smaller focus groups for ongoing input from the different tourism sectors are beneficial—for gaining input, identifying specific businesses, strengthening partnerships, and distributing information on progress. Reporting progress back to community members helps insure the ongoing participation needed for improvement.

Cultural tourism is a particularly sensitive type of tourism. Culturally-rooted communities in rural areas, as well as urban neighborhood communities, are struggling to maintain their traditions and community identity. Initiatives to teach culture require resources. Although the cultural exposure may seem like an "interesting attraction" to those larger communities providing referrals—in actuality, small communities need real economic benefits to teach and continue their way of life, and these benefits are only achieved by referrals to specific businesses.

The difference between viewing culture as an "attraction" versus maintaining a "way of life" may become a serious cultural rub. Culture is a way of life in the viewpoint of traditional communities, not something to be used for profit. Serious tourism issues arise out of this difference in perception. Chapters later in this book address these issues and suggest how to resolve them.

Understanding such sensitivities in rural and culturally unique communities requires a realization of the wide range of impacts created when groups are considered an "interesting attraction" for referrals. Indigenous communities tend to be concerned about privacy impacts that prevent the practice of culture. Setting clear boundaries about dates for community closure reduces impacts. For example, Taos Pueblo in Northern New Mexico (USA), a UNESCO-designated World Heritage Site offering tours, closes the traditional plaza to visitors for one month during the winter to allow for private religious practice (www.taospueblo.com).

Rural Hispanic communities tend to be concerned with the problem of exposure to outsiders, who may want to buy land and "move in," pushing out traditional agrarian lifestyles. Asian communities frequently want the public to understand their contributions and the diverse cultures they represent. African-American communities want visitors to understand their interpretation of history. Both contributions and correct historical interpretation come from tourism messages expressed by cultural groups during planning and development stages.

THE POWER OF LINKING

Linkages are the most effective way to create a referral network. How to bring balance into the process? Guiding rural and traditional communities to see both their strengths and needs for improvement is a benefit to complementary linking.

PLANNING PROCESS:
Internal and External Linking

Internal Linking:

- *Who retains knowledge of your cultural arts and foods?*
- *Who in the community can tell stories and interpret local history?*
- *Where are the most appropriate places to tell your story or create exhibits?*
- *How will youth and elders become involved?*
- *Which community businesses need support to deliver services to visitors?*
- *How can entrepreneurs become involved delivering services?*

External linking:

- *See your community in relation to surrounding communities.*
- *What are your historical connections?*
- *Which businesses complement each other for a full range of visitor services?*
- *Where are business niches for providing visitor services?*
- *How does transportation support visitation alternatives?*

A first step in the planning process involves conducting an asset or resource inventory, as detailed in the next chapter. Often communities overlook their strengths. One of the most frequent ways visitors are lost to a local network is by referral to areas outside of the local community or region, due to a lack of services essential for an extended stay. While collaboration of this type is good for a region, the ideal is an overnight stay locally with expenditures in locally owned businesses, then referring the visitor on to another stay in another community within the regional network. The Neah Bay Chamber of Commerce, located at the Makah Nation in Washington, USA, is an example of tribal and non-tribal local businesses working together in a referral system. (www.neahbaywa.com).

Later chapters in this book build upon the notion of cooperation in determining visitor interests, marketing, product development, and evaluating visitor satisfaction. These expensive tasks become easier on a cost-sharing basis. Effective tourism development joins businesses and entrepreneurs together to achieve a larger concept through small-scale linking.

Another level of effective collaboration involves planning together. When communities and regions identify possible gains, anticipate negative impacts, and develop strategies for moving ahead together, the power of the draw is increased. An even greater level of collaboration occurs when a common theme is identified by a group and businesses adopt the theme. "HandMade in America" is a successful example of a non-profit organization promoting the theme of craft and culture for community and economic development (www.handmadeinamerica.org).

The immediate referral without a stay results in costs to the community, without benefits. By conducting a thorough assessment of the local tourism system and then educating visitors about local opportunities, referrals within the network strengthen local enterprises.

DEVELOPING A VACATION CONCEPT

Once complementary network strengths are understood, it is possible to develop itineraries that link together specific attractions, service businesses, and transportation to form vacation concepts. Unlike city stays, where visitors assemble their own itineraries from hundreds of choices, the rural stay requires enough activities to constitute a draw.

Determining the Effective Links

Meeting a balance of visitor interests makes the most innovative combination of links. Examine statewide and regional visitor surveys closely during the planning process as a guide to potential tourism niches. For example, understanding whether a community's visitors are more attracted to recreational opportunities or shopping is important to foster successful enterprise development.

Look for natural connections, such as historical trade routes, cultural art tours, or combinations of cultural and scenic beauty points of interest. Once these connections are identified, tapping into a combination of resources—such as economic development and arts programs for teaching, interpretation, enterprise development, and marketing—increases the long-term stability of a tourism effort. Long-term commitment to a viable idea, coupled with cultural and ecosystem restoration, correlates well with sustainability.

Connecting the Links into Itineraries

The tourism draw to an area depends upon the variety of available activities and how well they are linked. Highlighting the uniqueness of a region historically, culturally, and ecologically is possible through interpretation and informative marketing. Once a tourism resource inventory or a plan is completed according to the methods described in Chapters 3 through 6 (or by using other traditional cultural processes), then linking complementary activities, services and enterprises into appealing vacation itineraries is possible.

Visitors prefer more than one itinerary option—such as educational, shopping, and recreation-oriented visits. Multiple-day visits are encouraged with several itineraries. Effective itineraries include:

- Attractions
- Services
- Educational opportunities
- Local ecosystems
- Tours
- Driving times
- Transportation options
- A map linking offerings
- A calendar of events

Emphasizing smaller-scale businesses, such as bed and breakfast lodging and restaurants featuring local foods, creates the itinerary of greatest local benefit.

A local community is best prepared to provide accurate and fascinating interpretation. Conveyance of a message through a vacation itinerary motivates and excites the visitor for a journey to a specific location. This message is created by identifying "out-of-the ordinary" activities, unique foods, restful lodging, places of scenic beauty—and interpreting them in relation to the message. Tools for interpretation are visitor guides, brochures, and websites, or if on a low budget, a simple photocopied flier.

The vacation perceived as a struggle to find services and activities repels visitors. Either they don't return for a repeat visit or leave the region early in search of a more interesting or scenic experience. Since word-of-mouth referrals are an extremely effective way of advertising, the experiential vacation requires excellent customer service. The attraction to small-scale links, whether rural or urban, increases the visitor's ability to connect with local people and learn about local cultures or other ways of viewing the world, foods, and local history.

Sustainable Benefits

Certain cultural groups are cautious about tourism. This hesitation may be advantageous when applied to reducing privacy impacts and avoiding exploitation. However, hesitating is detrimental if a failure to engage happens. Non-participation with the tourism industry means tourism is "done upon" the community by the standards and procedures of the industry. Then, the community is reactive to what the industry sends.

A proactive stance toward tourism works in favor of community needs and desires. For example, a strong need usually exists for diversification and product development if local artists and other cultural entrepreneurs are to realize a fair chance at marketing their work. New options in contemporary art may attract young artists. By learning the visitor profile and visitor interests from tourism data, the basis for a community to develop services and new products to sell becomes understood. In other words, an equitable exchange requires internal support to survive.

Benefits to communities attracting both cultural and ecotourists are likely to be increased respect, appreciation of the educational experience, and involvement or support beyond the visit. These two tourism market segments tend to be conscious of the visitation "travel ethic,"[3] whereby visitors are expected to adapt standards of behavior which respect the cultural and natural surroundings. Essentials to sustainability in tourism are: 1) deciding proactively upon the desired market, 2) attracting the market, and 3) managing visitors in a way that reduces negative impacts. Rather than feeling inconvenienced by regulations, visitors usually feel at ease when they understand the cultural boundaries.

One challenge to sustainable tourism is physically managing large numbers of tourists while providing a good interpretive experience. Quality visitation experiences involving sharing and reciprocation increase the guest appreciation of local cultures. In turn, visitors are likely to be respectful of natural resources, purchase more, and donate to local programs.

As a largely untapped benefit of tourism, donations are part of reciprocating. Culturally oriented programs such as training in the cultural arts may be supported by donations from visitors. Yet, a donation program to support these needs must be carefully structured, with recipient projects clearly designated and a tax exempt status provided in the form visitors are accustomed to when donating. For some visitors, contributing and knowing they are making a difference is part of the satisfaction gained in visitation.

TOURISM AND ECONOMIC DEVELOPMENT

There is a basic distinction between business development and economic development—one that is repeatedly misunderstood. Business development is specific to individual enterprises. Business planning, capital, employee training, and marketing are all components of business development—which in turn contributes to a local economy.

What is termed "economic development" refers to a whole system of interconnected businesses, entrepreneurs, and traditional economic activity. If considered in a holistic perspective, all resources, including natural and environmental, are addressed. When a development project is envisioned as a hub, or connecting a broad range of rural and culturally diverse communities, the economic impacts will be far reaching.

A community's internal economy will benefit from the interest generated by entrepreneurial participation, and a broader range of fascinating, handmade or locally grown goods for sale. Cultural traditions are then strengthened. For rural and traditional communities, economic development cannot be quantified in dollars alone.

In small-scale local economies, true economic development only occurs when specific factors work in unison: as economic multipliers increase; as leakages to the outside economy are reduced; as traditional items are produced; as traditional bartering and subsistence systems supplement cash income (thus reducing dependency on full-time employment); and as cottage industries flourish and support extended family units. This scenario contrasts sharply with large-scale business development focused entirely on profit margins and the number of jobs created.

True economic development takes a great deal more time and effort than larger-scale business development. A solid yet flexible foundation is created through expertise expanding in local communities and diversification of the economic system. In other words, internal strengths or capacity of a community develop over time, and dependency on external development and management expertise is minimized.

Entrepreneurial Niches

The starting place for understanding the regional tourism system is to assess the offerings, gaps in services, and niches for potential development in a region. Without a complete range of services and activities in a regional tourism system, the visitor draw will be weak and the stay short.

Understanding the regional tourism system builds a foundation for assessing niches appropriate for new development. Does the existing tourism system represent a good balance of services and attractions? Or, are services missing, causing visitors to leave at critical points in the day or to leave dissatisfied? If individually owned businesses complement non-profit and government services, a solid foundation is created for future tourism development.

Businesses that complement each other within a region form a strong economic system. An effective planning process asks participants to look at both the economy of the region and their local economy. This analysis identifies the gaps, called "business niches." The hub concept for development—or a primary visitor intake point providing referrals to small-scale businesses—encourages local residents to see the niches available for entrepreneurship and to develop small businesses providing services and products.

Models for assessing impacts point to the importance of identifying community-preferred business forms as well as addressing unacceptable forms and limits. Some appropriate limits concerning the commercialization of culture as defined by Jennifer Craik,[4] necessary for a community to consider, are:

- Impacts on arts production and cultural development;
- Characteristics of the souvenir industry;
- Character and performance of cultural tourism initiatives;
- Acceptability of new cultural activities and products;
- Creation and featuring of heritage sites and attractions;
- Indicators of cultural pride;
- Indicators of cultural stimulation (e.g., cultural arts); and
- Changing educational and skill profile of the community.

Considering value-added in a culturally appropriate way, such as information or packaging local foods and products, expands opportunity. For example, assembling gift packs of local foods with a food history, recipes, and eating bowls or a handmade placemat, creates a unique product and supports several entrepreneurs. **Value chains** occur when products pass through activities of a chain in order, and at each activity the product gains some value. When based upon traditional economic lines of distribution, this is important for sales benefitting many entrepreneurs in the chain.

In Chart 2.2, an example of linking within a Native American (USA) community is illustrated. Entrepreneurial niches perceived on a regional level lead to a unified vacation concept. Linking for referrals is fundamental to economic development and builds a stronger attraction for business to a region as a whole.

Chart 2.2 TRIBAL ECONOMY NETWORK

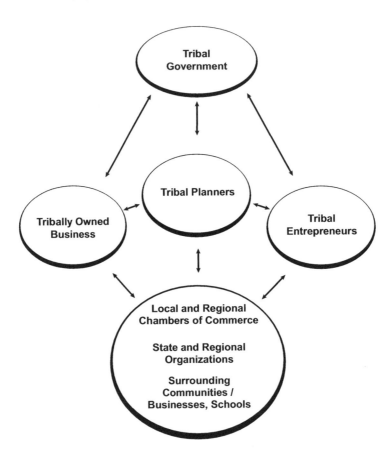

INCREASING ECONOMIC MULTIPLIERS

Small communities lacking a broad range of services experience a high level of economic leakages outside of their local economy. Economic leakages occur when dollars are spent outside of local economies due to the lack of services within a region. An economic multiplier is the number of times a dollar is recirculated in a local economy. When leakages occur, the economic multiplier is small. The higher an economic multiplier, the stronger the economic base within a small economy. Regional linkages providing referrals increase a multiplier effect.

There are two markets to consider in tourism, the internal community and those outside of the community or region. Tourism may bring a large enough supplemental market to a small community to justify basic services such as gas stations, convenience stores, laundromats, grocery stores, and clothing stores. Combining external and internal markets therefore brings increased benefits to a community. Additionally, service-oriented businesses tend to generate the highest multiplier effects from tourism.

> ***Visitor purchases plus local purchases hold the potential of a sustainable market for an enterprise.***

Frequently, rural communities do not realize what treasures their local culture and local economy are in the visitor's eye. These are a part of local everyday life. Yet, a satisfying experience to the visitor is the everyday, the authentic. Assistance from outside of the community may be useful in pinpointing these unique local strengths.

As an example, bed and breakfast lodging operations offer potential for the rural farm house or empty nest family. Staying with a family gives personal connection to the area, an opportunity for local interpretation and guidance to other links in the tourism network. Farm stays present fascinating experiences for travelers, and hold the potential for generating enough additional income to sustain the farm. Whether information about the farm or a u-pick-em experience is provided, "value-added" is perceived with the lodging experience. Link farm stays, and a fascinating itinerary is created. In Europe, considerable governmental assistance to farm stays has resulted in less farm land lost to development, in addition to a linked referral system.

Diversification is the key to creating economic multipliers. Balancing larger-scale with small-scale industries creates additional employment niches and encourages small supplier enterprises for larger businesses. Additionally, developing opportunities for cultural entrepreneurs works well with cooperative and extended family-based cultural values. For these reasons, it is beneficial to encourage a complementary approach to economic development. When all businesses in a region see themselves working toward a common tourism goal, a linkage is formed to encourage cooperation for other community needs. The creation of a cohesive community or region may become a long-term economic development outcome.

ORGANIZING FOR EFFECTIVE TOURISM

In summary, regional-level cooperation is a vital ingredient for small-scale and locally owned tourism. A regional- or local-level organization or committee is valuable for coordinating: 1) planning, 2) implementation of projects, 3) interface with the tourism industry, 4) creation of promotional pieces or websites, and 5) evaluation of impacts and redirection—all in an interrelated process. In particular, ecosystem impacts, infrastructure, transportation, and related businesses are easier to view comprehensively within the regional context.

Structuring for Success

Collaboration, either through informal meetings or by forming a tourism association, unifies a voice to be heard and included in decision making. Regional, state and national level organizations supporting economic efforts desire to link with rural areas, yet may express frustration in trying to connect with individual businesses and entrepreneurs. To be effective and link for a unified concept, these larger groups need to connect within a common direction and organize communication channels with specific information on businesses and entrepreneurs. Increased cultural understanding is an outcome of network relationships.

A strong factor in community success is linking to the industry. Structuring within the community or region to address the larger picture of tourism development and community needs, rather than business development only, is essential for increasing economic multipliers. Small-scale management, empowering and coordinating small groups, produces additional jobs for local people. When the value of cooperation is perceived—then strengthening internal capacity through sharing experience and skills becomes a culturally-based economic development goal.

Bringing together the arts, culture, and tourism entities of a region to discuss culturally and environmentally appropriate development has far-reaching implications. By addressing projected national trends and designing strategies to link to these trends, a community or region of communities may enhance a niche in cultural tourism. Alignment is also created in the planning process to support community artistic and cultural needs, while maximizing tourism gain and protective measures.

Essential to long-term viability is constancy of effort. As leadership changes in communities, successful ideas are sometimes dropped. This pattern constitutes a frequent waste of local resources. Long-term commitment to viable ideas with a good cultural fit emerges by forming a committee to continue efforts.

Benefits of Planning

In summary, achieving an approach tailored to individual communities increases receptivity to tourism, sets boundaries for tourism, and inspires the community to proceed. Planning enables participants to see the positive aspects of their community, ways of protecting what is treasured, and the potential for determining who will visit and how they will be educated to respect the community. The next chapter guides the analysis of a tourism system—to recognize local assets, identify the missing parts, and develop the basics for an outstanding visitor experience.

Sustainable development is local, within a regional context. Listening to the community vision, and proceeding realistically, start with small scale projects and effective linked networks.

COMMUNITY-BASED SOLUTION
Restoring a Traditional Welcoming, Makah Nation,
Neah Bay, Washington (USA)

The Makah Nation is a traditional Native American fishing village, maintaining a lifestyle closely tied to land, sea and the arts. The Tribe is known for wood carvings and finely woven basketry, as well as shell and silver jewelry. Tourism provides the majority of tribal members' livelihood through fishing and recreational tours, art galleries, commercial fishing, lodging, and food service.

The Makah Cultural and Research Center began in 1979, to house and curate an archaeological collection from the village of Ozette. Cultural items were preserved when the contents of four houses (55,000 artifacts) buried by a mudslide in the late prehistoric period of the Makah people (300-500 years ago) were excavated. Artifacts from the Ozette site helped re-establish the Makah's treaty rights by providing evidence of the Tribe's historic reliance upon whaling and fishing for sustenance. Ozette is regarded as a gift from the past and an invaluable opportunity to fully utilize the collection to study culture and revitalize traditions.

Today the center is presenting a "living museum" concept, emphasizing direct contact with tribal members and their cultural arts, storytelling, demonstrations, and exhibits of student artwork. Language preservation efforts include classes and activities immersing youth in Native language and culture.

A traditional welcoming was recently restored in the community through the completion of two 14-foot carved welcome figures located on the main road into the village at the Makah Cultural and Research Center. Carver Greg Colfax interprets this renewed tradition: "Long ago, welcome figures were put up by chiefs to welcome guests to their village, to their houses, and to their potlatches. Some of the figures represented humans, some represented ancestors, and some represented the mythical origins of their family. In this case, they are welcoming guests to the village. The man and woman represent the husbands and wives of this village, welcoming guests to our territory." Symbolic designs on the carved figures tell cultural stories.

Success factors in Makah tourism include two intake points for visitors (a museum and a visitor center), cultural arts teaching programs, a strong language teaching program, a tour program and implementation of a recreational permit which generates financial support to the tribe. The Neah Bay Chamber of Commerce offers promotion to entrepreneurial businesses regionally and coordination with tribal government. (www.makah.com)

FURTHER READING

Chambers, Robert. *Rural Development: Putting the Last First*. London, UK: Longman, 1983.

> Perceptions of rural poverty are often misinterpreted due to the gaps between outsiders and those inside the culture. This text addresses methods for outsiders to learn, useful surveys, a new professionalism, and techniques for practical action such as research and development leading to transfer policies.

Hall, Derek, Lesley Roberts and Morag Mitchell, editors. *New Directions in Rural Tourism*. Aldershot, UK: Ashgate Publishing Limited, 2005.

> Tourism, as a potential element of development and regeneration, requires new strategic thinking to achieve sustainability and niche marketing. The interrelationship between local and global issues is illustrated with case studies from several countries.

Mason, Peter. *Tourism Impacts, Planning and Management.* Oxford, UK: Elsevier, 2008.

Much of tourism planning and management takes place in relation to tourism impacts. Economic, socio-cultural, and environmental impacts are considered with a focus on education, the role of interpretation, and sustainability.

Spenceley, Anna. *Responsible Tourism: Critical Issues for Conservation and Development.* London, UK: Earthscan, 2008.

Policies and institutional activities are considered in relation to responsible nature-based tourism, economics of wildlife tourism and ecotourism, and the ecological impacts of tourism in relation to South African examples.

Wurzburger, Rebecca, Tom Aageson, Alex Pattakos and Sabrina Pratt, editors. *Creative Tourism: A Global Conversation. Santa Fe, NM*: Sunstone Press, 2010.

Creative tourism offers visitors the opportunity to develop artistic potential through active participation and is one of the fastest growing trends in the global tourism market. Issues and sustainability factors are addressed with global examples from New Zealand, Spain, France, Canada, Egypt, Scotland, Italy, China, and the United States.

3
BEGINNING THE PLANNING PROCESS

Moving forward with an eye to the past reflects the wisdom of time-honored traditions.

The skills of listening, assessing and discussing create a solid path for small-scale tourism. Throughout the planning process, the challenge is bridging from community expression to cultural interpretation—without becoming lost or overwhelmed with the details of assessment. Arriving at a unique experiential concept representing a culture is not an easy task, but one that requires careful attention to cultural views, hesitations, and boundaries for sharing.

Before generating ideas for new tourism projects, a first step is to identify existing activities, amenities and services. This is the community participation stage of the planning process. Gaining a thorough understanding of the current local tourism system is the first, and often overlooked, phase for community-based tourism.

Planning is a means of designing strategies to maximize the benefits of moving forward, while protecting resources. An inclusive planning process is central to identifying needs as well as opportunities, shaping future tourism programs and initiatives. Designing strategies for expanding the potential from tourism—cultural, artistic and financial—while protecting a community's identity and historical resources, is essential to the planning process.

> **Framework for Integrating Culture**
>
> - Recognize traditional planning processes used in the culture.
> - Start with cultural values.
> - Base the gathering of community input on traditional, cultural ways of involving community.
> - Identify resources and economic forms currently working well.
> - Assess concerns and solutions from within the community.
> - Gain intergenerational participation.
> - Develop a vision consistent with cultural values.

When the scale of tourism is too large or resources are not adequate, the usual causes are a lack of participation and assessment at the planning stage. The foundation for culturally appropriate participation is created from the collective background, cumulative experience, and families participating together.

A valuable question concerns: "Which comes first, assessing community views or completing a resource inventory?" The order of the steps recommended in this chapter is not always a set sequence. For example, assessing resources before beginning the participation phase leads to a better-informed set of questions to ask. Even when the planning comes entirely from within a community, not all community resources may be readily perceived at the beginning.

Failure to assess resources leads to two types of misperception. The first misses potential by not realizing all resources, such as natural beauty or local skills. Lack of forward movement from a belief in a deficiency of resources is the likely outcome.

The second misperception over-estimates readiness by not assessing and not seeing the gaps in services or experienced personnel, resulting in projects too large for the community's management capacity. This misperception also results in a lack of forward movement due to an inappropriate scale match to available resources in the community.

Frequently, the community is not aware of what exists locally and may suggest duplicate services and businesses. Or, the community may not be able to see the potential for existing businesses and amenities. Planning as a process creates awareness of what exists and generates community enthusiasm for moving forward.

PLANNING AS A PROCESS

Where to start? A possible initial question asks: "What are time-honored traditions for planning in your community?" Another is: "Which cultural values guide community involvement, earned livelihood, and respect of nature?"

Viewing planning as a process, the role of the planner is to listen, to ask questions, to listen again, and then to provide guidance. As the community shapes a direction and a pace suitable to culture and resources, desired outcomes become a reality. The ongoing participative process provides encouragement, points out progress within a culture's own terms, and assists in securing resources, bringing community involvement along.

A value-based approach to planning and data collection: 1) sets a consistent direction for tourism, 2) is inclusive of resource conservation, 3) interfaces with other economic development initiatives, and 4) builds alliances and linkages for tourism development. Once internal directions are known and clearly expressed, communication external to the community is likely to be effective.

The term ***stakeholder***, used extensively in planning, refers to groups with a concern in the outcomes. Creating a tourism committee with representation from stakeholders participating in tourism—local government, enterprises, artists, entrepreneurs, and all age groups including elders and youth—guides the process through planning to implementation. Monthly meetings are advised, to keep involvement steady.

As a planner, I always take time to listen to community members who are opposed to tourism. These people care about environment, culture, and possible strains on community resources. They want to be heard and their concerns may be translated into strategies to prevent negative impacts. This group tends to be clear about the type of visitor they don't want and cultural boundaries for sharing information.

Although a plan on paper may not be part of a traditional process, a written document supports a tourism team working together, and is valuable for communicating with tourism partners. Those optimistic about tourism see potential positive benefits. This group is the most productive for generating business ideas and discovering ways of linking, both within a community and to other communities. A clear vision of desirable markets, such as heritage, recreational, or ecotourists, then emerges. Once a guiding committee is formed, following the steps in this chapter will lay a valuable foundation before project ideas are solidly formed. Enthusiasm generated by such a group moves projects forward.

Chart 3.1 CAPACITY-BUILDING FOR TOURISM

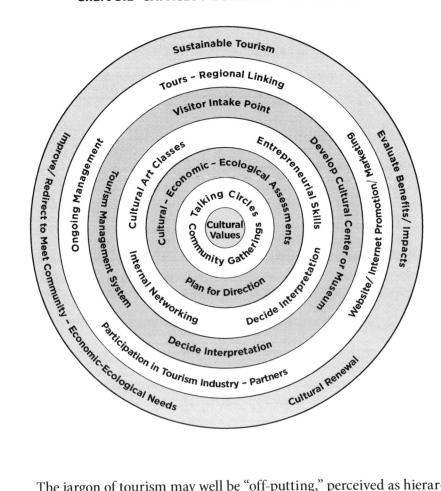

The jargon of tourism may well be "off-putting," perceived as hierarchical in orientation. Caution should be heeded with terminology used. Only through careful thought in the planning process will community decisions be reached regarding which aspects of culture are appropriate to share with the public, which aspects should not be shared to avoid exploitation of culture, as well as those "gray" areas that might be appropriate if visitor education increases respect for local culture. Issues of cultural relevance and respect are valuable to communicate to the tourism industry and urban partners. Solving these furthers cultural understanding.

With that caution stated, this chapter will use the term "asset" carefully. A local word may exist that is more appropriate than the term "asset."By identifying and listing offerings or resources, a community is in a better position for careful consideration of both negative and positive impacts that tourism might bring. In Indigenous cultures, sacredness is associated with plants, animals, and places. These relationships are particularly sensitive—and discussion with other cultures is sometimes prohibited. Conversations may need to be private, from within the culture, and not recorded on paper to retain privacy.

One positive outcome of an inward and extensive planning process is what might be termed "community esteem," sensing internal capability or the ability to move forward. A frequent comment after a resource inventory is "I didn't know we had all of this." Perception is as important for protection as it is for utilizing local resources. Scenic beauty is often taken for granted in the everyday setting. As community awareness of local offerings is heightened, needed protections as well as possible forward actions are easier to see. And sometimes this awareness brings a decision to not participate in tourism, or to participate away from the community.

A community feeling confident can move forward.

A culturally-based data gathering and assessment stage is central for understanding the challenges in moving forward and the needed improvements. Addressing these challenges with adequate community input builds a strong foundation for tourism and serves as a watchful guide for identifying community preferences.

As mentioned earlier, traditional communities sometimes feel more comfortable in their discussions about tourism if they speak with other communities similar in size, culture, or regional location. Comparing opportunities, challenges that arise, and solutions to those challenges, increases confidence to proceed. A solid community-based foundation for tourism is useful to set a target for the appropriate number of tourists the community is able to host per year, the type of tourism, and return desired.

ASSESSING COMMUNITY VIEWS AND CONCERNS

Development usually implies change, either forward movement or recovering economic forms that worked well in the past. Traditional communities—such as rural, tribal, and ethnically distinct urban neighborhoods—frequently are wary of change, with good reasons. Sustainable development respects tradition, land and animals, sets an appropriate pace, and listens to desired directions. A gradual process is valuable for resolving community ambivalence.

Explaining an assessment to the community initiates a dialogue for awareness of valuable cultural and environmental resources to protect. Significant questions then emerge. Where should tourism be located? What are the acceptable boundaries or restrictions to tourism? How will community privacy best be protected? What kinds of jobs do community members want? Answering these questions leads to a focused approach to tourism.

Physical impacts are essential to assess. How many visitors can a community's infrastructure (water, sewer, environmentally sensitive areas) sustain? Land use planning and environmental impact studies are tools for considering the extent of tourism regarded as sustainable and ways of containing visitors—or managing away from ecological and culturally sensitive areas.

The land use plan assesses the physical qualities or characteristics of land, evaluates demographics, and defines use needs, including acreage and location. Topics often included are: population, agriculture, archaeological and cultural sites, boundaries, buildings, fishing, flood control, forests, lakes, rivers, timber, historic sites, housing, irrigation ditches, landscaping, land status, minerals, roads, sacred sites, sewage lines, sewage treatment, soils, topographic data, traditional use areas, vegetation, water lines, water rights, water supply, and water quality.

If these prior studies have been completed for a community, it is possible to summarize the resources and limitations during the community discussion. Then, a basis is formed for both the potential of development-appropriate areas and those that require protection. Not disrupting traditional land use patterns supports sustainability. Maintaining a sense of place, both historically and ecologically, is central to community well-being.

Agreement on direction is an aligning point for community involvement in sustainable development. Restricting or focusing tourism in a specific geographic location protects both environment and resident privacy. When a community perceives tourism as an intrusion, visitors sense this discomfort and are, in turn, less satisfied. A favorable community attitude underlies successful tourism.

Diversified levels of business development are a key factor in community satisfaction. A frequent source of friction within a community occurs when local government planning addresses only larger-scale enterprises. A more diversified approach is inclusive of individual entrepreneurs and small businesses as well as larger businesses. Including the smaller-scale of service and supplier businesses strengthens a tourism system from within, creates jobs, and increases economic multipliers. When businesses of different scales work together within a tourism system, the visitor experience becomes cohesive.

LISTENING AND TALKING CIRCLES

Listening to cultural concerns and needs is an opportunity to observe patterns and connections. For some cultures, a meeting may look more like a "gathering," with discussion in a circle. For many egalitarian cultures, a respectful meeting allows time for everyone present to speak. Multi-generational participation encourages a wide range of perspectives, and discussion at several intervals "fine tunes" the process.

> *Listening skills are central for perceiving opinion and understanding desired directions.*

In the initial phase of cultural tourism, qualitative methods are valuable for addressing retention and restoration, before growth and commercialization. My last book, *Planning for Balanced Development*, explains methods for conducting interviews and surveys. In addition to surveys and needs assessments, community opinion about desired directions is gathered through public meetings or gatherings.

Meetings may take different forms cross-culturally and the appropriate form is crucial to determine before scheduling. For example, in mainstream planning practice, meetings involve a set agenda and procedures to numerically quantify opinion. In many rural and Indigenous cultures, meetings involve getting together informally or formally, to build consensus.

Using the wrong match between method and culture usually results in a lack of the participation-building necessary to later carry out projects. Or, even worse, use of the wrong method could alienate the entire community or segments of the community. For this reason, it is important to take time with leaders in the community to determine the most effective way of eliciting opinion.

Proceeding with cultural sensitivity and interaction through the planning process—including all groups or stakeholders in the community—is well worth the investment of time. True community involvement allows the time for thorough internal community considerations. Giving the space for discussions that need to occur privately weaves the tapestry of cultural richness and strengths.

In traditional communities, the interrelationships between ideas are complex and difficult to record. Drawings rather than long bulleted lists may be more effective, since interrelationships are more easily seen visually, by connecting ideas. Circles showing process and continuity are often preferred in traditional communities.

Gathering Community Input

Size of the community sometimes determines which methods will work and appropriate combinations of methods to gather community input on needs and desired directions. These are useful individually, or in multiple approaches:

- Informal discussion;
- Community meeting/gathering;
- Focus groups interested in a topic;
- Interviews;
- Surveys conducted at meetings, in households, and businesses;
- A survey within another community survey, such as economic development; or
- Periodic feedback discussions.

If a number of surveys and studies have been already conducted in the community, planning sessions will be enhanced by summarizing results. This leads to depth in the discussion of potential strategies and solutions, by avoiding repetition. Traditional methods of gathering community input, such as storytelling, are important to include in the process—these stories reflect long-term, multi-generational concerns of the culture.

A community survey complements talking circles, community meetings and small group discussions. Assessment of local skills may be addressed in the community survey. The sample community survey presented in the next chapter is useful either at a community gathering or as an interview format.

Choosing the most effective set of data-gathering techniques requires understanding the community as well as existing tourism resources. Taking the extra effort to go to several locations within a community or a region is valuable for securing the best range of opinion. Depending on whether the culture is individualist versus consensual in decision making, this stage of community input may take several months. Consider this effort as time well invested. Thorough community input saves years in the long run by preventing stalled projects, either from lack of community agreement or availability of adequate resources.

The most effective approach of the technical assistance provider or facilitator within the community is to ask questions. After everyone has a chance to speak, state "This is what I heard, ____." And then, "Is that what you meant?" Fine-tuning the input is essential and creates rapport with community members.

A collaborative method may identify alternative scenarios. To the greatest extent that a community perceives the possibility of multiple outcomes, there will be less hesitation to generate ideas for options. In-depth questions come from an understanding of the culture and rapport with the community.

Holding the Community Meeting

Community meetings are an effective way of gathering input, for people respond well to the sense of being heard. Because of this personal involvement factor, surveys alone rarely contribute to consensus building. And in a culture with consensus-based decision making, gatherings are the way.

Starting with an identification of community and cultural values reassures community members of a planning process tailored to their needs and capabilities. Where meetings are held is another factor for good attendance. Community and cultural centers, rather than government offices, tend to be inviting. Ethnically distinct groups are sometimes best reached through church locations and small neighborhood meetings.

Attention to cultural traditions or protocols increases participation. For example, providing food is a supportive aspect of the meeting tradition in numerous cultures. Meetings may be perceived as "cold" or not supportive without this basic amenity.

To create a process of discussion and feedback, several methods may be used in combination:

- One or more smaller talking circle sessions are useful for identifying concerns, issues, and possible benefits from tourism involvement.

- One larger participation session is necessary to attract the community-at-large. Results of the initial discussions, presented to follow cultural protocols, are a respectful part of the process and focus the larger discussion. A community visioning session held in a venue significant to culturally-based tourism increases receptivity. Presenting examples to emphasize regional approaches to tourism and interpretation, as well as win/win situations created in other locales by similar cultures, heightens community confidence.

- If the results of a larger gathering are followed up in additional, detailed community sessions, specific issues can then be explored in depth. This is a good way to obtain substantive feedback on the issues. Continual feedback to the community after each step encourages continued participation.

- Small focus group sessions, designed to sample different cultural points of view and culturally diverse organizations, encourage individuals to speak more openly than in a large group and focus the conversation on specific issues.

- Interviews with local or local government officials and additional sessions with neighborhood groups identify resources and connect with larger regional efforts.

- A balance of qualitative methods for listening and exchange includes qualitative data, essential to interpret the quantitative or numerical data collected for surveys and marketing efforts.

One successful approach is to hold a larger venue meeting at a community or cultural center plus several smaller, focused meetings. Inviting all interested groups or stakeholders to the larger meeting furthers the ideal synergy that occurs when different groups interact. However, it is my experience that many culturally-rooted communities do not attend these meetings unless the communication is that local planners and governments will be truly listening and direct benefits will be coming.

Also, those who do come to large meetings outside of the community sometimes are not the primary stakeholders who make decisions. Lack of forward movement then results.

These are a few pointers for organizing an effective meeting.

- Announce the meeting at least two weeks in advance, and then again a few days before the meeting as a reminder.
- Use methods appropriate to all age groups in the community—such as newspaper ads, fliers to households, internet messages, and word-of-mouth.
- Keep the meeting at a predetermined time length, unless the group indicates a flexible duration.
- Schedule meetings for a balance of timing to fit community needs for inclusion, e.g., evening, afternoon, weekend.
- Observe local protocols for persons speaking first—this tends to be a political leader, a religious leader, or an elder. A prayer is sometimes the protocol for opening a meeting.
- Prepare a summary of meeting results and distribute the main points at the next meeting or in the local newspaper or newsletter, keeping the feedback loop ongoing.
- To encourage sustained participation, distribute information about the planning steps ahead, community benefits and concerns—use the local newspaper, radio station, or community newsletter, if making information public is culturally acceptable.

- Serve food, generously.
- Provide child care.
- Encourage intergenerational involvement.

> *Gaining participation requires knowing what factors inspire a gathering in a particular community.*

In rural areas, the newspaper is often a weekly and may only be effective for the advance notice. Small community, organizational, and tribal newsletters may be monthly.

INTERGENERATIONAL INVOLVEMENT

In culturally traditional communities, involving elders is not only respectful, but also insightful. Elders recognize the possible negative impacts from tourism and bring cultural factors to the forefront of the discussion. Elders' perceptions of impacts into the future pertain to sustainability and are based on knowledge of the past, efforts tried and succeeded, as well as those that failed. Keep in mind the pace of discussion appropriate for elders, allocating time to listen to historical examples, potential difficulties with tourism, and positive ideas.

Elders tend to bring culturally specific participation and planning processes into view, when encouraged to speak. Particularly if elders gain the sense of being heard, they are likely to come forward.

Include youth, for they are imaginative and without limits on new ideas. Additionally, youth will be the generation to perpetuate desired projects to be pursued after the planning. Working in an educational setting or after-school programs is a way of involving younger generations.

Youth involvement in the course of planning may lead to fun project ideas for teaching responsibility, arts, food preparation, and other skills. For example, some traditional communities are developing business clubs for high-school youth, with field trips to outside locations, such as markets, festivals, Native American pow-wows, and museum shows. These groups teach cultural appropriateness of selling and entrepreneurial skills at a young age, in preparation for later employment, or as a part of a family business. Youth will participate if they sense respect for their input.

FROM MEETING TO ONGOING PARTICIPATION

Successful data gathering from meetings includes these factors:

> **Attendance:** Although a minimum of twenty to twenty-five people is desirable for a small community, the quality of participation may be more meaningful than numbers. Attendance may increase for subsequent meetings, if meeting results are distributed (through a summary or word-of-mouth) and demonstrate progress on issues considered important to the community.

> **Representation:** Geographic differences, age groups, and ethnic groups represent different points of view. Also invite businesses, local government, and federal or state agencies surrounding urban or rural areas—to include a range of tourism partners. Focus group meetings are useful for gaining in-depth information from stakeholders who represent different points of view or hold specific knowledge of the tourism-related subject.

> **Full participation:** More than one meeting may be needed to include adequate representation, to inform on issues, and to allow enough time for community member input. Always allow enough time at the beginning of the meeting for a summary of the last meeting or meetings, to bring new attendees up-to-date on the progress.

> **Follow-up:** Continue with feedback and development. Gaps in the planning process lend a sense of "not enough result" for the time invested in meeting attendance. Giving priority to a pressing issue, such as cultural preservation or environmental impacts, tends to increase continued participation. Setting a schedule for meetings and focus group sessions in advance gives community members options for attendance and the feeling of momentum.

> **Deliver immediate benefits to the community:** Visible benefits will encourage participants to "stick with the planning process," even in the early stages. Examples are postings for businesses and entrepreneurs on websites, inclusion in regional guides, creating a local visitor guide, an artist database, a business directory or guide, or a brochure. Explaining these coming

benefits during the initial phase will increase participation. "Giving back" intermediate results to the community encourages ongoing involvement.

OUTLINE FOR TOURISM PLAN

An outline for the tourism plan sensitive to cultural concerns could include the following topics:

    Executive Summary
- I. Introduction
- II. Location / Regional Network Concept
- III. Community / Culture/ Values
- IV. Community Profile/ Assessments
- V. The Tourism System
- VI. Key Issues
- VII. Tourism Readiness
- VIII. Tourism Goals and Objectives
- IX. Market Overview and Trends
- X. Strategies to Capture Market Share
- XI. Needed Promotion
- XII. Partnership Opportunities
- XIII. Developing Working Relationships with Tourism Partners
- XIV. Product Development
- XV. The Transportation System
- XVI. Potential Environmental and Access Impacts / Protections
- XVII. Funding Opportunities—Sources Leveraging
- XVIII. Personnel Scenarios for Managing Tourism
- XIX. Recommended Phases, Steps and Development Timelines
- XX. Tourism Program Operating Budget

    Conclusion

A thorough analysis of the tourism system looks at both regional and local levels, with a community assessment seen within the context of the regional network. The outline above includes both levels.

EXPLORING KEY ISSUES

Key issues or concerns are identified in the beginning of the planning process. Addressing these concerns helps build support within the community and is useful in preventing unwanted negative impacts. Identifying key issues surrounding the sharing of culture is often the pivotal point for moving ahead with cultural tourism.

Privacy and historical accuracy are likely to be important issues in the design of cultural tourism. Particularly if a visitor or cultural center is seen as a hub for cultural group activity, interpretive exhibits and referrals to communities—these issues need to be addressed. Setting cultural boundaries, such as which audience is allowed for specific topics, is frequently an outcome of defining key issues in traditional communities. These issues, briefly mentioned earlier, are summarized with solutions.

> **What are the stories different cultural groups want to tell?** Stories interpret local views for cross-cultural understanding. Telling cultural stories appropriate for the public to hear, or only in the restricted season for the type of story, enhances the authentic experience. Eliciting community opinion on those stories and points of interpretation will be central to public meetings and interviews.

> **How will historical accuracy be furthered?** Cultural groups are often frustrated with the lack of accuracy in publications, exhibits and public events. Interpretive materials are important for a community telling the story from a local viewpoint—or even more interesting, from multiple viewpoints.

> **How will cultural privacy be protected?** The comfort level with tourism is highly related to maintaining necessary levels of privacy for internal, protected information. For example, neighborhoods and cultural groups in the Southwestern United States voice their dissatisfaction with the invasion of privacy to practice culture, the loss of historical significance to areas, and with culturally invasive questions asked by tourists. Learning about issues and suggested solutions is a way of designing educational materials for tourism that encourage culturally sensitive visitation.

- **How will increased income be generated from tourism and jobs created, without necessarily increasing the numbers of tourists?** Providing in-depth educational experiences is one way of increasing per-tourist expenditure. Extending visitor length-of-stay is another variable for increasing expenditures, if the community has both the capacity and the desire for visitors to stay overnight. Repeat visitation resulting from an educational experience and friendly customer service are others.

- **What is the community's capacity for tourism and tourism management?** Planning must address capacity related to infrastructure, such as water, sewage, and solid waste, as well as management capability. Negative impacts from tourism occur most frequently when capacity does not match the scale of tourism development.

- **How are multipliers from tourism dollars created?** Identifying and preventing leakages, such as the purchase of imported goods for sale (rather than locally made), increases the multipliers resulting from tourism. When local producers and suppliers are given first preference, additional jobs are created and the profits from sales stay within the local economy—creating a greater multiplier effect. Entrepreneurs providing lodging, food production, food service, as well as the art and culture sectors, then benefit.

- **How will urban/rural linkages be enhanced?** Steps involved in planning create networks, itineraries, and supply sources. Linking local resources with statewide and national tourism organizations and initiatives is another way of enhancing the development and promotion of these linkages.

When these key issues are explored during public participation for relevancy, ongoing involvement is encouraged. In Chapter 6, which covers steps to complete the tourism plan, tourism issues are illustrated in relation to goals and work plans.

ANALYZING THE TOURISM SYSTEM

While this section may sound straightforward, most communities never take the basic step of assessing their resources or "assets." Knowing what exists is the starting place for building upon strengths and improving existing services or activities. Authentic interests in the eye of the outsider are regarded as a part of everyday life and frequently are not recognized by the community. By assessing offerings, gaps in services, and niches for potential development—interrelatedness and cooperation among the elements of a tourism system become evident.

The Resource Inventory

The tourism system framework—including attractions, activities, services, transportation, information, and promotion—builds a foundation for assessing niches appropriate for new development. Additionally, specific topics that work cross-culturally are suggested by Jana Prewitt in the *Tribal Tourism Toolkit*.[1] Resources to look for in a community's service system, with cultural considerations added, include the following.

ATTRACTIONS AND ACTIVITIES

Cultural and Heritage: museums, cultural centers, public exhibits, performing art centers, artists, entrepreneurs, storytellers, demonstrators, speakers, cultural art galleries, historic sites and buildings, historic churches, missions, books, DVDs, entertainment, outdoor and indoor markets, and archaeological sites (if access allowed).

Events: festivals, pow-wows, art shows, seasonal celebrations, feast days (with restrictions), animal honorings, plays, parades, concerts, historical re-enactments, sports events, and traditional running.

Natural areas: geographic features, rivers, lakes, waterfalls, parks, islands, scenic landscapes, fisheries, nature reserves or sanctuaries, mountains, boundaries, and monuments.

Recreation: fishing, canoeing, kayaking, swimming, horseback riding, golf, casinos, boating, bird watching, bicycling, hiking trails, hunting, games, skiing, playgrounds, and gardens.

SERVICES

Welcome centers, guided tours, shopping, traditional or regional foods, gas stations, auto repair, lodging (hotels, motels, bed and breakfasts), camping, spas and resorts, snack bars, infrastructure (water, restrooms), sewer, safety, emergency, health services, roads and electricity.

TRANSPORTATION

Airlines, car rentals, bus lines, ferries, shuttles, tramways, bicycle rentals, and boat rentals.

INFORMATION

Visitor centers, cultural committees, tourism staff, tour guides, artists, entrepreneurs, business owners, grant writers, event organizers, craftspeople, demonstrators, singers, dancers, and fundraisers.

PROMOTION

Websites, visitor guides, vacation planners, brochures, rack cards, travel magazines, recreational guides, referral companies, Chambers of Commerce, Convention and Visitor Bureaus, web designers, feature writers, and related social media.

Interdependence between the elements of a tourism system is central to understand. For example, cultural resources are impacted if cultural boundaries for the sharing of information, as well as physical boundaries for visitation, are not defined. Natural resources are impacted if basic services such as restrooms or trash containers are not in place.

Not only do all of the basic services and attractions need to be present for tourism, but also the parts of the system need to work well together. Understanding a tourism system is essential for maintaining balance in a sustainable scenario. When individual-owned businesses complement non-profit and government services, a solid foundation is created for future tourism development.

Coordination is the underlying need for an effective tourism system: even culturally-based enterprises such as museums need effective lodging, food service, and transportation to be reached by the public. As an underlying principle to tourism development, a coordinated approach is likely to draw community and visitor.

PLANNING PROCESS:
Identifying Resources

Ask the tourism group or planning committee to identify each local resource—whether a service, attraction, geographic location, event, recreational opportunity, or cultural interest. Include elders and other keepers of the traditions.

List local resources, under these categories:

Tourism Resource	**Strength**	**Limitation**	**Ecological Concern**
Attraction/activity:			
Events and calendar			
Recreational opportunity			
Special cultural interests			
Services			
Transportation			
Information			
Promotion			

Are there gaps in local resources?

List regional resources, under these categories:

Tourism Resource	**Strength**	**Limitation**	**Ecological Concern**
Attraction/activity:			
Events and calendar			
Recreational opportunity			
Special cultural interests			
Services			
Transportation			
Information			
Promotion			

Are there gaps in regional resources?

The resource inventory forms a solid foundation for strategies to move ahead with tourism development. In other words, before linking, the components in the tourism system must be known. Individual businesses sometimes market in a publication without showing how they interrelate to other businesses or where basic amenities such as lodging and food service are available. This approach presents a disjointed image of offerings to potential visitors, much less effective than a unified approach.

Completing the resource inventory is valuable for determining capacity to accommodate visitors and improving existing resources. The gap between existing services and needed services only becomes clear once current assets or resources for tourism development are identified. Chart 3.2 illustrates a sample inventory.

Restrooms are rarely talked about, yet factor-in heavily for satisfaction in the visitor experience. Finding a public restroom is sometimes a challenge in rural and tribal locations. Parties with small children, baby boomers, the elderly—and yes, every person traveling needs a restroom. When restrooms are not provided, the visitor moves on to the next locale and spends shopping and meal dollars in that location. The local community loses the potential income benefit and incurs the expenses of traffic.

Giving the community a preliminary, short version of the resource or asset inventory (information on businesses, activities, and amenities) serves several purposes. First, the resource inventory helps the community visualize an appropriate starting place or scale that matches community capability and resources. Second, suggestions on how to create a vacation concept will be based on complementary resources. This gives the community a chance to add to the inventory and creates a feeling of contribution. Third, a structured session tends to steer the conversation to a focused direction.

Why is an assessment urgent? A whole region is affected by gaps in a tourism system. One unhappy experience—whether at lodging, a meal (or lack of food service), or an unfriendly atmosphere—will affect vacation planning for the whole region. Word travels quickly.

Although a community may have highly developed elements of a system, these parts do not necessarily function in sync as a coordinated system. A large number of businesses representing a distribution of attractions and services constitutes a strength for tourism.

Chart 3.2 SAMPLE TOURISM SYSTEM INVENTORY

ATTRACTIONS/ACTIVITIES

Visitor Center
Historic Church
Museum & Cultural Center
Creative Entrepreneurs, Inc.
Native Tours

Arts Businesses:
Arts and Crafts Cooperative
Creative Arts Studio
Red Horse Trading Post
Native Jewelry
The Pottery Studio
Road Runner

Indigenous Marketplace
Turquoise Trading Post
Native Carvings
Basket Cooperative
Traditions Enterprise

Calendar of Events:
Youth Art Show	May
Tribal Fair	July
Pow-wow	August
Winter Art Show	December

INFORMATION/ VISITOR EDUCATION

Visitor Center
Websites, tribal and tourism

Orientation at the Visitor Center
Tribal newspaper
Radio station
Electronic newsletter

SERVICES

Food Service:
Native Foods
Healthy Path Restaurant
Red Rock Bakery
Garcia's Grill
Local Foods Grocery
Sunset Co-op

Lodging:
The Inn at Spring Creek
Barbara's B & B

Gas and Vehicle Service:
Fast Stop Gas Station
Red Rock Service Station

Other Services:
First National Bank
Police Department
Fire Department

TRANSPORTATION & INFRASTRUCTURE

Native Tours operates a mini-bus system and serves as an alternative to high impact tour buses coming into the village. Reservations are made at the museum.

Air travel into the HUB airport is 90 miles away. Southwest Tours provides tour bus transportation from the airport to the community's Visitor Center.

PROMOTION

Tourism website
Tourism brochure/rack card
Visitor Guide
Highway billboard

The critical factor in effectiveness is availability of detailed information on businesses, to provide referrals for the public as elements of a cohesive system.

THE SCOT ANALYSIS

Seeing the strengths, challenges, opportunities, and threats that change could bring, helps identify gaps. The SCOT (an alternative to the commonly known SWOT[2] analysis) assesses Strengths, Challenges, Opportunities, and Threats. Many communities do not want to talk about "weaknesses," or will talk about them and then balk at the weaknesses appearing in the written plan. It is best to call them "challenges."

- **Strengths** can be expanded. Identifying strengths is a good starting place for the community to become confident and inspired to move forward, both for preservation and new innovation.
- **Challenges** are areas in need of improvement. Strengthening the weaker links becomes a priority for the successful project.
- **Opportunities** are beneficial areas to develop. These identified opportunities link the community to resources and are the basis for strategy.
- **Threats** that change might bring, addressed in the beginning, help prevent negative impacts. In particular for Indigenous peoples, resolving threats to maintaining cultural privacy is fundamental— for cultural sharing to unfold.

This framework is valuable for anticipating the positive gains and potential negative impacts of tourism development. Chart 3.3 illustrates a sample SCOT analysis.

Chart 3.3 EXAMPLE SCOT ANALYSIS

STRENGTHS:

- Scenic beauty
- Excellent air quality
- Unique history
- Local Native American culture and arts
- Hot springs in the area
- Mountains - hiking trails
- Fishing, hunting, skiing
- Several National Forests and National Parks
- High traffic counts
- Comfortable lodging available
- Services, such as restaurants and local clinics
- Federal agencies support local efforts
- Unique local foods
- Talented local artists
- Art shows and pow-wows attract visitors and create a market for community members

CHALLENGES:

- Local historical interpretations depict a negative image
- Training in business management, customer service and hospitality are lacking
- Resources for development are in short supply

OPPORTUNITIES:

- Local federal agencies, towns and tribes could collaborate to create an interpretive or visitor's center
- With an increased market from tourism, the total market for local services would increase
- Cooperative efforts could increase the likelihood of obtaining funding for needed projects

- Tourism increases cultural pride and marketing opportunities for the cultural arts
- Tourism is a means of bringing local groups together
- The pride gained from the interest of outsiders raises self-esteem

THREATS CHANGE COULD BRING:
- Cultural privacy could be impacted/must be maintained
- Highway traffic increases could impact residential areas
- Intellectual property rights must be protected
- Local towns have mixed feelings about an increase in tourism due to the danger of visitors "moving in" and driving up land values

CONDUCTING THE SKILLS INVENTORY

Building internal capacity depends upon recognizing local skills and assisting community members to expand those skills. The incentive of planned projects holds potential for inspiring people of all ages to develop new expertise. Youth are encouraged to stay or come back to rural areas after education when they perceive a place for themselves in the future. Specific knowledge of skills present in the community informs discussions on training and entrepreneurial opportunities—the essentials for widespread economic gain through tourism.

To strengthen an internal effort, identify people willing to be involved in a tourism effort and inventory their skills in:

- Community development
- Hospitality
- Lodging
- Food services
- Entrepreneurial skills
- Technology
- Marketing
- Management
- Specific services (e.g., food, lodging, guiding)

- Arts
- Generating funding

Chapter 7 details steps for creating a skills database. Often in rural areas, community members have dreams of their own entrepreneurial project, yet do not see a means of securing adequate resources or skills. Through community participation, entrepreneurs begin to see the possibilities through a collaborative effort.

DEVELOPING A TOURISM VISION

Picturing a specific future, or a vision, pulls people together to create a common focus. There is not necessarily one common vision. Several visions within a community or a region may be expressed. If a negative vision surfaces, the specifics are valuable for determining potential negative impacts. The essence of planning is to document the different visions and determine where the intersections of these visions exist as a basis for cooperation.

When to conduct a visioning process does not always have a standard answer. Common planning practice calls for visioning at the beginning of a project. In this section on strategic planning method, several notions about the timing of planning steps are questioned and examined in terms of differences in community worldview.

Envisioning how tourism might look in a community may become more specific in the middle of a planning process, once resources and activities are identified. Or, visioning might be best conducted at two different points—at the beginning of the strategic planning process to determine a general picture of potential tourism-related activities, and then later after the SCOT analysis when goals are forming. Repeated visioning exercises may better produce specific ideas when they occur at different points.

Cultural note: The appropriateness of visioning may vary from culture to culture. I find this technique to work very well with Indigenous cultures, particularly with an eyes-closed participant approach and the planner leading with questions. For some cultural groups, religious considerations may view creating a vision as not within the realm of personal power. A difference may exist between allowing a vision of the future to arise, rather than shaping the future.

PLANNING PROCESS:

Create a Tourism Vision

Ask participants to close their eyes. Guide them to a vision by asking the following questions. Then, encourage a discussion of the perceived vision.

- *See your community in the future.*
- *What are community members saying to each other about visitors coming to the community?*
- *How are cultural values central to the visitation?*
- *How could visitation encourage cultural teaching programs?*
- *What activities are visitors engaged in?*
- *What products are they purchasing?*
- *Which new businesses will be developed as a result of tourism?*
- *How is the community linking to other communities in the region?*
- *What resources does your community have to develop tourism?*

Several visions are likely to be represented at the sessions. Working toward a unified vision forms the basis for an intersection between needs and opportunities, or where common ideas and actions take place. Special needs of population segments may be incorporated into the vision statement. With this step, care is taken to identify resources. Then, with community participation strategies, link these resources to the potential of a local tourism industry—consistent with the community vision.

A circular or feedback process with community input improves the outcome, particularly if the original vision is too large for the community. Or, once the asset inventory is conducted and small, locally owned businesses are identified, the goals may be fine-tuned to include ways of supporting entrepreneurs and artists in a strong tourism network. A sample vision statement follows:

Our community extends traditional hospitality, promotes authentic arts, interprets our unique heritage to visitors, and conserves our natural resources in respect for Mother Earth.

Participation in forming a vision leads to long-term involvement and the potential for recognizing local skills. Once a vision for the future is clear, community members may express their ideas for creating businesses, protecting their environment, and preserving traditions. The connection between forms of culturally appropriate business development concerning the arts, culture, and tourism are then easier to consider in relation to technical assistance, training, promotion, and financing for small-scale business start-up or expansion.

ACHIEVING BALANCE

A value-based approach recognizes internal community reasons for engaging in business, assesses existing entrepreneurial activity, and strengthens already existing economic activity—according to community-determined directions. Assumptions made from one culture to another include individual versus group ownership. Central questions include: "How will benefits be shared" and "Who is allowed to learn?" Integrating community perspectives throughout tourism development is fundamental to sustainability.

The perceptive match between community involvement, project ideas, local resources, and environmental capacity usually determines the success of tourism. It is important to devote adequate time to initial participation, data gathering and assessment to ensure a foundation for community benefits.

Planning as a process is the time for realistic assessments, building partnerships, and enhancing internal capacity to overcome the isolated style of development that tends to occur with rural and traditional communities. In the early stages of planning, community participation begins to focus the effort. Then a narrowing of options becomes possible as the participation phase progresses and needs are perceived. Specific topics to be considered throughout planning in relation to sustainability are presented below.

Chart 3.4 SUSTAINABILITY TOPICS

CULTURAL/ SOCIAL:
- Cultural values
- SCOT analysis
- Tourism vision—several generations
- Key issue definition
- Potential positive gains from the interface of culture, arts and tourism
- Cultural arts being taught
- Arts at risk of being lost/needs for teaching
- Cultural heritage site identification
- Constraints and opportunities for cultural entrepreneurs
- Methods for accurate cultural interpretation
- Historical and heritage concepts
- Needed community facilities
- Short-term and long-range cultural and social goals

ECONOMIC:
- The tourism system
- Key issue definition
- Identification of community linkages
- Skills analysis/training programs
- Traditional economy strengthened
- Inclusion of entrepreneurs
- Market analysis/visitor survey results
- Strategies for urban/rural cooperation
- Identification of venue needs
- Short-term and long-range economic goals
- Suggestions for cooperative action
- Strategies for urban/rural cooperation
- Concerns with commodification

ENVIRONMENTAL:
- Land Use Plan
- Environmental Impact Assessment (EIA)
- Infrastructure assessment and projections
- Protection of sacred sites
- Access and protection for gathering areas
- Species protection
- Environmental protection measures needed
- Evaluation plan for assessing impacts and redirecting

ACTION PLAN:
- Short-term and long-range goals
- Project definition
- Timelines for cooperative action
- Staffing needs/responsibilities
- Budgetary needs for implementation

A COMMUNITY APPROACH

The optimal outcome of this initial phase of tourism planning is the formation of a realistic vision for tourism involvement. Internal discussions, which have helped to identify community opinion, strengths and weaknesses, as well as local skills and resources, also are useful for forming direction. Such a solid foundation not only guides a plan, but also begins the process of internal capacity-building.

Internal discussions also are useful for inspiring a sense of influence over tourism, the formation of enterprise concepts, scale of tourism, and the kind of tourists that would enhance a community's traditional economy. Visitors bring impacts with them. Some of these are positive, such as expenditures. Others may be negative, such as introducing a different set of values—as well as privacy, infrastructure and environmental impacts.

A significant part of tourism planning is determining potential impacts and strategies to enhance the positive, while mitigating or preventing the negative. The end result of this process is a managed tourism plan. Yes, impacts are reduced by thinking through boundaries, whether cultural or environmental, and educating visitors. Tourism brings interaction between different cultures, and holds the potential to either erode or encourage local cultural values. Planning and management make the difference.

"Cultural heritage management" is the term used in reference to physical sites and monuments with consideration of history and cultural significance in time. For example, the protection of sacred sites, focal to Indigenous communities, must be included in these considerations. Cultural heritage "assets" refer to landscapes, historic places, sites and built environments, in addition to less tangible cultural practices, knowledge and living experiences.[3]

Overall, the field of cultural heritage management suggests limiting visitation to lessen potential negative impacts. Yet, communities with the cultural ties to these sites and few job creation opportunities frequently want visitation. The resource inventory can identify levels of needed protection for sites and cultural privacy.

Success factors used to protect culturally significant places are:

- Limiting access, by restricting the location of, or focusing tourism activities;
- Defining types of information appropriate to share through community participation; and
- Effective visitor education, explaining sensitive areas (physical and cultural) and appeals for public cooperation.

A combination of these approaches is usually highly successful, since the majority of visitors focused on culture want to be educated. A preliminary resource inventory assists the community to determine a scale that matches resources. Adding to the resource inventory and refining, with community input throughout the stages of planning, create a functional database useful later—for preservation efforts, interpretation, and economy building.

The next two chapters focus on the methods for analysis of community opinion and the tourism market. Finding the good match between these perspectives forms the basis for sound community decisions regarding tourism. A careful consideration of tourism markets is useful for community decisions regarding an appropriate group of visitors to attract, cultural boundaries for sharing, scale of enterprises, ways of including entrepreneurs, and assessment of needed redirection.

Chapter 5 discusses sources of tourism data and how to interpret available data for a tourism planning effort. These sources are useful to identify trends, yet rarely assess the local, small-scale and cultural market. For this reason, Chapter 4 introduces the methods needed to conduct a community-based, focused visitor survey. These approaches are complementary and essential for a community-specific approach.

COMMUNITY-BASED SOLUTION
Ganados del Valle, Los Ojos, New Mexico (USA)

The Hispanic mountain village of Los Ojos faced decades of out-migration due to the erosion of a traditional economy tied to the land, also resulting in the decline of cultural traditions. To create a positive cultural future, planning identified traditions in need of renewal as well as options for culturally-based employment.

Land tenure changes had severely affected the traditional economy. In 1848, when the United States annexed New Mexico, the pattern of cooperative land tenure fundamental to community grazing rights and sustainable grazing was disrupted by the practice of fencing off the common grazing lands into an individually owned pattern of land tenure for the introduction of commercial livestock production and export marketing. Increased dependency on a cash economy led to out-migration and long commutes for employment.

In response to the planning effort and dedicated community involvement, Ganados del Valle (Livestock Growers of the Valley), an economic development organization, was formed in 1983. By 1991 the organization had created thirty-five new jobs and organized agricultural support programs in co-op breeding, grazing, and financing—establishing itself as a model for culturally beneficial and environmentally sound rural economic development.

Tourism provided the market. Tierra Wools, a weaving co-op, has revitalized the Rio Grande weaving tradition. By using the local wool from the nearly extinct Churro sheep, improved biodiversity resulted as well, by bringing back the species to the region. Combining overlapping market niches, cultural tourism attracted visitors looking for the non-commercialized setting for cultural experiences. And the growing demand for natural fibers and high-quality handmade items provided a second opportunity. Tierra Wools also sells handspun wool yarn, finished with natural dyes.

Success factors include further overlapping of products. Pastores Lamb (now Shepherd's Lamb) markets meat directly to homes and restaurants, and sells at farmers markets. Rio Arriba Wool Washing offers services locally and regionally.

Support from Ganados del Valle to local residents includes technical assistance in marketing, product design, management, business finance and livestock management, as well as a loan fund. Los Ojos is restored economically through tourism and the export of weaving (clothing, rugs), sales of lamb, renovation of historic buildings, as well as bringing back the Churro sheep. After two decades, a local economy is re-established with increased cultural practice.[4] (www.handweavers.com)

FURTHER READING

Gunn, Clare A. with Turgut Var. *Tourism Planning: Basics, Concepts, Cases.* New York: Routledge, 2002.

>Tourism planning concepts and basics are explained, to include assessments, addressing environmental concerns and ecological issues.

Guyette, Susan. *Planning for Balanced Development.* Santa Fe, NM: Clear Light Publishers, 1996.

>This introduction to culturally-based, sustainable strategic planning emphasizes ways of merging cultural preservation with economic development.

Mill, Robert Christie and Alastair M. Morrison. *The Tourism System.* Dubuque, IA: Kendall Hunt, 2009.

>An introduction to factors influencing the market, characteristics of travel, transportation, tourism impacts, policy, regulation, marketing, and promotion.

Prewitt, Jana. *Tribal Tourism Toolkit*. National Association of Tribal Historic Preservation Officers, 2002. (www.nathpo.org/Toolkit/NATHPO.pdf)

>This online resource tailors the tourism planning process to tribal culture, including data-gathering topics also applicable to other cultures.

Smith, Linda Tuhiwai. *Decolonizing Methodologies: Research and Indigenous Peoples.* New York: Zed Books, Ltd, 1999.

>New approaches to research are discussed as a basis for research with Indigenous peoples—that is respectful, ethical, sympathetic, and useful.

Wilson, Shawn. Research is Ceremony: *Indigenous Research Methods*. Halifax, Nova Scotia, CAN: Fernwood Publishing, 2008.

    Relationships are the Indigenous reality; Indigenous research maintains accountability to these relationships through careful selection of topics, methods of data collection, forms of analysis and the way information is presented.

World Tourism Organization

    The archive (http://unwto.org) contains several documents useful for planning sustainable tourism.

4

COMMUNITY AND VISITOR SURVEYS

Taking the time to secure input from both community and visitors creates a solid foundation for tourism decisions.

A survey is more meaningful than simply gathering numbers. The well-designed survey produces both qualitative and quantitative, or numerical, information. By combining the results from community surveys and visitor surveys, visitor interests may be matched with community preferences—pivotal for attracting people, designing an educational experience, and expanding community benefits.

The community survey—the survey conducted within the community—reflects cultural priorities, local activities, needs for cultural privacy and boundaries, and preferences for employment. This survey is a means of securing opinions and suggestions for moving forward—for deciding whether tourism is wanted, identifying potential tourism projects, securing funding, designing training programs, and for marketing locally made items.

Community surveys, whether formal or informal, are an important way to encourage community participation in tourism. Qualitative processes are useful for determining cultural or topic-relevant questions for quantitative data gathering. Effective interpretation of quantitative data also becomes enriched through descriptive qualitative data, information to provide community-based context.

> **Framework for Integrating Culture**
> - Encourage participation in community surveys through culturally-based activities.
> - Choose a survey method compatible with resources.
> - Determine needed community training and technical assistance for full participation in the survey effort.
> - Provide interpretation for quantitative data.
> - Include demographic questions in the visitor survey, to understand the visiting culture.
> - Focus questions to determine visitor interest in current offerings and desired offerings.
> - Thank the respondent in a way appropriate to the culture.
> - Provide guidance on cultural questions for visitor survey efforts outside of the community.
> - Share the results with the community, business owners, and entrepreneurs.

The visitor survey, conducted from on-site in the community or at a broader geographic level, will indicate visitor preferences and concerns, as well as demographic data. The visitor survey provides the foundation for building the match between visitor interests and what the community desires to offer and is able to offer. Training may be required for community members to most effectively participate in delivering the visitor survey and gathering the best information possible through visitor contact at a survey location.

QUALITATIVE AND QUANTITATIVE APPROACHES

The cultural difference in quantitative versus qualitative approaches rests with the intent of the outcome. When surveying within the community, quantitative approaches intend to discover a majority opinion, useful for moving ahead quickly. Qualitative methods for gathering opinion range from talking circles, small group or focus group meetings for discussion, interviews that invite opinions to be expressed, to open-ended questions on surveys.

Quantitative methods prevalent in the tourism industry for assessing visitor preferences include visitor surveys, market studies and impact assessments. Collected numerical or multiple choice response data are frequently presented without interpretation. Statewide and regional visitor surveys are largely quantitative and tend to lack specificity of questions for local use, as well as interpretation for a particular community. While such studies yield valuable generalized data, lack of interpretation may limit practical use.

Quantitative survey methods hold potential bias inherent in the structuring of questions, ranging from assumptions in the starting place to the response options stated. Cultural significance in the questions is important to the usefulness of the responses, for both qualitative and quantitative data. Being aware of possible bias strengthens choice of method, structuring of questions, and interpretation.

In contrast, qualitative approaches emphasize discussion, identify desired directions, note opinions, and allow a broad range of information and views to be discovered. Why is the approach used in research so significant? As Margaret Kovach points out in *Indigenous Methodologies*,[1] research creates policy and policy generates programs. Resources, technical assistance, and services—all are based upon research outcomes.

Qualitative methods provide context for interpretation, tend to be process-oriented rather than goal-oriented, and are useful for building consensus. Process carries an invaluable benefit for actually moving a community forward. Qualitative methods elicit opinion and support participation that is contextually relevant. In Indigenous terms, this participation is called "bringing the community along," and refers to cultural capacity-building. Quality-of-life related to connectedness of family and culture is not measured in dollar output alone.

Complementing each approach with the other is useful for reducing bias in tourism decisions. For example, conducting a planning process in a gradual way can include small focus group sessions to determine the starting place and the appropriate questions to ask on a survey.

The depth of the survey, in relation to the community's offerings and potential, helps tailor a tourism approach suitable for the community. Then, matching the results of the community survey with the visitor survey, the market analysis (Chapter 5), as well as the resource and skills inventories (Chapters 8, 9), shapes a tailored tourism plan with form, scale, and timing appropriate to culture and community. Several survey types and complementary studies support sustainability:

Cultural/social	Community Survey
	Skills Assessment
Economic	Visitor Survey
	Business Survey
	Tourism System Analysis
Environmental	Tourism System Analysis
	Carrying Capacity Analysis
	Impact Analysis
	Land Use Plan

Potential ecological impacts to address include—protection of native species, fragile areas, water quality, sacred sites, gathering areas, plants and soils used for the practice of cultural arts, and access for community members. In other words, not sacrificing resource protection for economic gain is central to sustainability.

This chapter addresses methods for both the community and visitor survey. If hiring a planning consultant, insist on a survey tailored to the culture of the community and the ecology of the locale.

CONDUCTING THE COMMUNITY SURVEY

Forming a small committee (with the emphasis on "small") is valuable for constructing a survey instrument tailored to the community. The survey might be designed by three to five people with experience in tourism, guided by a planner. Representation of different viewpoints in the community underlies an effective committee, to make certain that different possible scenarios for tourism are covered. Large committees tend to develop long questionnaires that do not secure a good response rate.

Even though the large committee approach may be tempting in a consensus-based culture, form the survey with a small group, then test it with a larger group and secure feedback for needed revisions. Testing the survey with a minimum of ten community members furthers insight as to the wording of the questions, thoroughness of questions, and time required to ensure completion.

Sample community surveys are useful for gaining insight on content and structuring questions. However, relying on an entity outside of the community for survey design may lead to a standard survey not tailored to the specific community—unless involvement and feedback occur with every step. Take the time to compare possible questions, modify questions, and to develop additional community-specific questions to increase cultural relevance.

Interviews may be more effective in some communities, yet take more resources and people hours to conduct than surveys. The one-on-one connection between interviewer and respondent is personal and encourages valuable comments beyond structured questions. Time invested at this point will determine the usefulness of the data for projects that benefit community-based enterprises and encourage cultural learning.

Common sources of bias in community surveys are:

- Cultural questions not addressed;
- Small-scale, entrepreneurial topics not included;
- Survey too long, failure to complete;
- Concerns of all cultural groups not included;
- Questions reflect industry bias of continued growth;
- Traditional economy not addressed, or tourism as one part of diversified income streams for family support; and
- The options of no tourism or limited tourism not addressed.

Survey sampling methods are generally developed with urban communities in mind. A rule of thumb in the urban setting is a minimum 10% response rate. For the smaller community, a higher response rate is needed to secure representation and is feasible when local cultural offerings are woven into the survey method. A 100% household response rate is not very likely, yet between 50% and 80% is possible for the small community.

Several places appropriate to collect survey data from the community include:

- At a tourism planning meeting;
- At a pot-luck dinner to discuss tourism issues;
- At a cultural center or museum community hub;
- At other meetings in the community;

- At a community events, such as festivals or county fairs;
- Through local businesses used by community members;
- In the local newspaper, with a designated drop-off place;
- On the community's website (as a supplementary way of collecting surveys); or
- Household interviews, if funds are available.

Offering a drawing with a prize, for those returning the questionnaire, is a valuable strategy for obtaining a good response rate. Protect respondent confidentiality by assigning a number to the questionnaire, then keeping a master list in case follow-up is needed.

A survey effort is a good opportunity to gather data on other community needs such as economic development, job training, social services, or cultural center and museum development. A caution—if a comprehensive survey tries to cover numerous topics, tourism is likely to receive only brief coverage in the questions.

Keep the survey concise, to increase the completion and return rate. And always thank participants for their time at the end of the questionnaire, in a traditional language—bilingually, if applicable. The following sample community survey emphasizes the qualitative, open-ended question to continue the idea of a listening approach with the community.

Example 4.1 TOURISM ASSESSMENT COMMUNITY SURVEY
COMMUNITY TOURISM SURVEY

Name:_____   Phone #: _____

Occupation: _____   E-mail: _____

Address: _____

Please take 15 to 20 minutes of your time to give feedback on the appropriateness of tourism and potential as a means of employment.

1. Which cultural values are important to you in creating employment?
2. Do you approve or disapprove of tourism as a means of creating employment and furthering cultural understanding?
3. What concerns do you have about tourism as a local industry?

4. Are there possible solutions to your concerns?
5. Describe the potential benefits from tourism.
6. How can community resources (cultural & natural) be protected?
7. Are there community areas where visitor access should be restricted?
8. Are you interested in starting an entrepreneurial business?
9. Do you have prior experience in:
   ___ food service
   ___ lodging/bed & breakfast
   ___ gallery or gift shop
   ___ tour guide
   ___ entertainment
   ___ vending, outdoor markets
   ___ other relating to tourism _____
10. Are you an artist? If yes, list the arts:
11. Do you have agricultural products to sell?
12. Do you sell your arts or other products?
13. If yes, would you need a small business loan?
14. Are you interested in training for any of these areas?
    ___ food service
    ___ lodging/ bed & breakfast
    ___ art gallery or gift shop
    ___ arts – traditional or contemporary
    ___ tour guide
    ___ entertainment
    ___ customer service
    ___ marketing
    ___ financial management
    ___ taxes
    ___ vending, outdoor markets
    ___ other topics relating to tourism _____
15. Are there ecological areas and gathering places that need to be protected?
16. Describe your suggestions for tourism management, if tourism were developed.
17. Would you like to serve on a tourism committee?
18. Any other comments or areas of concern?

Thank you for participating!

Keeping Momentum

Following up with a report is the link between data gathering and community involvement, since feedback to the community inspires continued participation. Distribute results through small local newspapers, organizational and tribal newsletters, or as a handout at the next participation meeting. Survey data are valuable for addressing sustainability factors concerning economic gain, retaining culture, and minimizing the intrusion—while caring for the local environment. As a reminder of community opinion, periodic reports keep the discussion and participation ongoing.

In the ideal tourism development scenario, a community survey or other data sources are compared with visitor interests to determine entrepreneurial niches. If the expense of conducting a visitor survey is a barrier when first considering tourism, then an initial step may be to compare community opinion with broader regional visitor surveys indicating visitor interest.

Examining existing regional, statewide and local surveys is beneficial to give the community background information. However, a point of caution: a survey is only *as effective as its design*. Surveys adapted from other regions or countries may not ask the questions relevant to a specific community. Therefore, discuss the survey results with the local community and ask whether the necessary questions have been addressed, to guide ongoing data collection.

The downside of using generalized data is that specific entrepreneurial niches for culturally-based businesses are usually not perceived. Planning for a local visitor survey at a future time, when resources are secured, improves targeted enterprise development as well as marketing efforts. The more focused the survey to local offerings, the better the match between community expertise and visitor interest.

THE VISITOR SURVEY

"Where do they come from and what are they looking for?" These questions underscore the appropriate match between visitor interests and what the community offers. A well-designed visitor survey puts the power into effective tourism development and marketing. Knowing what visitors want is fundamental for developing products, attractions, and services.

There are two paths to securing data. Visitor data collected locally, tailored to a specific community or region are called ***primary data***. Surveys already collected by another source, such as national, state, or a larger region are known as *secondary data*. Both types are valuable to a tourism effort. This chapter addresses methods for conducting a survey and the next chapter points to secondary sources of tourism data.

The first major decision is whether to conduct a visitor survey in a local community or whether to collaborate with other communities regionally. Using both routes is ideal. Collaborating with tourism agencies to suggest culturally-based questions yields a broader sample, often at no cost. And, conducting a community-based survey, as resources for a survey effort become available, targets business opportunities with community-specific questions.

The use of standard industry questionnaires for visitors frequently leads to a generalized—and sometimes not community-relevant—set of questions in a survey. While standard demographic data for visitor surveys are valuable for comparative purposes, targeted questions on visitor preferences provide useful data for implementation of visitor amenities, activities, lodging and food service that are compatible for the community.

Understanding visitor preferences increases tourism benefits. When new business development matches visitor interest, visitation and jobs increase as well. Understanding of local history and culture expands also. To target a specific tourism market, local businesses must be responsive to visitor needs. Assessing visitor characteristics and intent relates to design of the mutually beneficial visitation experience.

The majority of state and national visitor surveys collect data in urban areas, missing rural differences. Numerous surveys assessing the international market are collected on planes, rather than in the regions visited. Using urban survey results indicating potential visitors, plus conducting a community-specific survey—is useful for determining the right "cultural fit" between visitor interests and the desired direction of the community. The majority of visitors will start their trip in an urban area and then explore a region. Understanding the characteristics of visitor interests in both environments is valuable for creating the tourism draw to a community.

Comparative Data

Exploring market strategies from similar regions and their successful efforts in attracting a market draw provides a beneficial comparison. Decisions about the specificity of data needed (national, state, regional, local) relate to the type of business targeted and the uniqueness of the local community. A survey developed specifically with local attractions and products in mind produces data useful for development.[2]

Using a few standardized demographic questions from national or regional tourism surveys (such as residence or point-of-origin, age, number in party, and number of nights stay) facilitates the comparison of data from one region to another. From this type of survey question a community learns how similar or different their visitors are, compared to visitors regionally, statewide, or nationally.

When designing a visitor survey, using a combination of standard questions, plus questions addressing local offerings, increases the ability to compare local and regional differences. This is basic for understanding local visitors as well as how to attract visitors from the larger market.

Participating in larger survey efforts (such as regional or national) is valuable for suggesting questions relevant to a specific culture. For this reason, becoming familiar with larger survey efforts and taking the time to participate will bring local benefits. To find opportunities for participating in broader surveys, ask Chambers of Commerce and tourism organizations about their planned market research program. If there are none planned, explain the benefits and initiate the discussion for a collaborative regional effort, where stakeholders participate and share the costs.

Choosing a Survey Method

Several options for conducting the visitor survey are: the survey card given to the visitor (an intercept survey), an interview form, or an electronic survey (on-site or via website). While website surveys are sometimes easier to collect, keep in mind the limitation that respondents are browsing and only may come. A survey of visitors who come to the community location tells more about the desires and experience of actual visitors.

Choice of a method depends upon budget available, staffing available to assist, and processing expenses. Both web-based and on-location surveys are useful. The questionnaire handed to the visitor, or located in a visible place, is low-tech and easy to place in several locations—while yielding both quantitative (numerical) and qualitative (open-ended) responses. An interview conducted in person requires extensive staff time. Chart 4.1 compares the advantages and disadvantages of several survey methods suitable for tourism data gathering.

Chart 4.1 SUMMARY OF VISITOR SURVEY METHODS

QUESTIONNAIRE:

Advantages:

- Concise
- Quick completion time
- Can be placed in several locations
- Low cost
- Structured responses are easier to tabulate

Disadvantages:

- Needs to be short in length, fewer questions, to encourage visitors to complete
- Questions need to be worded with great clarity to ensure consistency in response interpretation
- Expense of coding and processing

INTERVIEW:

Advantages:

- Provides opportunity for detailed questions and responses
- Time to include extra questions
- Respondent less likely to quit before survey completed
- One-on-one opportunity to guide visitors
- Best results if a "perk" is offered, such as a discount

Disadvantages:

- Takes longer than the questionnaire method
- Trained staff needed to interview
- Tourists are in a relaxation mode, reluctant to take time out from their vacation time
- Offering a "perk" for completing has costs

ELECTRONIC, ON-SITE:

Advantages:

- Staff time at site is minimal
- Tabulation does not require data entry, saving time for processing
- Faster for visitor to answer questions
- Speedy to process or tabulate results
- Easier to collect a larger sample size

Disadvantages:

- Expense of the electronic system
- Usually placed in fewer locations, due to cost of units
- Survey processing software is costly
- Lose a broader sampling capability if fewer locations
- Less personal, some visitors do not respond well

WEBSITE:

Advantages:

- Large sample easier to collect
- Low cost once website is developed
- Easier to collect a sample from a wide geographic area
- May serve as an informational tool about services and events

Disadvantages:

- Limits the sampling—surveys only potential visitors inquiring, rather than based on an actual visit
- Needs to be short in length, for web surfers are likely to click through quickly

Electronic surveys are the most up-to-date method. An on-site computer terminal programmed with the survey provides automatic data entry and fast tabulations. Small communities may still consider conducting a visitor survey, even if the electronic method is not within a local budget. There are advantages to the personal method of an intercept survey or the interview, such as direct contact with visitors and the opportunity to elicit additional information through a conversation. Issues, needs, and a perception of what is liked about the current community offerings are identified in a discussion!

Focus groups are another method frequently utilized by larger-scale tourism studies, such as those conducted at the state level. For a smaller community, coordinating local efforts with state studies is useful to further the inclusion of cultural or rural content questions. Focus group input tends to be expensive, for participants are generally paid for their time.

Other low-cost ways to gain focus group type data are comment cards, or notes on visitor comments—at museums, businesses and visitor centers. If front-line employees with direct visitor contact are given a short set of questions and take notes from interactions, useful information can be collected to further survey interpretation. These interactions are useful for documenting the satisfaction level of visitors or difficulties experienced with the tourism system.

Constructing the Visitor Survey

A broad range of questions identifies basic demographic characteristics and visitor interests—useful for both tourism development and marketing. Tourism surveys identify the following:

- Visitor primary residence, or "point-of-origin;"
- Age of respondent;
- Source of information obtained for trip planning;
- Specific activities desired while staying with the community;
- Interest in historical interpretation;
- Topics for exhibits or demonstrations;
- Types of products desired;
- Where buying products currently;
- Planned spending on products and services;
- Specific tours;
- Lodging type;
- Food choices—especially cultural;

- Household income;
- Satisfaction rating on local businesses and activities; and
- Suggestions for improvement.

There are several factors in designing the survey "instrument," as the list of questions is called. A few pointers are to:

- Agree on an appropriate length at the beginning of the process (number of pages and respondent time);
- Decide on general topics of importance;
- Look at regional and state surveys to make basic demographic questions compatible;
- Condense questions whenever possible;
- Brainstorm additional questions;
- Work together to shorten questions; and
- Format questions to condense.

The survey should be of a length that can be completed in ten to fifteen minutes, as visitors want to continue enjoying their vacation. Consider the following in survey design.

Introduction A concise explanation of the purpose of the survey emphasizes the importance of the respondent's time. Relating to an improvement in services for them is helpful for aligning visitors. Explain the amount of time completion of the survey will require. This increases the response rate, particularly for visitors occupied with the details of a vacation.

Focus Decide upon a short list of topics, such as: basic demographics, cultural content, purchase favorites, food choices, lodging preferences, and satisfaction with the visit.

Brevity A greater percentage of the short survey will be returned.

Clarity Questions should be worded clearly and be brief in length. Avoid wordy explanations or tourism jargon.

Interest	Topics appealing to visitors will inspire them to complete. Gathering input from community businesses, visitor centers or museums who regularly interact with visitors, lends good direction for framing relevant questions.
Comment	At least one open-ended question and comment space should be included for visitor suggestions or comments on service.
Thank You	Thank the visitor for taking the time to complete the questionnaire. If a perk or discount coupon is offered, mention the details here.

Return Information

Include clearly stated information on the place to deposit the completed questionnaires. Some visitors will take the survey away from the surveying location (regardless of the instruction) and will need information on the return, including a mailing address.

Expressing Appreciation

A frequently omitted part of the survey is appreciation for the visitor taking the time out of a vacation to participate. The survey card or electronic survey should always include a "thank you for your time" statement at the end, along with the information for returning the questionnaire. The well-designed survey, coupled with a friendly attitude toward the visitor, will inspire visitors to return—with anticipation of a new adventure in the future. A bilingual expression of gratitude for participation is intriguing to the visitor, if applicable. Whenever possible, thank the visitor in person.

Example Survey

A brief survey conducted at several American Indian tribal settings is presented in this section. This sample survey was printed on cardstock, front and back, to provide a substantial writing surface. Cultural content questions are relevant, particularly if the community is designing a museum or linking closely to artists and entrepreneurs.

Example 4.2 SAMPLE CULTURAL TOURISM VISITOR SURVEY

(community) _____

Please help us to improve visitor services by taking
10 minutes to complete this short survey.

1. Primary residence:
  City/Town: _____
  State: _____
  Out-of-country
  Country: _____

2. Age (check one)
  ___ 18-24   ___ 45-54
  ___ 25-34   ___ 55-64
  ___ 35-44   ___ 65-74
  ___ 75 or older

3. How many nights will you be staying on this trip? _____

4. Number in party:
  Adults ___ Children ___

5. Interests while on Native lands:
  ___ Learning about tribal history
  ___ Eating Native American foods
  ___ Learning about Native culture
  ___ Recreational/outdoor
  ___ Art demonstrations
  ___ Tours
  ___ Museum
  ___ Arid agriculture
  ___ Casino
  Other _____

6. How did you learn about us?
  ___ Visitor Guide
  ___ Website/social media
  ___ Brochure
  ___ Chambers of Commerce
  ___ Newspaper/magazine
  ___ Atlas/map
  ___ Family/Friends

7. Which of the following interest you?
  ___ Educational materials
  ___ Arts/cultural demonstrations
  ___ Family activities
  ___ Current tribal issues
  ___ Website
  ___ Virtual museum
  ___ Traditional feast meal
  ___ Tribal events

8. Which food(s) interest you?
  ___ Locally grown foods
  ___ Native American foods
  ___ Salads
  ___ Low-fat/low-cal
  ___ Burgers/pizza
  Other _____

9. Which of the following interest you for purchase?
  ___ Baskets   ___ Painting
  ___ Carving–stone, wood
  ___ Clothes   ___ Food products
  ___ Drums
  ___ Dreamcatchers   ___ Music
  ___ Jewelry
    ___ shell ___ silver ___ bead

  Other _____

10. **What do you plan to spend on lodging & food on this trip?**
    Lodging $_____   Food $_____   Casino $_____   Arts $_____

11. **Are you interested in tours?** ___ Yes ___ No
    If yes, what type of tours? ___ Art ___ Walking ___ Natural Areas
    ___ Historic Sites ___ Birding ___ Cultural/Museum
    Other _____

12. **Is a tribal location your primary destination for this trip?**
    ___ Yes ___ No

13. **Where are you staying?**
    ___ On-reservation ___ Off-reservation

14. **What type of lodging?** ___ Cabins ___ B & B ___ Hotel
    ___ Motel ___ RV ___ Campground ___ Friends/relatives

15. **Would you be interested in lodging at a tribal location?** ___ Yes ___ No
    If yes, which type? ___ Motel ___ Hotel ___ B&B ___ Campground
    ___ Cabins ___ RV Hookups ___ No Hookups

16. **Were restroom facilities adequate?** ___ Yes ___ No

17. **Is more visitor information needed at this site?** ___ Yes ___ No

18. **Is parking adequate?** ___ Yes ___ No

19. **Are picnic facilities adequate?** ___ Yes ___ No

20. **Was customer service adequate at this site?** ___ Yes ___ No
    Comments:

21. **What is your combined household income?**
    ___ less than $20,000   ___ $50,000 to $74,999
    ___ $20,000 to $29,999   ___ $75,000 to $99,000
    ___ $30,000 to $39,999   ___ greater than $99,000
    ___ $40,000 to $49,999

22. **How satisfied are you with your visit to tribal lands?**
    ___ Very ___ Somewhat ___ Not very

23. **Comments or suggestions regarding your experience on tribal lands:**

Thank you!
Please return this form at the tribal museum.
(address)

The questionnaire, handed to the visitor or located in a visible place, is low-tech and easy to place in several locations. Sensitive questions such as income should be placed at the end of the questionnaire; if a respondent feels offended at the question, the majority of the questions are already completed and the survey will be returned. If sensitive questions are placed at the beginning, the respondent may stop early and dispose of the questionnaire.

A flier or sign posted at the surveying site may be useful to further align the visitor. Communicate the importance of the survey to the community's efforts in improving visitor services. This step encourages visitor cooperation, for the prospect of an intriguing return will motivate participation. Also, communicating the importance of buying locally to generate needed income to residents is basic to creating benefits.

TRAINING IN SURVEY PROCEDURES

The amount of employee or volunteer training necessary will vary according to the type of survey conducted. For questionnaires, a brief orientation on the purpose of the survey will encourage staff attention to the project. To assist the staff in being effective, explain each question and the intent for collecting each type of information. Outline for staff the possible responses, particularly for questions where more than one response is possible.

The intercept survey conducted at a community location is either handed to visitors by employees or volunteers, or placed in a location for visitors to pick up. Asking employees—at lodging, the restaurant or the museum admissions desk—to encourage visitors to fill out the questionnaire increases the sample. A basket or bin with a sign must be made available to hold the completed questionnaires.

If using the interview method, training must be in-depth to ensure that all survey workers will ask the questions in a consistent way. Conducting practice interview sessions improves results. Time the length of interview sessions for each interviewer to make certain that the survey time required is consistent and fits within the initial estimate. Keeping the length from ten to fifteen minutes will increase survey participation and consistency to the survey.

Scheduling the Survey

Conducting the survey at a time of year when tourism is at peak in the community area supports an adequate sample. Not all visitors will want to take time out for a survey, so the "response rate" will only be a percentage of visitors.

Yet, seasonal differences in visitor preferences do exist. The most frequent mistake made in visitor surveys is starting too late in the tourism season for a particular locale, and then not collecting an adequate sample size during that tourism season. If possible, extend the survey into the additional seasons, starting at the beginning of each season, to reach different tourism markets in the sample.

Families with children tend to come in the summer, when school is out of session. Baby-boomers and retirees tend to come in the fall. Schedule the survey carefully, considering the existing workload of tourism staff and the flow of visitors during the visitation season.

The Survey Pilot

Bridging cultures with survey questions can be a challenge. Knowing whether other cultures understand the survey questions requires a trial run. Give the questionnaire to ten visitors and ask them for feedback. An intercept locale where visitors will be spending time, such as a tour or in a restaurant waiting for a meal to arrive, is ideal for feedback.

Or, test the survey with the personnel of a local Chamber of Commerce or a Convention and Visitor Bureau. Staff members experienced with the local tourism market are likely to have a broad knowledge of visitor interests and ways of communicating with other cultures—valuable for focusing the survey to only the essential questions.

Where to Survey

The best results for the location of the survey are places where visitors will stop for a period of time, or where they are "clustered," such as:

- A visitor center
- On a tour
- At a museum
- A place of lodging
- At a restaurant

Places where visitor information is displayed are likely stops on the visit and where visitors are usually receptive to taking a short time out of a busy day. Again, the "exchange" is a primary reason for the visitor to take the time for the survey.

Visitor Survey Sample Size

Determining an adequate sample size is neither a precise undertaking nor easy. Small communities tend to receive a smaller number of visitors. The larger the sample possible, a more accurate picture of visitor preferences will likely emerge from the survey. Yet, obtaining the larger sample is expensive in terms of staff time for the gathering and data processing time. The benefit of actually completing a survey versus trying for a huge sample must be weighed carefully.

- Look at the sample sizes of visitor surveys conducted in the region.
- Decide on a sample target at the beginning of the survey.
- Sample size should represent a broad number of categories of visitors to the community, such as recreational tourists, ecotourists, and cultural tourists.
- Balancing the number of completed survey forms collected at each different collection site (e.g., visitor center, museum, lodging, restaurant, hiking trail, a tour, or at a marina) will increase the representative sample for each of the groups coming to a community.

Aim to collect 1,000 surveys minimum for a small community sample, but no less than 500. The type of visitors to a community varies widely, particularly in the difference between casino players, recreational visitors, and those seeking cultural activities. The larger the sample, the greater flexibility for summarizing the responses by category, such as the place collected, or activities. Income level, intended level of expenditures, type of lodging preferred, and type of food preferred are other categories valuable to cross-tabulate, or summarize by categories. For planning purposes, learning about these sub-samples gives information on the potential niches for developing new businesses.

Motivating the Visitor to Respond

People on vacation do not wish to spend time away from "play." Their escape from a fast-paced world burdened with paperwork and computers should be relaxing. If an exchange occurs during the survey, such as valuable visitor information, then the survey respondent is likely to take the time to finish the questionnaire. At the start or completion of a tour is an excellent time to ask for visitor participation in a survey. Asking for the survey in proximity to available visitor information will appear as a fair exchange.

Placing a survey or a comment card in lodging rooms is an excellent way of collecting data. Evening relaxation time often presents the opportunity to introduce an activity. If a visitor education piece (brochure, visitor guide, or even a single sheet of information) is placed by the survey, visitors will be more likely to respond. Some businesses, such as casinos, offer free tickets or small gifts in exchange for the member sign-up survey. The exchange should be pleasant and subtle—just a reflection of appreciation of valuable time given on a vacation. Regard each new stop on the journey as an opportunity for visitor education.

THE IMPORTANCE OF INTERPRETATION

What do all the numbers tell us? This question is the common response of community members, planners, town councils, tribal councils, community developers, and funders—who see page after page of numbers and charts with no text. Interpretation through text ties the numbers to their significance for a particular community, region, or state.

Keeping the data analysis basic enables users of the data (e.g., local governments, tribal governments, Chambers of Commerce, or business owners) to readily apply the data in practical ways. Most local governments, funders, or tribal councils will not want to struggle through page after page of dense statistics. Attractive bar graphs with percentages of responses, and a brief discussion of the meaning of the numbers in direct relation to the community, will have the best impact.

Sample Interpretation

In this section, sample charts follow interpretation in italics for several data sets. Note: "N" equals the sample size.

Chart 4.2

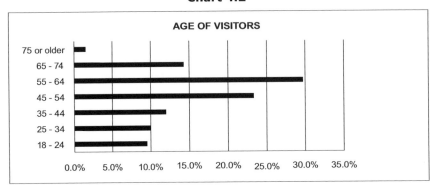

N = 949

In Chart 4.2, the age range of visitors shows a high concentration of baby-boomers and retirees. A total of 55.0% of respondents are in the 45 to 64 age range, and 16.0% are above 65 years of age—for a total of 71.0% above the age of 45. Understanding the age range of visitors is valuable for planning visitor activities. Interests of baby-boomers tend to be educational experiences and shopping.

Chart 4.3

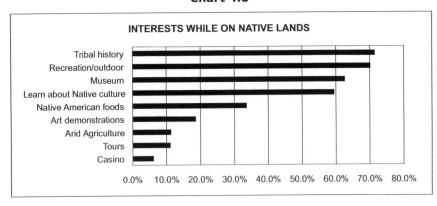

N = 949

Knowing visitor interests assists the community in developing activities. The question, "Interests while on Native lands?" yields data relevant for tourism planning. Chart 4.3 reflects the leading activities as tribal history, museums, learning about culture, outdoor recreation, and the traditional feast meal.

By holding a community meeting to present visitor interest to entrepreneurs, awareness of niches for product development can lead to increased jobs in the community. Developing materials on tribal history (e.g., visitor guides, books, talks on the arts or history, videos, DVDs, and demonstrations) is a way of educating the general public and presenting positive images of Native contributions.

Chart 4.4

FOODS OF INTEREST

Food	Percentage
Native American foods	~65%
Locally grown foods	~60%
Salads	~35%
Lowfat/ lowcal	~22%
Burgers/pizza	~22%

N=949

Chart 4.4 presents the top ranking food choices as Native American foods, locally grown foods, salads, and lowfat/lowcal. A meal can have added educational benefits with interpretation. When information about tribal history and tribal foods is included on the menu—the meal becomes an educational experience. Education about food offers the opportunity to communicate a lifeway. Food service is an essential tourism draw, leading to increased expenditures in other local businesses, such as lodging, museums, casinos, and art galleries.

Information on products visitors desire to purchase can yield insights on niches for entrepreneurial activity. Shopping opportunities (Chart 4.5) identify the five highest levels of product choice as: stone carvings, jewelry, baskets, jerky, and paintings.

Chart 4.5

PRODUCTS OF INTEREST TO PURCHASE

- Carvings
- Jewelry
- Baskets
- Jerky
- Paintings
- Clothes
- Music
- Drums
- Dreamcatchers

0.0%   10.0%   20.0%   30.0%   40.0%   50.0%

N=949

Of the jewelry options, silver ranks first, shell second, and bead third; all ranked high. A breakdown of jewelry preferences indicated 32.8% with an interest in silver jewelry, 17.0% in shell jewelry, and 16.0% in bead jewelry. Other items for purchase mentioned are: books, paintings, photos and postcards, tote bags, coffee mugs, and DVDs.

Interpreting the Numbers

Understanding the significance of the numbers contributes to the likelihood of sustainable development. In these examples, specific visitor interests identified the market niche for several businesses. The intersection between what the community wants to share and what the visitor seeks is the point of a potentially harmonious tourism scenario. Good interpretation, based on questions well designed for the community or region will indicate potential for new business niches and new product lines by matching local skills with visitor interest.

Gap analysis determines the difference between what travel markets seek and the amenities provided for them in the region. A gap is the point of opportunity to provide a unique offering, either through business niches or interpretation. Assisting local entrepreneurs to develop businesses expands the direct benefits of tourism. Providing summaries of survey data on specific visitor interests to entrepreneurs and businesses, plus technical assistance, enables community members to target niches for product development, specific visitor markets, and to be effective with promotional dollars. Any marketing and distribution of promotional pieces on the part of the local community would greatly benefit the development of these enterprises, whether owned by a local government, tribe, or individual.

Frequency of Survey

Since travel trends are constantly changing, repeating the local visitor survey every two years is recommended for staying informed of visitor trends and as a way of measuring visitor satisfaction. The first survey is the learning curve—taking more time and community cooperation to design the survey, to gather the completed surveys, and to process the data. A subsequent survey effort should use most of the original survey questions, to allow for comparison and identify shifts in visitor attention over time.

If results were shared with the community and specific development outcomes (e.g., training, capacity-building, businesses, marketing pieces) are visible, then community businesses and organizations are likely to assist with repeat surveys.

SHARING SURVEY RESULTS

The power of the survey depends upon the number of people who actually use the data to improve or develop visitor services. While this may seem like a basic practice, rarely do community members obtain access to the data or instruction on how to use the data for development purposes. Visitor data are valuable for:

- Assessing visitor satisfaction and improving services;
- Planning new services, including the business plan for financing or need for phased development;
- Determining new niches for tourism development;
- Completing tourism plans;
- Designing museums and interpretive centers, based on visitor interest;
- Determining effective marketing strategies;
- Learning where to place marketing materials;
- Designing effective websites and use of social media;
- Learning about products or cultural art preferences for purchase;

- Determining a correct pricing range; and
- Justifying both need and potential in funding proposals to develop visitor services.

To extend use of the survey, these are ways of sharing results with the community:

- An article in the local newspaper or newsletter displaying charts and a brief explanation of the meaning of the statistics in relation to the community;
- A brief report, separate from a plan, suitable for distribution to local governments and businesses; and
- A community meeting using a slide show, data summaries, and explanations of potential use for development purposes, as well as information on funding sources.

To achieve the greatest result, utilize all methods. Training explaining the stages of development—from data collection to direct use in generating resources—is the most useful end result for small-scale approaches.

Once a local community completes a valuable visitor survey, there may be a tendency to keep the survey results confidential. Reconsider. The power of a visitor survey resides with sharing the results. As communities and regions share data, an improved perception of the visitor profile is reached. All local communities in the region benefit through the ability to develop amenities that link together, meeting the needs of their visitors. Recognizing visitor concerns and levels of satisfaction is the path for designing a mutually beneficial tourism setting.

STRATEGIES FOR INCLUSION ON LARGER SURVEYS

Several levels of surveys can work together to give a broader profile of tourism opportunities. Whether to be included in a larger survey effort or to conduct a smaller community-based survey is not an either/or choice. National level or international surveys indicate broad, long-term potential for a draw to a region. Statewide tourism surveys bring the data closer to home in terms of immediate potential, and usually describe regional differences.

Surveys conducted by cities, Chambers of Commerce, or Convention and Visitor Bureaus show the profile of the immediate, existing market. Does this sound like a great amount of data? All of these levels are needed for in-depth interpretation, in terms of the broad sweep of characteristics—such as point of origin, gender, travel party size, average length of stay, average amount of expenditures, general interests, and type of lodging preferred.

The category of data generally missing is specific interest in cultures and cultural activities. Culture with a capital "C" is included, such as museums, concerts, and galleries; however, culture with a small "c," those local small-scale events, artists, and enterprises are usually overlooked for questionnaire content.

Solutions abound for inclusion. When participating in tourism organization meetings in nearby towns and cities, or local universities, ask for the local community or culture to be included in the range of questionnaire topics. Effective strategy generates alignment. Rather than focusing solely on community needs (and never in a demanding tone), point out the regional or state benefits of including local culture for increasing the cultural tourism draw. Point to the overlap in markets, such as geotourism, where recreational, ecotourism and cultural tourism intersect. Attending state or regional tourism conferences is a way of gaining input into a broader level visitor survey.

Space on a questionnaire given to several separate questions may become an issue. One solution is to suggest a ranked-interest response, covering many attractions in the state or region.

In this example, total scores for each interest would be added and then divided by the number of total responses, producing an overall average score for each topic. A ranking for all of the interests is then easily determined, based on the score of each.

Remember—the more specific the solution suggested for inclusion, the greater likelihood of an implementation. If possible, ask for a breakdown or cross-tabulation of demographic questions by specific topics, to further target the community's market effectively.

Example 4.3 SAMPLE CULTURAL SURVEY QUESTION

Please rank your level of interest in the following offerings of our State, with 5 representing the highest level.

Level of Interest

Scenic beauty	1	2	3	4	5
Hispanic culture	1	2	3	4	5
American Indian culture	1	2	3	4	5
Museums	1	2	3	4	5
Festivals and Events	1	2	3	4	5
Recreation	1	2	3	4	5
Shopping	1	2	3	4	5
Outdoor Adventure	1	2	3	4	5

FROM SURVEY TO ACTION

Community members often see the potential of tourism in terms of jobs, sales, and promoting cultural understanding. When visitor interests are made available to the community, ideas for entrepreneurial opportunities start to emerge. For example, local entrepreneurs are likely to perceive innovative business ideas, once new business niches are defined by a visitor survey. Good survey interpretation, based on questions designed well for the community or region, will indicate potential for new product lines, matching local skills with visitor interest.

Hold a community meeting where visitor survey data are presented, with training on using data for a business plan. This guides community members to generate ideas for business niches using local skills. These are the elements of an effective implementation stage to the survey. Applying survey data—for tourism plans, business plans, economic development plans, visitor center plans, museum and cultural center plans, community comprehensive plans, and strategic programmatic plans, as well as to funding proposals—carries the survey results to practical community applications. Forwarding the survey to work directly for the community is the basis for making the sizeable effort of a visitor survey worthwhile.

The sustainable benefits of improved tourism are both intangible and tangible. Intangible results include ongoing progress in terms of improved visitor understanding, respectful behavior, and incentive for visitor return. A community will then appreciate the process of assessing and improving. Tangible results such as number of visitors, jobs, new businesses, dollar impacts, and improved services for community members, will foster community interest in earned livelihood through tourism. Then, community support is likely to come forth for future survey efforts.

COMMUNITY-BASED SOLUTION
Zuni Tribe

The Zuni Tribe, located in New Mexico (USA), is a Native American community well known internationally for turquoise and silver jewelry-making, particularly in the intricate channel-work style. In this "village of artists," 85% of families earn a living in the cultural arts. While the community relies heavily on tourism for income, tensions regarding visitation tended to run high due to privacy impacts, particularly to the Middle Village plaza area during ceremonial times. Protection of cultural information is also a strong community concern.

Tourism planning carried out the intention of determining better ways of targeting the market by learning visitor preferences, while designing a strategy to manage tourism. Economic leakages to sales in cities, rather than purchases locally, were occurring due to lack of a local business and entrepreneurial directory.

Through tourism involvement, several forms of data-gathering assisted the community in setting direction. Community meetings determined the most acceptable and desired topic for visitor education to be tribal history. Determined in a visitor survey, the leading visitor interests included history, the cultural arts, and cultural foods. By comparing community interests with visitor interests, a good match between history and the arts emerged, encouraging the community to move forward with tours.

Outcomes of the planning process included the creation of a visitor center intake location and a tour enterprise to manage tourism. An educational website and a visitor guide (*Experience Zuni*) communicate visitor etiquette—explaining restrictions and locations where visitation is allowed, as well as restrictions on photography. The visitor guide features a traditional greeting and directs travelers to businesses in the village, keeping sales local. And the website features additional information on Zuni arts and artists. (www.zunitourism.com)

FURTHER READING

Morrison, Alastair. *Hospitality and Travel Marketing.* Delmar, AU: Thomson Learning, 2009.

    Explanations on the relationship between marketing and the tourism industry include details on research and analysis, surveys, market segmentation and trends, product development, communications, pricing, and evaluation.

Kotler, Philip, John Bowen and James C. Makens. *Marketing for Hospitality and Tourism.* Upper Saddle River, NJ: Pearson Education, Prentice Hall, 2009.

    Understanding the role of marketing in strategic planning relates to surveys, understanding buyer behavior, market segmentation, targeting, promoting tourism products and managing marketing.

5

ANALYZING THE MARKET

Visitor expenditures expand the local market for basic services, increasing community benefits.

One of the basic components of tourism success, marketing, is frequently under-estimated in small communities. The marketing section of the tourism plan includes market research, analysis, and promotional strategy. Based on specific data, strategies for reaching potential visitors and attracting them to a community or region for a vacation concept can be developed.

Two markets comprise the total potential for tourism-related businesses, the internal market of residents and the external market of visitors. Addressing both markets holds the possibility of improving the economic conditions of a region, by expanding the overall market potential necessary to increase businesses in the local economy. Collaboration with tourism partners is key.

What are the primary barriers to marketing? Planning ahead, time, and funds may be seen either as obstacles or as a focus for creative, rewarding, and low-cost opportunities. Attracting visitors to a community depends upon learning about potential market segments, their characteristics, and preferences. If a community has engaging cultural activities and cultural arts—and is willing to share some information with the public—then cultural tourism may be a good fit. If not, and the community has scenic beauty with public access, then recreational tourism may be a better fit. An interpretation of history from the community's viewpoint adds an additional cultural appeal to either.

> **Framework for Integrating Culture**
>
> - Identify potential markets.
> - Research the characteristics of those markets.
> - Find the best match between resources or activities, and market interests.
> - Decide which markets can support cultural goals, while fostering respect for cultural boundaries.
> - Identify messages clearly with a unifying concept or brand.
> - Link small enterprises and determine ways of supporting the network through collaborative marketing.
> - Begin the visitor education process about culture through informational content in marketing.
> - Determine what does not "sell" or commodify culture, but rather shares an experience.

The potential market with little local competition is a good market niche. Yet, this market may not be appropriate or desired by the community. Exploring choices in market potential creates a basis for community decisions.

ABOUT MARKET RESEARCH

The first stage in market research asks the question, "Who is out there with interests aligned to our offerings?" This determines existing and future customers. The second stage of market research addresses the questions, "What are others doing to serve the market?" and "Who are the competitors and who are the complements?" Then, once the potential market is known, targeting occurs. This contributes to a focused approach. For example, is the low end to be reached, or the high-end profile who want custom-made products? Or, is authenticity going to be the feature that will attract potential clients? In the case of handmade cultural items, authenticity is one of the most frequent draws to attract clients.

There are several sources of visitor data available to answer these questions. A broad-based approach to marketing is less effective for tourism than an approach identifying one or a few market segments—such as cultural tourists, recreational tourists, or ecotourists. Overlap between markets is powerful to identify, for subsequent marketing efforts are more proactive when designed to appeal to several markets with interests in common.

Finding the best match between potential markets and community preferences leads to a good "community fit," or "cultural fit" in culturally distinct communities. This chapter presents an optimistic approach to marketing, with strategies for effective networking, as well as maximizing no-cost and low-cost marketing opportunities. Reaching out to the public with informative promotion enhances visitor education, creating results beyond the profit motive.

Due to the isolated location typical of rural and Indigenous reservations or reserves, several markets must be cultivated for economic development success through tourism. A public relations effort is needed to develop a regional market. Emphasizing the importance of local culture as "value added" to the economic development efforts of the local region as a whole is a strategy for creating alignment with other communities.

Marketing with educational content improves cultural understanding and encourages purchases. If a community lacks resources for public relations, collaborating regionally for inclusion is an effective intermediate alternative.

PLANNING PROCESS:

Key Questions for Marketing Research

Assessing markets is a basic step. A good tourism plan or a stand-alone marketing plan examines market data and targets marketing efforts by answering the following questions:

- *What type of tourism market are you trying to reach (e.g., cultural, recreational, ecotourists)?*
- *What economic strata are you trying to attract (e.g., students, middle income or high income)?*
- *What geographic region or country are you trying to reach?*
- *Does a particular market segment seek out your region?*

- *Are these potential visitors focused on the activities, art items, or products you currently have?*
- *What other activities, products, or lodging interest them?*
- *Who is the most attentive to learning about and respecting your culture?*
- *Where are they from?*
- *When do they make decisions?*
- *Why do they buy from community businesses, or why not?*
- *Who are the competitors and why?*
- *What is the uniqueness or competitive edge of your offering?*

These are a few of the larger-picture questions in market research. Knowing the answers to these questions helps identify the businesses with high potential in the tourism plan.

Marketing research is usually conducted by a planner, an economic development specialist, a business owner, or a hired marketing firm. If a consultant is hired, the best results will come from an interactive process between business owners, community members, and the consultant. When gathering primary data through a survey at the community location, a combination of several sources collaborating is the most useful. Techniques used for gathering marketing data include: conversations with actual clients, on-site surveys, mailed surveys, internet follow-up surveys, and examining larger studies conducted by counties, states, or other governments.

Conducting marketing research through a local visitor survey, as detailed in the last chapter, is effective for understanding current visitors. In primary marketing data collection, key questions are determined for gathering data, covering both visitor characteristics and preferences. Then, these questions are asked of all clients or potential clients.

One of the common mistakes made in tourism development is to proceed on a "personal favorite" business idea of someone in the community, without carefully assessing market potential. Using a list of potential business ideas generated at a community meeting as the only basis for business decisions is one common pitfall in business development. Identifying clusters of entrepreneurial businesses that can feed into, or supply a new business, is important to overall jobs or earned income in the community. These are called *supply chains*.

Smaller businesses often overlook market analysis and marketing strategies, losing substantial income. Frequently, information on the best promotional techniques is determined by asking customers how they were reached. A small community must reach selective markets for its marketing dollars to be cost effective. Therefore, the effort of determining and reaching markets improves both community satisfaction and enterprise success. The message must be precise and the media appropriate.

Positioning tourism offerings in the marketplace requires securing a worthwhile attraction in the prospective client's mind. Market research will yield the answers. To this end, the questions to ask are:

- What type of client am I trying to attract?
- How will culture be presented and protected?
- What dollar range are these clients willing to spend?
- What promotional approach is likely to appeal to that client?

> *Finding the intersection of several tourism markets is integral to market analysis.*

Overlaps in markets can enhance or broaden cultural tourism opportunities. For example, cultural tourists drawn to museums and learning about history may also be fascinated with animal stories or stories about place, in addition to buying local arts. Explaining the importance of animal designs on artwork would bring an out-of-the-ordinary experience to this market segment. Or, offering a recreational activity such as a traditional canoe tour may be enhanced with stories about local ecosystem preservation activities, as well as offering miniature canoes or t-shirts with a canoe design for visitors to purchase. Keeping in mind multiple intentions with visiting families is a way to discover the intersection of markets.

Expanding the seasonal market is possible with the overlap of markets. As another example, recreational fishing trips in the summer season and ecotourism birding in the winter season, as well as cultural festivals in the summer and fall, are possible combinations for marketing efforts to extend the visitation season.

Understanding target audiences, the overlaps, and ways of attracting that group of customers is at the crux of effective marketing to reach the potential market. "Develop it and they will come" rarely works for tourism.

MARKET DATA SOURCES

Finding data is sometimes a challenge. When internet connection is available, access to a number of studies may be located free-of-charge online. Chambers of Commerce generally share their data freely. Depending on the source, some data may cost a steep fee. The United States is an example where the majority of national level studies are now industry-privatized, and only available at a high fee per report. Solutions for securing useful data include attending tourism conferences where data are presented and noting the latest trends indicated in tourism survey data.

There are national, state, regional, and city databases to explore. Being creative in locating data may compensate for lack of budget to purchase data or to conduct surveys. Identify the markets and assess the potential for a community on these levels: 1) local, 2) regional, 3) statewide, 4) national, and 5) international—then relate the levels to each other to determine tourism potential. Local sources of data include:

- Visitor surveys;
- License plate surveys;
- Business records;
- Lodging surveys;
- Guest registers;
- Sign-in books; and
- Interviews with businesses.

Of the tourism data sources, organizations such as Chambers of Commerce are the quickest and least expensive to approach. Others require membership participation or sell studies. If the community cannot afford the price for study purchase, look for summaries of these in organizational market studies. Internet searches are a valuable way to locate market data, if the source is reliable. Organizations providing data include:

- Tourism organizations;
- Chambers of Commerce;
- Convention and Visitor Bureaus;
- Tax and Revenue Departments (gross receipts reports);
- State or regional departments of tourism;
- Economic development organizations;
- National parks and national forests;
- National departments of tourism or commerce;
- Industry-specific state or national business organizations;
- Tourism trade shows (international); and
- The World Tourism Association (international).

Websites for major tourism organizations are listed in Appendix A. Market data covering a large region yield generalized data leading to a visitor profile. The more localized the data, the more specific questions can be tailored to local cultures, scenic attractions or ecosystems. Look for the following types of data from each source:

- Place of origin (shows where to market effectively);
- National and regional differences in interests;
- Age, indicating market segment;
- Lodging preference;
- Products desired to buy, product selection and development;
- Income levels; and
- Attraction and activity preference.

Such data are useful to focus the target market for project and business concepts. The survey detailing offerings in the region yields data useful for specific development purposes. The most common flaw in existing data is an inadequate survey sample. Collecting data from several sources will allow for cross-referencing results, yielding a greater sense of accuracy in the overall market assessment.

Of the no-cost, low-cost, and costly ways of marketing—those containing specific information on activities provide the most effective way to interest cultural travelers. One frequent and serious omission in the marketing section of a tourism plan is not identifying the actual businesses and services in the tourism network. Without this specific information, marketing efforts are limited in impact.

ASSESSING A RANGE OF TOURISM MARKETS

Market segmentation organizes knowledge about potential customers and selects for specific attention those groups whose needs and wants are a best match for the community. These groups are called **market segments** and cluster by age, gender, point of origin, interests, and income levels. Market data related to cultural tourism include the following categories.

1. **Culturally oriented travelers** are drawn to authentic local cultures and museums. More than half of the U.S. adult population indicates inclusion of at least one cultural, art, historic, or heritage activity or event while on a trip in the past year. There are over 100 million adult historic/cultural travelers in the U.S. alone.

2. While **ecotourists** seek outdoor activities, this market segment also tends to be engaged in sense of place, local ecosystem knowledge, cultural stories about animals, plants, and water, as well as land conservation efforts.

3. A recent concept in the tourism market, **geotourism** sustains or enhances the geographical character of the place being visited, including its environment, culture, aesthetics, heritage and the well-being of its residents. The emphasis is on sustainability and authentic travel experiences that travelers are seeking today.

4. The **market for international tourists** to the U.S. is recovering and growing. International travelers spend $116 billion, with over 62 million visitors. Market potential is defined by knowing characteristics of visitors from different countries. For example, the German market holds potential for Indigenous communities. Germans tend to take longer vacations and have an interest in tribal activities such as pow-wows and festivals, as well as

purchasing tribal art. The French are interested in history and collecting tribal art. These markets also seek opportunities to learn about cultural renewal efforts and language teaching. Potential visitors from other countries will be discovered by reviewing country-specific market studies. These travelers collect both traditional and contemporary high quality art and tend toward either the short visit (e.g., Japanese visitors) or a longer visit (e.g., German).

5. The *minority traveler* is an expanding market segment. Hispanic, African-American, Asian-American and the growing American Indian middle class are groups drawn to other cultures and history. These travelers seek to understand local interpretations of history and gain educational experiences for their children.

6. The *business traveler* is a valuable market segment. Consider government employees, social services personnel, health service providers, consultants, and contractors. Business travel to a rural community often rounds out the tourism season, when lodging and food service are made available. Otherwise, this market segment lodges and dines elsewhere while working with the rural community and dollars are lost to the local economy. The business traveler tends to be a repeat customer.

INTERPRETATION OF MARKET DATA

What is the meaning of the numbers in visitor data? This significant question is not answered in the majority of tourism survey reports. Moreover, interpretation is critical for indicating different opportunities, depending on a specific locale and set of existing businesses. For this reason, a person familiar with the region or community should conduct, or at minimum, participate in the interpretive process.

Identifying tourism niches meeting visitor preferences, while meshing with desired community directions, is at the core of interpretation. Potential for a tourism draw is defined by matching activities with appropriate age, interest, and income levels.

After tourism market targets are identified, strategies must be developed to establish a tourism draw, while keeping in mind the protection of cultural privacy and fragile environments. To start and to focus, complete a page on each of these topics:

- What do we have to offer?
- Who comes already?
- Whom are we trying to attract?
- What do we need to add or emphasize to attract them?
- How will we attract them?
- When will we be ready?

These questions sequentially focus the approach.

Identifying the market segment desired and when readiness will occur are vital questions in relation to establishing community or cultural priorities. One approach in tourism is to attract as many as possible, whoever will come. Such an approach leads to a lot of "traffic"[1] with few local expenditures, plus negative cultural or environmental impacts. This approach is costly, both in terms of marketing and dealing with impacts.

THE MARKETING SECTION OF THE TOURISM PLAN

Through tourism planning, a community outcome determines clear directions for attracting visitors. Some may not necessarily want additional tourists, but rather would like to target a specific market, such as the cultural tourism market—a segment that tends to be respectful of local culture, appreciates authenticity, and spends more on locally made items. Summarizing trends, rather than just listing existing data, forms a useful basis for decision making.

Initially, an assessment of the market is part of the tourism plan. As economic development through tourism progresses, a detailed marketing plan will be needed—targeting specific market segments, types of marketing, timelines, and costs. A market analysis is the first step in determining whether the market exists for specific business enterprises. Generally, a market analysis section in a tourism plan anticipates a period of two to five years. Tourism markets change annually, as economic conditions in a region or a country fluctuate. In recent years, fluctuations seen are dramatic, correlating with rapid shifts in worldwide economies.

After the tourism plan, an annual re-examination of the market supports the fine-tuning of businesses in the tourism network. The current market position of tourism businesses is assessed, and in the market section of the tourism plan, segments of the market are targeted. The market analysis establishes a strategy for market entry, strengthening, or expansion. Emphasis should reach beyond promotion, to other strategies that will reach the desired market.

The level of detail addressing the market will depend upon these major factors:

- Time and funds available for the tourism plan;
- Whether resources are available to complete a detailed marketing plan;
- Whether business plans following the tourism plan will focus on both individual business and collaborative marketing efforts.

Sections for the briefer analysis in a tourism plan should address:

- Analysis of the tourism market or market overview;
- Estimate of market share (size of the total market the community or enterprise intends to attract);
- Summary of the tourism draw;
- Detailed strategies to tap different market segments;
- A unifying concept or brand;
- Market slogans;
- Potential for collaborative marketing with local businesses;
- Potential for collaborative marketing with surrounding communities;
- Package or self-guided tour potential;
- Internet and social media strategies;
- Website outline;
- Cross-marketing strategies;
- New promotional pieces needed;
- Suggested improvements to current marketing pieces;

- Action plan (tasks and timelines); and
- Detailed marketing budget.

List data sources in the tourism plan for reference purposes.

The market strategy addressed in the tourism action plan is stated by event, activity, deadline, and person responsible. A calendar is also useful to include in the plan, to serve as a guide for employees of the business. In addition, a market strategy is useful for addressing ways of training staff in marketing skills.

What does marketing cost? An annual percentage of approximately five percent to ten percent of the business's profits should be set aside for continued promotion, depending on the type of business. For the small entrepreneurial business, a lower budget is possible by pooling marketing efforts among several businesses. Effectively spent dollars target the primary audience desired to purchase the tourism offerings.

This is why market research, then monitoring the marketing effort and evaluating annually, determine marketing effectiveness. Strategy and timelines should be included for this step. Are sufficient funds available to draw the desired customers? If not, revising the marketing strategy to determine the most effective plan for tapping low-cost and no-cost opportunities is a next step.

DESIGNING THE TOURISM DRAW

Matching local offerings with visitor preferences is central to marketing an effective vacation concept. And effective, targeted marketing informs the visitor of specific offerings available, putting ease into the vacation experience. Marketing dollar value is increased when visitors learn about specific tourism offerings. For this reason, a cohesive or unifying set of information sources—or a link to a website detailing information needed for a complete vacation concept—will be the most inviting to a potential visitor. Networking communities together is effective for enhancing the draw, if well-designed, specific itineraries are developed.

Marketing Strategies

A strategy is a focused direction to get a result; a successful marketing strategy for tourism frequently blends a mix of goods and services to be offered. In this way, if one tour or art item does not sell well in a particular month, others may sell, thus producing consistent income for the business. Maintaining quality is another important marketing concept, as consistency of quality underlies the reputation of the business.

> *A marketing plan updated annually is an essential business management tool.*

Pricing is also central in the marketing process. For this reason, understand who the competitors are and the pricing used in their businesses. Finally, promotion is another element in designing a marketing strategy. This is the one area of business development most neglected in rural and reservation areas. In other words, many good businesses are formed but not promoted adequately.

A good market strategy: 1) considers cultural appropriateness, 2) increases sales and profit, 3) causes a gain in market share, 4) lowers marketing costs, and 5) unifies marketing efforts in a community. A marketing section of the plan should be easy to follow, and realistic about the potential market. Tourism strategies include:

Strategy 1   Attracting the cultural tourism market by emphasizing authentic cultural arts, museums, festivals, and demonstrations in promotional materials.

Strategy 2   Marketing a peaceful retreat concept to the urban professional.

Strategy 3   Expanding the tourism season beyond the summer months through additional marketing for cultural tourism, birders, peaceful retreats, and small conferences.

Strategy 4   Marketing several businesses together, creating synergy between the businesses.

Strategy 5   Marketing collaboratively with regional communities, to enhance the visibility of local cultures as "value added" tourism offerings.

Often businesses fail when the market projections in a business plan were skewed to fit the "ideal market" rather than the one actually existing. Depending on the budget available for development and the size of the community, a detailed marketing plan is completed prior to the business plan, with findings integrated into the business plan.

Frequent questions asked by visitors in their decision making are:

- Will we be comfortable on our vacation?
- Is there enough to see?
- Is the cost within our travel budget?
- Will we learn from the experience?
- Are there unique shopping opportunities?

Attracting visitors to a community does not translate automatically into expenditures. Visitors will ask, "Where are the activities?" Networking and sharing tourism data within a region generates an increase in overall tourism expertise for a region. Information embedded in the promotion increases the effectiveness of marketing. Example marketing activities include:

- Improving customer service to increase word-of-mouth referrals;
- Utilizing local visitor centers and rest stops to distribute tourism information pieces;
- Providing maps and business brochures in the foyer of museums and other local heritage facilities;
- Assisting regional communities to attract small conferences, through website information on facilities;
- Developing specificity in marketing pieces, such as a travel guide and website, to match community readiness;
- Seeking and allocating funds for low-cost media coverage and promotional opportunities, such as visitor guide ads, to promote the "genuine" or culturally-based experience;
- Pooling resources and securing matching funds for a marketing collaboration expands potential for ads in larger publications—initiated by such agencies as Chambers of Commerce, Convention and Visitor Bureaus, and state tourism departments;
- Creating educational website visibility, providing descriptions needed to link for an entire vacation concept—with information

on lodging, food service, transportation, and other visitor amenities, as well as history and cultural arts;
- Cross-linking social media to reinforce multi-media results; and
- Organizing representation at international tourism trade shows.

The marketing section of a tourism plan is valuable for designing strategies and estimating costs. Effective marketing strategies will target the determined market on a statewide, regional and national basis.

Cross-Marketing

The most effective method of promoting is cross-marketing. When businesses in a region or community combine resources to market together, their potential strengths for a vacation concept are optimized. Using this method, the draw is increased to local activities focused on culture, recreation, and scenic beauty. Markets, sometimes unlikely together, become linked through a common theme. For example, ecotourism customers extend their stay to attend a museum, particularly if exhibit interpretation addresses cultural views toward the environment.

Cross-marketing creates a win/win situation. Effectiveness of cross-marketing may be seen in two ways—reducing cost and achieving an extended distribution of marketing materials. By expanding the market range, while carefully planning to minimize negative impacts, focused or targeted tourism development is achieved. This is a very different concept from mass tourism, attracting all who are willing to come.

Promotional materials encouraging vacation planning around a combination of cultural activities and facilities, arts, lodging, and food service—are appealing to cultural tourists—and tend to increase length-of-stay, plus encourage an increase in the family segment of clientele. As educational activities are added, family appeal increases. Sharing costs of marketing materials among participating businesses is a useful strategy when funds are limited.

A self-guided tour concept can be communicated, cross-marketing several enterprises. Packaged tours may be a later stage of business development for a community, yet the basics of showing a unified concept must occur early in the planning stage to create the effective marketing draw. The concept of *relationship marketing* involves networked linkages between participants within the tourism system, which enhances the visitation experience. Visitors then become actively engaged in related exchanges with providers.[2]

Counting Visitors

Is the local visitation number factual, an estimate, or the unspeakable wild guess? Unless the community requires a permit, charges a fee, or controls transportation through a tour company or community-owned vehicles, exact annual counts are not possible. Visitation numbers are usually an estimate, calculated with a method to improve accuracy. Use caution when projecting the market from estimated numbers, especially when using these statistics to plan a tourism-related business. Within the tourism industry, estimates are confusing when stated as fact.

Conducting a count can be expensive. Therefore, look for counts at surrounding parks, facilities near the community, visitor sign-ins, and traffic counts (a mix of resident and visitor vehicles). Actual visits versus the sum of people at stops are not necessarily the same, due to double counting at multiple locations. State- or county-conducted traffic counts are a valuable and readily available source of information.

Lodging records are often used for estimates. Sign-in books are another less costly way of counting visitors, effective for one location such as a museum or a visitor center. A more expensive, yet more accurate way of tracking visitors is to install a counter in a visitor center entrance. Selling a permit for visitation is one source of accurate counts, if entrance can be controlled.

THE UNIFYING CONCEPT OR BRAND

For marketing to create an effective draw, a unified and specific concept must be defined. Although the concept of a ***brand*** is a current trend in tourism, cultural tourism efforts should be careful to avoid commodifying culture, people, places, and representative cultural arts—by focusing on "product" without interpretation.

Value-based characteristics such as friendliness and generosity may be incorporated into the brand concept to create unique visibility. Rather than seeing a brand as a product defined with a logo, this newer definition of brand concerns a unified perception of a locale to visit. Identity is added to the visitation experience and culture is an important part of the concept.

A brand is an accumulation of characteristics that form a destination's image and identity.[3] One advantage of a defining concept is ongoing distinction. A short statement repeated on all marketing pieces, websites, and social media unifies the draw. Small-scale experiences benefit from a unifying concept. Branding statement examples are:

- Different views, endless discoveries
- Travel our historic route
- Learn, experience, see the authentic
- Traditional guides—learn to be in nature
- The source for Native arts

Product branding complements and reinforces the broader brand concept. Each gives strength to the other, in the overall tourism draw. Some cultures have an adverse reaction to the brand concept. A response during one tourism planning process in a Native American community—"Sounds too much like cowboys." If branding is not a culturally acceptable term, or seems to commodify culture, use the concept of a unifying theme.

> *Branding is a way of creating an image to stay in the memory of potential visitors.*

Connoting an experience and feelings for the people or locale is a better approach than isolated bits of information on businesses or natural features. A brand is sometimes described as a promise and a vision of the destination. Smaller communities working together within a region create a destination image that draws visitors to spend several days of their vacation time. Defining the distinct elements characterizing a region gives identity to a range of activities, the elements of a brand concept.

The vacation concept providing a good tourism market draw requires five days to one week of activity options. By linking smaller enterprises together and defining a unifying set of characteristics, a regional tourism identity is created. This may happen by two different methods: 1) describing elements of a satisfying vacation experience, based on existing characteristics, or 2) identifying a theme with existing and future potential—then deciding as a community to further develop that theme.

Here are a few ideas on desirable vacation experience characteristics, to point the way.

Restful:

- Clean air;
- No traffic;
- Comfortable lodging;
- Familiar foods; and
- A peaceful retreat.

Educational:

- History;
- Authentic cultural arts;
- Activities for children;
- Opportunities to learn history;
- Cultural experiences (museums, arts); and
- Opportunities to experience another culture (culturally diverse lifeways and foods).

Recreational:

- Adventure;
- Scenic beauty;
- Access to outdoor activities;
- Opportunity to learn about regional species;
- Discovery in nature; and
- Contributing to preservation efforts.

Seeing a region's strengths from the eyes of an outsider may be difficult for local communities. Differences between states, regions, and cultures, as well as the urban/rural destination, must be understood in relation to the preferences of several markets. For this reason, hiring a marketing consultant with experience working within different markets is useful.

❖ ❖ ❖ ❖ ❖

PLANNING PROCESS:
Develop a Unifying Concept

- *Describe the unique character of your community or region.*
- *How are values expressed in your hospitality tradition?*
- *What does the region want to offer?*
- *Condense these ideas into a unique, concise statement.*

❖ ❖ ❖ ❖ ❖

A *logo* is an artistic design that represents a tourism concept or a product. When a logo reflects the marketing statement and is used on a letterhead, business cards, and invoices, it becomes a visual symbol to remember one or more businesses. Create a distinctive image that appeals to several target market segments. The logo should be unique, appealing, catchy, and memorable. Place a copyright or trademark on the logo to keep others from using it.

"Is the concept working?" should be a continual inquiry relating to sustainability. Measuring effectiveness of the brand concept is valuable for redirecting the concept or improving upon the elements that are working well to attract the desired visitors. A high level of customer satisfaction plus the concrete brand concept give the visitor a specific recommendation to pass along to friends, co-workers and relatives. Word-of-mouth recommendations are the least expensive and most effective form of advertising.

Not providing an experiential vacation concept leads to the loss of potential visitors. For example, if a rural community is adjacent to hiking areas, creating a sense of the "adventure" is more effective than just listing facts about the forest. Storytelling is another way of adding interpretation in traditional communities. All details of a cultural story need not be included if this is private information. A brief version with the message may create the sense of discovery.

Several factors significant to the success of a brand,[4] defined as repeat visitation and/or referrals, are:

- Satisfaction (delivery on the experience);
- Value (price and quality);

- Image (brand's personality and reputation);
- Convenience and availability;
- Service and hospitality; and
- Quality products available for shoppers.

Working together to create a brand is known as *co-branding*. By partnering with well-known areas, either rural (e.g., wine country, fishing and hunting areas, tribal arts, national parks and forests) or urban to rural and tribal collaborations, communities starting their tourism development may realize a benefit from a brand concept rather quickly. Communicating with a state tourism department or program on an ongoing basis furthers inclusion in their branding. A win/win situation is created by "tagging along" to make an already successful concept even more attractive with increased offerings.

When businesses have a theme in common, the learning experience from each enhances the overall knowledge gained from a vacation concept. This result is engaging and exciting to the visitor.

Integrated Marketing Communications

A coordinated effort between different media for marketing, or *integrated marketing communication* (IMC), is useful to outline in the tourism marketing plan. As the internet becomes a significant part of everyday life in the countries most likely to purchase leisure or educational travel, opportunities increase for:

- Travel reservations;
- Purchase of tour packages;
- E-businesses (before and after travel); and
- Increased opportunities for small businesses.

Through the internet, visitors are now becoming knowledgeable of a community, culture, services, and other businesses pre-visit. To maximize the advantages of visitation, providing a way for visitors to purchase locally made items post-visit increases benefit to the local economy.

A few of the internet resources useful at the publication time of this book are: websites, blogs, UTube, Facebook, Twitter, LinkedIn and other social networking sites. The strength of using these web resources rests with the interface between those used, to reinforce the message and the reach of contact. Viral marketing, using a "send to a friend" button on the website, targets better than mass marketing due to shared preferences. Effective use of the internet is becoming an ever-increasing source of low-cost promotion.

DIVERSIFYING WAYS OF MARKETING

Promotion is at the core of tourism success. Along with good management and adequate capital, there are several means of securing promotion at low cost. A small community is able to develop a financially balanced approach to promotion—by first outlining no-cost and low-cost strategies and then adding those of increasing cost each subsequent year. Capacity-building grant funds may cover some marketing costs in the budget. This strategy gives the community a chance for the first stages of promotion, until profits are generated to pay for expanded promotion.

Visitor Recommendations

If service is good and the cultural tourism experience is worth the trip, then word-of-mouth marketing is effective. Marketing materials for visitors to take back home as souvenirs and pass on to other potential visitors—along with positive comments and social media connections—reinforce the referral marketing strategy.

Media Connections

Communicate with local media through press releases, event notices, and story content for free coverage. Staying in touch with reporters, columnists, and assignment editors encourages them to contact the community directly when a story idea emerges. Consider guest television and radio appearances, and post the links to interview video clips online via social media.

Local Tourism Publications

Local marketing draws more visitors already in the area, full-time residents, and part-time residents to cultural offerings. Advertising dollars are a wise investment for cultural enterprises, since cultural tourists are seeking contact with authentic cultural experiences and people, a unique experience, and an opportunity to purchase genuine art items. These publications are often posted online in addition to availability in hardcopy. Inclusion in the calendar of events section of local and state travel planners is usually available at no charge.

The following list of publication types represents excellent opportunities for inclusion in articles and calendars:

- Travel planners;
- State visitor guides;
- Publications of local newspapers;
- Regional guides;
- Getaway guides;
- County guides;
- Festivals and events calendars;
- Guides from urban Convention and Visitor Bureaus;
- Bus schedules with maps;
- Heritage publications;
- Websites; and
- Video kiosks.

These are vital sources to consider. Exposure in these publications draws a large number of visitors at no cost to small communities. Purchase ad space as revenues increase. Travel planner publications reach visitors as they plan their vacations. This point of contact is the most effective for reaching travelers as they decide their expenditures.

One caution—timing is crucial. A vacation concept must be running smoothly and well managed before securing this degree of marketing exposure. Negative cultural and ecological impacts tend to occur when many visitors come before readiness in local capacity is in place. Word travels rapidly in the travel industry and reliability is a crucial factor for continued referrals.

Inclusion in Travel Guides

Working with local travel writers for inclusion in visitor guide articles is a high-impact, no-cost means of marketing. There are two ways to utilize the visitor guide avenue of marketing. One is to be included in travel articles in existing guides. This is generally a good first step to pursue since the discussion space allocated to articles provides greater coverage than the small advertisement and the cost is free. Articles usually do not cover the topic of one business only, but rather a regional concept or group of businesses.

The second is the purchase of advertisement in these guides. This strategy does cost; purchase over the long term is necessary, since repeat advertising is the way to secure attention. Cost-sharing ad space among several linked businesses is an effective method for collaborative marketing. If locally made products and authenticity issues are covered, local cultural groups will benefit to a great extent. Most travel guides are now also published online, maximizing international reach.

The Brochure

A brochure may either be printed in color on glossy stock, or simply produced on a copier or printer as a starting place. A brochure informs the public of offerings and may also provide information on cultural context. Brochures are generally three panels, an 8 ½" x 11" page folded, or four panels on an 11" x 17" page.

Effective content includes: 1) traditional welcoming, 2) community—short description, 3) visitor etiquette in brief, 4) list of main activities, 5) map showing location in a regional and national context, 6) website links to a directory of community entrepreneurs and businesses, and 7) a membership/donation panel for cultural arts teaching, language classes, or a cultural center or museum (4th panel). For hardcopy distribution, a brochure rack creates visibility. Networking with other communities or businesses for a larger brochure rack in a place visible to tourists supports linkages and encourages a longer stay in the region.

Web links mentioned in the brochure provide the additional information needed to benefit from the trip. The brochure posted on the community website is valuable for both virtual users and on-site use. Posting on the website will become necessary over time, as marketing and visitor information shift increasingly to the internet.

Panel or Rack Card

A panel card is one-third the size of a brochure, usually printed on a heavier-weight card stock. The advantages of a panel card displayed in racks are the reduced cost compared to a brochure and a generalized draw to the community. The disadvantage of a panel card is less space to advertise specific enterprises. If the rack card motivates visitors to go to the website, a website link for the specifics will partially compensate for the lack of space.

Visitor Guide

The advantage of developing a community-based visitor guide is to give listings to entrepreneurs at a reasonable cost, thus increasing direct benefits to the local community. Although a visitor guide is generally an expensive project, there are several ways to reduce costs, particularly in the first years until ad sales build to cover the costs. A visitor guide may initially be printed in black on white on newsprint, with a color cover, and later expanded to color inside as revenues are generated. Increase the number of pages over time, as revenues increase.

Collaboration between several communities for a pocket travel guide or visitor guide reduces the cost for all communities and businesses involved. A four-color publication is the next level in cost and effectiveness due to the extra space for additional information. Include a locator map and increase distribution as the budget expands over the years, to locations beyond the local community as a means of increasing visitor draw. Placing visitor guides in lodging places increases referrals.

In a visitor guide, there is enough space to describe cultural arts in detail, with pictures and short biographies of people and brief histories of culturally significant sites. Remember to include: 1) traditional welcoming statements, 2) visitor etiquette, 3) a calendar of events, 4) a brief history, 5) festivals and art shows, 6) overview of authentic cultural arts, 7) heritage sites, 8) outdoor activities 9) geotourism-based itineraries, and 10) a clear locator map showing businesses and entrepreneurs.

Frequently, small businesses cannot afford to purchase advertising in publications. Finding a way to make listings for cultural enterprises affordable, or free-of-charge, benefits the larger tourism network as a whole. Some grant sources are available for assistance to small businesses, if the effort furthers a group of businesses in overall economic development rather than a single business. One strategy for securing funding is the teaching of marketing skills to enterprises and assisting them to place advertising.

DISTRIBUTION

Several distribution methods for marketing are important to outline in the tourism plan:

- Linking kiosks and visitor centers in the region, while providing visitor information (with excellent maps), increases the impacts of marketing.
- Placing brochures from individual businesses or small pocket travel guides from communities is effective at locations accessible to visitors arriving by air as well as by car. Other transportation sources, such as ferries and multi-modal routes should be considered. Web tools for travelers are used increasingly by the traveler en route.
- A concentrated effort to distribute brochures and travel guides at the gateway communities to the region will have the greatest impact.
- If each business carries copies of regional brochures or even a small business directory, then an itinerary concept comes to life—as one business forwards visitors to all of the others.
- An arts flier describing the authentic art-making process (available at gift shops and galleries) encourages sales of handmade items and encourages community members to learn cultural traditions.
- Fliers on art-making at festivals present a "value-added" dimension, or educational experience, to the event, encouraging an increase in the cultural and geotourism markets.
- Interfacing with the promotion for festivals and events results in additional marketing exposure.

Assessing the most effective distribution points for reaching visitors as they come into the community is useful for visitor education.

THE TOURISM WEBSITE

Addressing website structure and content connects market analysis to the steps needed to reach a specific target market via the internet. When local websites appear as a fragmented list (e.g., attractions, natural features, lodging, food service, calendar of events), they are boring. Unify local tourism elements with an experience concept to capture visitor interest. Excitement about a destination motivates potential visitors to plan and go.

> *More than access to one business, visitors seek experiences.*

The website must reach beyond lists and links, to communicate a cohesive visitation experience. Photographs, graphics, and clips of traditional music enliven a website. Visitors are asking, "What new knowledge, understanding, or feeling will I come away from the vacation experience holding?" This is the memorable vacation concept. A new appreciation of nature, a new interpretation of history, the feeling of contributing to a community effort, or the excitement of one-on-one contact with another cultural group—these are examples of the sought-after vacation experiences.

A contemporary dilemma concerns how to transmit information in a digital age, or how to use the internet in a cross-cultural, respectful way. Are stories on a website authentic, when not told in a listening circle? Some communities may object to this mode of presentation.

Yet, the internet is a venue for those not able to physically travel, or to prepare a traveler before the actual visit. Travelers provided with some depth on local initiatives feel connectedness; this is the experiential. Communities deciding internally on appropriateness of sharing information will become comfortable with the internet.

Generate Home Page Interest

As the number of websites for vacation options increases each year, so does the competition increase for moments of visitor attention. Potential visitors tend to browse several websites quickly, spending less time at each site than in prior years. For this reason, the home page must be both informative and inviting. Home pages need to be intriguing enough to reduce the bounce rate, or the number of people leaving early before exploring the entire site. The most frequent mistake made in website design is the assumption that visitors will stay and explore the entire site. Increasing visitor time spent on the home page and continuing through the site is central to drawing the visitor to the physical location.

Think creatively of the website as a visitation experience, not merely a way to post data. All the principles of hospitality should be applied, especially friendliness. Starting with a traditional welcoming or greeting is exceptional, whether in the local language or in the visitor's language.

Keeping the home page brief and uncluttered will capture attention. The buttons on the home page should relate to trip planning, such as:

- Explore
- Culture
- Activities
- Travel tools
- Itineraries
- Contact us

What are the community's offerings under the main categories? Pull-down menus will allow the visitor to navigate quickly. Travel tools include the weather, driving distances, and maps for all trip segments.

The home page will communicate well with fewer words. Images or photographs rotating in a slide show format are a way to communicate adventure and authenticity with few additional words on the page. Rather than paragraphs or long sentences, use keywords or phrases formatted for a quick visual scan.

Include the Essential Topics

To be effective, the website must give information needed for vacation planning, such as lodging, food service, attractions, and links to other communities. The next most important information set includes ATM availability, internet service, and cell phone reception. Preferences of the local market will determine which information items are of use to visitors, highlighting the importance of coordinating market research with website design. Keeping content current prevents visitor frustration, encourages them to come and stay longer, as well as return for the repeat visit.

If resources are limited, website development may be phased with continual expansion of information over time. Internet trends change every year, primarily with "surfing" habits. Reading tourism publications, attending conferences, and networking within the tourism industry, are ways of staying up-to-date with these changes.

One constant for tourism, rarely remembered for websites, is the vacation concept—showing visitors how to put together the pieces of information for an intriguing vacation. Consider these topics:

- History;
- Local calendar;
- Overview of communities;
- Etiquette for respectful visitation;
- Local services available;
- Links to other local businesses (especially lodging, food service, shopping);
- Links to Chambers of Commerce;
- Forests, parks, lakes;
- Maps;
- Photographs (scenery and cultural);
- Information on cultural revitalization efforts;
- Itineraries (scenic);
- Weather; and
- Visitor survey (optional).

When posting a calendar of events, a description of the events gives the potential visitor a better perception of what is offered, how long to stay, and whether the event will be the focal point of the visit.

Seasonal weather patterns are valuable for potential visitors to know, for bringing appropriate clothing and gear. A primary intention for providing information is to increase the comfort level of the future visitor.

When a website is effective, travelers will easily find the community. Changing search or tag words and experimenting with effective topics makes an enormous difference to success. Reassessing tourism market trends, both nationally and internationally, assists the tourism program or business to discover current visitor interests. Attending conferences, reading tourism reports, and obtaining information from state tourism websites are strategies for staying current. A list of resources in the tourism or marketing plan serves as a reminder.

The Appropriateness of Photographs

Some communities are more receptive to posting photographs of cultural activities than others. But in most traditional communities, photographs of some activities would not be allowed. After exploring this topic within the community, note restrictions on the use of photographs for media in the plan. Highly restricted activities could be described in a general way. Every marketing effort—whether a brochure, visitor guide, or a website—must respect the privacy wishes of the community.

Visitors will feel more comfortable when the policy on photographs allowed in the community is posted on the website. This web opportunity for visitor education prior to the visit is valuable for visitors to plan their equipment needs as well as their activities in advance. Profits accruing to photographers and not to traditional communities have long been a sensitive topic in cultural tourism. A brief, yet comprehensive policy is best to put in place. Options include:

- No photographs allowed as a possible policy;
- Photographs of some events;
- Photographs of some events, but with a purchased photography permit;
- Higher photography fee for commercial uses; and
- Permission only for special circumstances or restricted publication.

Fees tend to be higher for video privileges and the community may want to see the video and give permission for a limited use. The advantage of such a policy is community control over images. Avoid a cumbersome policy that travel writers and photographers will be reluctant to engage in, thus limiting free media exposure for local tourism offerings.

Protection for photos on the website is a consideration. Making photographs not downloadable and stating policy on use by the public will help protect culturally private images.

THE MARKETING BUDGET

A multi-media approach to marketing is necessary to reach those visitors planning vacations and using internet sources of information, as well as visitors already arrived who use both internet and hardcopy information. Younger demographic groups usually prefer the internet. When seen as a means of continued education for the visitor, well-designed marketing efforts further community intentions for cultural tourism.

Budgeting for marketing in the tourism plan ensures forward movement on the part of the community or enterprise, since this step is frequently omitted. In summary, typical marketing budget categories for a small, rural community anticipating a gradual enterprise start-up include:

- Rack card;
- Brochure;
- Website;
- Chamber of Commerce memberships (for distribution);
- Travel magazine and newspaper articles (no cost);
- Advertisements in visitor guides and travel planners;
- Tourism trade shows; and
- Distribution in kiosks.

Tourism Trade Shows

Participation in tourism trade shows allows travel agents and tour companies to learn about a community's offerings. Although these trade shows are expensive to attend, either sharing booth costs or participating with a regional, state, or national tourism organization, will cut costs substantially. Individually owned businesses tend not to promote by this method, highlighting the need for inclusion in a regional tour or tour concept. Travel agents participating in these shows are seeking an itinerary-based tour to book.

Marketing participation through advertisement in larger guides distributed at trade shows effectively reaches the agent booking tours. A list of the largest international tourism trade shows is included in the appendices.

SUSTAINABILITY

The challenge in cultural tourism is to create the bridge from popular demand to designing and marketing a unique, authentic experience of local cultures. Whether a tourism enterprise or set of enterprises succeeds often depends upon the quality of the market analysis. Variables central to sustainability include:

- *Size of market.* Scale of enterprises must not only match market potential, but also capacity and desired directions of the community, in order to benefit economically. Protecting cultural privacy is a factor for deciding the size of the desired market.

- *Characteristics of market.* A hasty market analysis, or one that relies on surveys not containing questions relevant to the community or culture, does not accurately assess a match between community, culture, and offerings—one factor resulting in enterprise failure.

- *Cultural fit.* If the community is excited about the idea or enterprise, community members will work harder toward the success, in terms of both visitor education and financial viability. Negative attitudes drive visitors away.

- *Educational value.* Informative marketing pieces are likely to be taken home as souvenirs, and shown to educate other potential visitors. Updated websites allow visitors to continue their learning experiences after their return, increasing the educational value of the visit.

- *Ecological protection.* Attract a respectful market and limit the market draw to the carrying capacity of the local environment, for the preservation of culturally significant plant and wildlife areas.

- *Readiness.* Matching pace of the market draw with internal capacity is crucial for drawing visitors to the community only when capacity for managing tourism is in place. Small-scale efforts are easier for ongoing assessment and improvement.

Educating the tourism industry on the uniqueness of a culture, as well as cultural boundaries for participation and the sharing of information, reduces potential negative impacts from tourism. Educational efforts, through participation with local tourism entities or training to the industry on cultural differences, help pace marketing to appropriate form, scale, and timing. Cultural understanding increases sustainability.

COMMUNITY-BASED SOLUTION
International Folk Art Market, Santa Fe, New Mexico (USA)

The International Folk Art Market (since 2004) provides a venue for artists to create and sell high-quality artwork and serves as an advocate for the preservation and transmission of folk arts worldwide. Now the largest international folk art market in the world, the organization presents an annual international festival highlighting some of the world's finest folk art, multicultural entertainment, ethnic foods, and educational activities for children and families. During the market, visitors observe artists' demonstrations at the booths and have many opportunities for interaction and cultural exchange, deepening their appreciation for diverse cultures.

The market serves as an advocate for the preservation, survival, and transmission of folk arts, and represents an innovative cultural enterprise model for international development, business skill building, and poverty alleviation. Facilitating the link between producers who may be marginalized and from rural areas in developing nations—and direct contact with new international customers who appreciate and value their traditions—is a central outcome.

With access to a market in an urban community known internationally for markets (e.g., Santa Fe Indian Market, Santa Fe Spanish Market), International Folk Art Market draws over 20,000 for the weekend. In 2011, there were 135 artists from 49 different countries across six continents. Expanded benefits from 54 artists from participant cooperatives represent approximately 20,000 artisans, positively impacting the lives of over 200,000 extended family members.

Success factors include location, bringing the profits directly to artists (participants retain 90% of sales), a system for tracking progress by documenting sales, partnerships strengthening the market (the Museum of International Folk Art, the New Mexico State Department of Cultural Affairs, and the Museum of New Mexico Foundation), as well as extensive training and use of 1,500 volunteers. (www.folkartsmarket.org)

FURTHER READING

Bernstein, Joanne Scheff. *Arts Marketing Insights.* San Francisco, CA: John Wiley, 2007.

    Cultural tourism is addressed as part of the presentation on using strategic marketing to define, deliver, and communicate value in the arts. Includes leveraging the internet and email marketing.

Middleton, Victor. *Marketing in Travel and Tourism.* Amsterdam, NL: Elsevier, 2009.

    This text on the special characteristics of travel and tourism marketing addresses: understanding the consumer, planning marketing strategy, the marketing planning process, marketing campaigns, and applying marketing—including case studies.

Morrison, Alastair. *Marketing and Managing Tourism Destinations.* New York: Routledge, 2013.

    This comprehensive text covers how marketing is planned, implemented, and evaluated in relation to issues, challenges, and expected new directions.

Sweeney, Susan. *101 Ways to Promote Your Tourism Business Website.* Gulf Breeze, FL: Maximum Press, 2008.

    Practical topics include planning the tourism website, designing the site to be search engine friendly, website elements that encourage repeat visitation, outlines for content, landing pages, increasing web traffic, online advertising, and maximizing media relations.

6

COMPLETING THE TOURISM PLAN

*A plan on paper supports
a tourism collaboration working together.*

Once community needs are understood and the market opportunity is clear, a foundation for tourism is created. Defining the steps to get a result, persons responsible, a time frame, and where to go for the resources, forms the basis for moving ahead as a group.

The previous three chapters covered data gathering leading into a plan. To review: forming a representative committee of all stakeholders in the community, securing community input, assessing the market, completing a resource inventory, identifying community strengths, recognizing cultural boundaries for sharing information, then creating a community vision for tourism —all are essential steps toward preparing a plan.

This chapter focuses on completing a written plan for the community to follow. This final step is valuable as a guide[1] for implementation. Keeping a group working together, moving forward, and showing the long-term planned benefit to the community, inspire continued participation. Funders and other resource providers respond well to a written plan.

> **Framework for Integrating Culture**
>
> - Identify projects compatible with community resources and cultural goals.
> - Create a team approach for planning steps to carry out projects.
> - Include all generations in project designs.
> - Ensure a scale and form for projects compatible with culture.
> - Define timing in a way that "brings the community along," developing expertise for management and ownership.
> - Design an evaluation plan according to cultural criteria for success.

ADDRESSING KEY ISSUES

Areas of concern are important to define early in the tourism planning process. *Key issues*, or those considered to be the most important by the community, guide the remaining planning steps. The following examples connect the strategy of cultural renewal to issues commonly defined during community participation.

Issue 1. Protecting Cultural Privacy

Privacy to practice culture is often regarded as the highest concern in relation to cultural tourism. Needs may range from closure of the community at times, to preventing unwanted photography of ceremonial activities. Protecting the privacy of individuals requires defining those privacy issues and addressing them with a managed tourism program in place.

Issue 2. Managing Visitation

Visitor education is necessary to protect privacy, as well as to expand economic opportunity for community members. Most visitors are aware of being respectful and guidance leads to this result. Attracting and educating the cultural tourism and ecotourism markets are the means of increasing the likelihood of respectful and caring tourists.

Issue 3. Protecting and Preserving Tradition While Generating Income

Tourism is frequently a stimulus for community members to learn the cultural arts. Encouraging an intergenerational approach to tourism programs expands activities available at traditional communities and enriches the visitation experience. Identifying artists and creating an artisan database establishes a solid foundation for arts learning programs and educational materials on the arts.

The need to create employment from culturally-based activities is linked to cultural survival, providing alternatives to out-migration from traditional communities. Earned income combined with traditional economic activities frequently supports rural families in the continuance of cultural lifeways.

Issue 4. Maintaining Authenticity

Protecting authenticity of traditional or cultural forms and preventing the unauthorized use of cultural symbols are other measures to reduce negative impacts. Educating the public about the value of handmade cultural arts and the history of the art enhances appreciation and the sense of cultural property. For example, preventing Native American arts made in copied cultural styles from being sold as "Native American made" protects the integrity of the market.

Issue 5. Environmental Conservation

In traditional communities, there is usually a strong desire to preserve cultural landscapes, environments that reflect the historical and cultural character of an area. Care taken with architectural styles and landscaping ensures consistency with the characteristics that give a cultural sense of place. Tourism-related programs that educate the public about local values and techniques in sound environmental practices will benefit other community programs.

Once issues are defined and strategies identified, participants are better able to create goals and objectives to guide a managed tourism program. These issues will not likely be resolved quickly, but rather will require long-term involvement.

DEVELOPING POLICY AND ETIQUETTE

Policy guides community direction for tourism development and management. Larger-scale versus small-scale, environmental protection, cultural privacy guidelines, community ownership, and procedures for informing the public on policy are topics valuable as guiding principles for tourism. If the community is divided on an issue, the policy formation stage provides a way of unifying opinion, or at least resolving differences. In communities where consensus is the traditional decision-making process, the specific cultural means of reaching consensus should be considered. Resolving a community's mixed feelings toward tourism can be facilitated by developing a tourism policy.

Each region and each culture within a region holds a different set of expectations regarding culturally sensitive or respectful behavior. To explore ways of designing a solution, include different opinions within the community. Consider the ways of benefiting from tourism while minimizing negative impacts. Visitors will feel welcome if the community is unified in policy.

PLANNING PROCESS:
Develop a Tourism Policy

- *What are traditional ways of welcoming and caring for visitors?*
- *How does tourism relate to our self-sufficiency goals?*
- *How will tourism support, rather than detract from, cultural retention?*
- *How many tourists can be managed in a year?*
- *How will this number of total visitors break down per season?*
- *Where will visitors be allowed in the community and surrounding areas?*
- *How will visitors be restricted geographically (to prevent negative impacts on residents and ecosystems)?*
- *What services will visitors require and how will those services be provided from within the community?*

- *How will local leadership and hospitality skills be fostered in sustainable development?*
- *How will the local community communicate and cooperate with the travel industry?*
- *How will privacy and cultural needs of the community be protected?*
- *What environmental protection measures will be needed?*

Intangible aspects of heritage are valuable to perceive in the policy stage. Those qualitative, difficult-to-quantify, benefits of tourism participation are central to both cultural revitalization and cultural survival. Ways of evaluating both qualitative and quantitative measures of success in cultural tourism connect to policy established in the early stages. Evaluation strategies relating to policy in sustainable tourism development are illustrated in Chapter 10.

Many traditional cultures teach protocols, thousands of years old, for taking care of visitors. Discussing these protocols for hosting visitors and deciding how to continue these traditions in current times delineates a contemporary way of welcoming. A statement of visitor etiquette provides a means of bridging the communication between community-determined policy and visitor education. Topics valuable for guiding the visitor include:

- A welcoming statement;
- Clear definition of where visitation is allowed and places off-limits;
- Boundaries on appropriate dress;
- Protocols on noise levels (e.g., silence during traditional dances, no applause);
- Protocols for being in natural areas (e.g., staying on the trail, not gathering or damaging plants, whether hunting or fishing is allowed);
- Photography regulations or fees;
- Events where visitors are welcome; and
- Thanking the visitor for coming.

When to define policy in planning and development is not a clear-cut question. Policy definition underlies key decisions, such as whether to participate or to not participate in cultural tourism. There is a positive tendency—once planning is carried out and everyone's opinion is valued and etiquette is defined—for participation to continue on some level.

Policy definition is likely to start at the initial stage of tourism planning and then run parallel to subsequent steps, as new aspects of participation in a tourism market are seen by the community. This is an interactive process to be fine-tuned and developed on a continual basis—as well as updated periodically by a community.

If the outcome of participation discussions regarding the tourism market is negative, and the desired outcome is no participation, the development of policy is a fundamental step. It is useful for the outside world—or even different groups within the community—to know the specific reasons why tourism is not desired.

Policy serves as education and is one of the best forms of insurance against negative impacts that are unintended or undesired. Deciding to not participate in a tourism market, or specifying limits to tourism, are meaningful communications with the tourism industry. A policy statement may indicate options for participating away from the community, or on the internet. Other options include setting aside a designated area at the edge of the community, or purchasing land away from residential areas. Stating policy in the tourism plan guides future actions.

Non-communication is likely to result in continual misunderstandings and exploitive (non-intentional or intentional) activities. Cultural tourism that is mutually beneficial to both the industry and community takes into account local values and ways of working with those local values.

Community conflict repels visitors. One potential outcome of a planning process is resolving mixed feelings about tourism. When efforts are in place to reduce negative impacts and to increase opportunities for community members in an equitable manner—there is likely to be more alignment with tourism. If community members do not sense an equal opportunity for accessing tourism benefits, complaining is likely to occur. Or, if privacy and traffic impacts are ongoing, community comments are likely to be heard in public. These tendencies affect tourism negatively.

Visitors love to learn. However, there usually are boundaries to sharing cultural information. When these cultural boundaries are adequately defined, and redefined over the long-term, the amount of information shared is in check. The easiest way to create a comfort zone in common is to educate visitors on respectful, non-invasive behavior.

Play detective. Ask curious visitors who like to converse what is most appealing and least appealing in the community. Then, share the information with the tourism group. Avoid criticism, and members of the tourism network will perceive the need for policy and collaborative improvement.

Another valuable way to gain ideas for tourism policy is to look at examples from similar cultures. Ask tourism managers about the successes and weaknesses of their policies. Find out if their situation, both geographic and cultural, is similar. Study problems in other communities and discover how they find solutions, to determine an effective tourism policy statement.

SETTING GOALS

Goals are long-term outcomes, effective for keeping the community working together on a common track. Having goals creates motivation and unity in the community. Goals may be process-oriented, as well as outcome-oriented, depending on the culture or the intended uses.

Goals are usually general. However, the more specific a goal, the easier it is to measure progress on that goal. *Objectives* are short-term steps that will be used to accomplish goals and "bring the community along." Between three to five goals provide a starting place.

Process-oriented goals tend to relate to capacity-building. Frequently, goals are result-oriented and not feasible for small-scale tourism in the long run due to a lack of continued community participation and internal capacity-building. Including both result-oriented goals and capacity-building goals produces the best scale and capability result. Continued attention and allocation of financial resources usually only occur if the community has placed a priority on specific projects. Effective goals address the five-year or ten-year time frame at minimum, and are useful for prioritizing projects according to capacity-building.

Where goals fit in the planning process varies from culture to culture. Tourism goals are usually set early, after assessments. This goal-setting point focuses the development, yet a caution to consider: goals may create "tunnel thinking," narrowing options too quickly. Be open to revisiting the vision and goals with the community toward the end of the planning steps, to see if other factors arise that would affect desired long-term outcomes.

PLANNING PROCESS:
Cultural Goals

- *Who should we include in goal setting (e.g., Tribal Council, Tourism Committee, Cultural Committee, museum staff, elders, and artists)?*
- *What are our community's goals for teaching and preserving traditions?*
- *What are our goals for language teaching and documentation?*
- *What are our employment goals relating to tourism?*
- *What are our reasons and goals for sharing cultural information with the public?*
- *What are our goals for creating a facility supporting both tourism and cultural retention?*

Context of Economic Development Goals

Recent priorities of local governments tend to focus on economic development, and specifically on creating jobs. To the greatest extent that the group concerned with cultural perpetuation is familiar with the community's economic development goals—and presents projects in a way as to connect to those goals—there is likely to be greater local government support.

PLANNING PROCESS:
Link to the Community's Economic Development Goals

- *What are the economic development goals of the community?*
- *Have economic development plans been completed?*
- *Is tourism included in economic development and land use plans?*
- *How will jobs be created by interfacing with other economic development efforts?*
- *How will tourism contribute to the community's economic development efforts (e.g., support for needed infrastructure, collaborative marketing)?*

Cultural Goals and Economic Goals Working Together

When different sets of goals have overlap and areas in common, people in the community are more likely to work together. Governments are often hesitant to support a program if it may become a financial liability and not sustainable. For example, learning about how decisions are made within the community and how to be included in the process supports the building of alliances for a cultural center or museum. Developing a plan of action and distributing copies to decision makers is a powerful step to gain support.

PLANNING PROCESS:
Meshing Economic and Cultural Goals

- *Where is there overlap of goals?*
- *Who are the decision makers for implementing goals?*
- *How do cultural goals contribute to a distinct economic future for the community?*
- *How will a cultural center or museum generate a portion of its annual income through business activities?*

- *What criteria do local government set for success of programs or evaluation?*
- *Do success criteria relate to a cultural future?*

The following sample tourism goals and objectives reflect community needs, visitor needs, and sustainable impacts. By evaluating results, redirecting, and sharing information on strategies that work, as well as those not working, tourism partnerships will be strengthened.

Example 6. 1   TOURISM GOALS AND OBJECTIVES

Goal 1: To improve visitor services, by:

Obj. 1.1   Creating an intake or interpretive center, to better educate and manage the flow of visitors;
Obj. 1.2   Developing adequate infrastructure, to include water, roads and sewage;
Obj. 1.3   Increasing basic services or amenities, such as restaurants and lodging; and
Obj. 1.4   Implementing an outdoor recreation program, to include trails, camping, hiking, and fishing.

Goal 2: To provide culturally appropriate information for visitors, by:

Obj. 2.1   Interpreting history from the point of view of local cultures;
Obj. 2.2   Developing a website with information on history, the cultural arts, and basic visitor amenities;
Obj. 2.3   Producing an annual visitor guide;
Obj. 2.4   Creating brochures for statewide use; and
Obj. 2.5   Working with local universities to produce books on cultural history, arts, and the people.

Goal 3: To support the local economy, by:

Obj. 3.1   Developing business services, to include a Chamber of Commerce, a small business development center and a business incubator;
Obj. 3.2   Increasing sales of local arts and crafts;
Obj. 3.3   Initiating a "buy local" campaign;
Obj. 3.4   Providing training and marketing for artists;
Obj. 3.5   Developing a marketplace; and
Obj. 3.6   Addressing authenticity issues.

Goal 4: To operate a managed tourism program, by:

Obj. 4.1 Developing a museum as a hub for visitor education and referral to local businesses;
Obj. 4.2 Protecting the privacy of community members;
Obj. 4.3 Developing and coordinating tours;
Obj. 4.4 Distributing visitor education materials;
Obj. 4.5 Updating the website, the calendar of events, and fees; and
Obj. 4.6 Connecting to a larger tourism network by joining tourism organizations, attending tourism conferences, and distributing marketing materials regionally, statewide, and nationally.

Goal 5: To increase sustainability of tourism, by:

Obj. 5.1 Furthering communication, cooperation and participation among tribal government, businesses and the non-profit sector;
Obj. 5.2 Encouraging conservation and protection of traditional land uses;
Obj. 5.3 Involving youth in tourism activities by providing entrepreneurial and sports opportunities;
Obj. 5.4 Evaluating community satisfaction, environmental impacts, and job creation annually, then redirecting tourism efforts as needed;
Obj. 5.5 Increasing economic multipliers by encouraging the recirculation of dollars in the local economy; and
Obj. 5.6 Sharing successes through presentations at conferences and mentoring other communities.

USING THE MARKET ANALYSIS

With a thorough market analysis as outlined in Chapter 5, the final plan matches the characteristics of different markets and the interests of visitors, identifying both the opportunities and constraints within a particular community. At this point in the planning, relevant sources of data will feed into project definition, to determine themes for the highest success potential.

Review these studies of visitor profiles for—place of residence, age, gender, educational level, income level, interests in culture and education, items to purchase, foods preferred, lodging choice, and spending intentions. The plan should give an overview of the market data most relevant to the direction of the plan, such as community preferences for the type of tourism desired, project ideas, and the size or scale of tourism envisioned by the community.

Community creativity emerges through this final stage of market research. Pulling together the pieces of a data puzzle to design tourism amenities encourages visitor expenditures, as well as community involvement. A thorough tourism plan will be useful later for economic development and business projections, as reflected in the next chapters. The market analysis step is frequently not given enough attention in business plans; the projections are only as good as the ability to attract the market.

DESIGNING PROJECTS

As valuable community ideas are generated in the ongoing community participation process—potential directions, activities, and cultural boundaries begin to shape specific project ideas. Projects contain activities guided by specific desired outcomes that occur within a designated timeframe. When project ideas are meaningful to the community, as well as to visitors, momentum will be achieved.

Once a direction is defined for moving forward, projects needed to carry out the direction and specific goals can be defined. On a positive note, community members are likely to participate when a project idea emerges, with steps and resources identified. The concept of a project is the way resources are generally secured; therefore specific, detailed concepts tend to align partners and funders. "Bringing along" a community involves the initial participation, feedback on progress, and redirection if necessary.

> *The project with the best cultural fit considers needs of the local culture, traditional ways of involving the community, and the speed at which projects tend to get accomplished.*

Now a caution—projects are one topic particularly sensitive to cultural bias. Making the transition from a vision to perceiving the path to get to that vision takes patience, especially if resources are scarce. The most common error in developing projects is overestimating the size or scope in relation to available resources.

Moving toward a vision is a gradual process in many cultures, phasing projects over several years. Community alignment with a project idea and desired cultural directions increases community participation, along with the likelihood of success. Cultural gaps usually occur between seeing a desired result or enterprise and the conventional funding structure of the one-year project.

The cultural fit of the one-year time frame may not work well due to multiple-year, progressive involvement needed to accomplish the vision and the community participation necessary to capture the qualitative and intangible aspects of culture. Flexibility in a project idea, integrating process-oriented outcomes as well as quantitative or number results, supports the definition of viable, sustainable projects. The questions in the following planning process bring forth a community discussion leading to realistic ideas.

Environmental impact assessments (EIAs) are completed for a specific physical project to determine both potential negative and positive impacts, biophysical as well as social. These studies are used to make decisions on whether to move forward with a project or to determine ways to proceed for minimizing negative impacts and increasing positive benefits.

PLANNING PROCESS:
Sustainable Projects

- *Think of a cultural tourism project related to community tourism goals.*
- *Who would be involved in the project?*
- *How long would the project take to complete?*
- *How could the project be phased into parts, or sequential steps over time?*
- *Is employment created?*
- *Does the idea support cultural retention or revitalization?*
- *What cultural processes or ways of working together will accomplish the project?*
- *Are environmental impacts anticipated?*

- *How is the natural environment protected or restored?*
- *Does the project work with local government?*
- *How are other community leaders involved?*
- *Are cultural entrepreneurs involved and supported through the project?*
- *What is the end benefit of the project to the community?*
- *How is cultural knowledge protected in the project?*
- *How is the experience of visitors enriched by the benefits to the community?*

Keeping in mind a balance between small-scale and larger-scale projects provides a range of business opportunities for local government and entrepreneurs. This balance is needed to increase economic multipliers. Well-designed, small-scale tourism uses visitor expenditures to increase those businesses providing basic needs and services to the local economy. A community will express increased satisfaction with tourism if an equal opportunity exists to tap into the benefits of the intrusion. Consider:

- Common intentions and goals, leading to potential cooperative projects for tourism development,
- Cultural boundaries for tourism development, identifying the types of information appropriate to share with specific markets;
- Business development potential for a wide range of services (including entrepreneurial opportunities for marketplaces, gift shops, and food service emphasizing local offerings, plus lodging);
- Dynamics between for-profit and non-profit sectors, to create a support network of tourism partners;
- Potential synergy between tourism and the arts;
- Long-range goals for funding tourism, arts and culture;
- Visitor access to local cultures and the arts;
- Effective visitor education;

- Promotional needs and suggested promotional pieces; and
- Short-term and long-range facility needs.

Project ideas presented in the written tourism plan should be at least one to two pages in length, summarizing the concept.

Example 6.2 PROJECT DESCRIPTION

Tourism presents a unique opportunity to create needed supplementary earned income, as well as to encourage cultural learning. Visitors to the area spend approximately $185 per day, but almost always in non-Native owned businesses. Access to land and capital is needed to start businesses, to further the potential of local entrepreneurs.

Four major employment barriers face the local community. First, is the lack of full-time local jobs, limiting ability to provide adequate support for families. Second, is the tendency for Native entrepreneurs to be severely underpaid for their products, with retail markup as high as ten times. Third, is the lack of training programs and product development assistance to translate local skills into higher-end marketable products. Fourth, workplaces encouraging Native language and reinforcing of cultural values are very rare.

Considering these factors, in addition to needs determined from a community survey, the Desert Mountain Tribe intends to develop a community-based entrepreneurial marketplace and business training support system for tribal members. This business idea for the Native Marketplace arose from community meetings as a way to bridge the gap between tourism opportunity and local talent.

The target is not solely income generation, but also cultural reinforcement, capacity-building, and community-building. Smaller steps will first be necessary to achieve this project in a manner that builds management and entrepreneurial capacity. The Native Marketplace enterprise is the first economic development step that will lead to a larger vision for job creation.

The business planning process examined comparable outdoor markets. They are very successful and tourists enjoy shopping in this environment. In the first year, tourist dollars will be secured primarily from the drive-by traveler. Tourists like to stop, interact and shop while touring the region. Direct contact with Native people is the draw. In the region there is only one highway. The Desert Mountain tribal community has a targeted market for making Native products an authentic specialty item.

By diversifying income options and utilizing the non-profit status of the Desert Mountain Tribe to secure grants and donations, the Native Marketplace will be able to provide needed training in entrepreneurial skills, excellent management, and site improvement. This plan outlines four income strategies: booth rental, site rental to art shows, grants, and a donation structure. This business planning process reflects an integration of Native cultural values to achieve a broad range of targets.

A competitive advantage will be secured over other outdoor markets in the region with a value-added educational experience. Fifteen booths will be managed in Year 1, and expanded to 25 booths in Year 2.

The Native Marketplace will offer to visitors—authenticity, the genuine experience of interaction with Native people, and an opportunity to support a traditional community. Community members will gain business skills, financial support, increased family values and enhanced cultural and spiritual values that are important to Native people. Additionally, the visitor will, for the first time, be able to locate the "original hosts" of the area and the opportunity to purchase original Native products, rather than copies. Visitors continually ask community members, "Where can we see authentic Native culture?" The Native Marketplace is a good solution for bridging market demand with opportunities for local Native people.

ADDRESSING SAFETY ISSUES

As the world becomes increasingly concerned about safety, communities need to plan and implement. Assuring visitors of safety measures already in place[2] will attract those urban or international visitors who constantly live with fears of violence in these turbulent times. The appeal of non-urban areas and smaller communities increases each year as the safer "getaway" becomes a feature to be highlighted in the design of tourism activities.

Does the community have scenic beauty, shopping opportunities, and safety? The first two assets tend to rank the highest on visitor surveys, nationwide. Safety is rarely asked on a questionnaire, but is frequently a decision factor in deciding to visit a particular region or itinerary.

Safety guidelines are valuable as a plan section, even if the community isn't a likely spot for terrorism. Erratic weather or forest fires sometimes leave visitors stranded. Snowstorms block mountain passes and rainstorms wash out small bridges and crossings. Is there enough lodging, water, and food to provide for a natural disaster? Assessing other weather-related disaster situations, such as earthquake, flood, hurricane, tsunami, and tornado conditions, plus letting visitors know that safety plans are in place—will increase the sense of ease needed by visitors.

Is there a local police force? Where is the nearest health care located in case of an injury or an accident? Is there a towing service nearby? These are questions of concern. Emphasizing safety in marketing materials enhances appeal of the community to potential visitors. Valuable guidelines and updates are given by Peter Tarlow.
(www.tourismandmore.com)

TIMELINES

Creating the realistic timeline for activities is sometimes a point of cross-cultural difficulty—or where the viewpoints of traditional communities and resource providers do not mesh together well. Communication following traditional ways of cooperation and working together is basic to understand in developing the time frame with a good cultural fit. Intangible aspects of culture typically take years beyond the one year time frame to achieve and these results are generally the most significant to a traditional community.

The following activities are examples for a community to explore, as these emphasize cooperation and targeted ways of working in collaboration.

Short-term (1-2 years)

- Work with neighboring cities, towns, tribes and businesses to increase the tourism draw (target number of visitors) to the local region.
- Complete a marketing plan, emphasizing collaboration of urban, rural, and tribal entities and local communities, to reach a greater potential geographic area.
- Create a targeted, staffed tourism program to improve community relations, market, and encourage local expenditures in locally owned businesses.
- Bring traditional artists together to decide which arts are appropriate for sale, and which should be for private (community member) use only.
- Develop new products through classes, combining community member skills with products visitors prefer.
- Correct misinterpretations of local history and culture to foster cultural understanding.
- Work with local newspapers for articles concerning traditional culture and events as a valuable form of free marketing.
- Work with statewide or local tourism entities to increase distribution opportunities, as well as opportunities to learn about promotion.
- Build alliances with local businesses to provide basic and complementary services for a vacation package concept.
- Connect to the surrounding museums and other cultural facilities to increase website links, with the likelihood of reaching a broader audience.
- Participate in sponsored FAM (familiarization tours), to increase exposure to travel agents and travel companies.
- Develop cultural activities open to the public, such as dances, art shows, festivals, and locally managed guided tours to attract the cultural tourism and international markets.
- Build a good inventory of traditional arts to draw the cultural tourism and international markets.

Longer-term (3-5 years)

- Collaborate and cost-share promotion with the surrounding towns or villages, to reduce costs and extend a regional concept.
- Target the RV and camper market through distribution of materials in national parks, reserves, and scenic areas, to expand market opportunities and increase sales.
- Collaborate with regional attractions, such as rural museums, urban museums, and lodging providers, to form an itinerary concept and create a tourism draw.
- Develop new product lines by packaging existing local products together.
- Provide information sheets about traditional history and cultural arts, as well as bio-cards on artists, to stimulate visitor incentive in paying a fair price for handmade items.
- Update an attractive brochure and maintain an informative website to attract a regional market.
- Link with other traditional groups for promotional efforts to create representation at international tourism trade shows, such as ITB (Berlin), Pow-Wow (USA), and JATA (Japan)—the most effective way to reach the international market.
- Keep restaurant service menus simple, and provide excellent quality, fresh foods. Visitors want to try local and ethnic foods, and want information about the local effort to preserve traditional diets, as well as nutritional information about local foods.
- Provide excellent ordering information at gift shops to expand product sales after visitation.
- Initiate an online order capability along with educational information on traditional culture for the website, to create ongoing learning results from a cultural center or museum. This additional information also encourages customers to purchase in support of learning center programs.
- Contact travel magazines in the country and abroad, to obtain inclusion in travel articles, at no cost.

- Work with local government to consider a unified tourism effort, linking businesses and cross-marketing all local businesses, to maintain a wider distribution of materials—while increasing cost-effectiveness.
- Use customer evaluation cards to learn the preferences of the tourism market coming to the community; tailor services and products to meet market demand if these preferences are a suitable cultural fit.

Linking with other communities involved in tourism is useful for gaining ideas on successful tourism initiatives.

Timelines keep a community group working together—by defining the steps to get a result, the person(s) responsible for carrying out the steps, partnerships and a time frame (see Example 6.3). Either a start date and end date are listed for each step, or three-month intervals can be indicated. Realistic timelines, identifying people to carry out the tasks and resources, are effective for keeping a community working together on forward movement for desired projects, as well as for aligning funders.

This step, sometimes missing in small-scale tourism planning, is essential for keeping the community moving together. The most common reason for projects falling behind or falling apart is the lack of teamwork in a community—one person cannot evolve a project effectively. Using traditional ways of working together creates a cohesive effort.

Keeping a team on track, cooperating and moving forward, showing the long-term planned scenario to local governments, tourism organizations, and to funders, will lead to quality collaborations. Balance between forward movement on a project and community comfort with the cultural pace is furthered by reviewing the timelines and progress every six months.

Tourism projects tend to not go beyond the planning stage when the concept is too large for the resources available or community capacity to carry out the project. Funders readily detect both of these reasons.

Example 6. 3   NATIVE MARKETPLACE PROJECT TIMELINE

Tasks	Staff Person	Start Month	Finish Month
Business Plan Completion			
Decide goals, objectives for business/ include community benefits	Tourism/ Market Manager	1	1
Detail market assessment/determine niches			
Staffing plan			
3-year income and expense statements			
Workplan for Marketplace Start-up			
Decide on eligibility and priorities for booths • Local community members • Surrounding communities • Additional vendors	Tourism/ Market Manager	2	2
Complete written vendor guidelines, eligibility			
Decide a phased rate for booth fees			
Detail an annual advertising breakdown			
Complete Operational Procedures			
Construct booth structures	Tourism/ Market Manager	2	2
Hold a meeting with vendors to review guidelines			
Register vendors			
Distribute vendor manual			
Coordinate with micro-loan funds			
Coordinate with local training resources/ tailor training to cultural styles and anticipated market			
Develop interpretive materials and vendor biographical cards			
Deliver training to vendors on procedures & sales techniques			

Example 6. 3   NATIVE MARKETPLACE PROJECT TIMELINE

Tasks	Staff Person	Start Month	Finish Month
Linkages with Tourism Associations for Marketing Share copies of the business concept with the Visitor Bureau and the Chamber of Commerce Attend meetings of local: • Chamber of Commerce • Visitor Centers • Visitor Bureau • Tourism Associations Agreements for distribution of promotional materials	Tourism/ Market Manager	2	12
Promotion Work with the Visitor Bureau & Chamber of Commerce to receive referrals Decide marketing slogans Decide linkages for marketing—newspaper calendars, radio, TV, hotels Work with local visitor guides to include articles on the Native Marketplace Design, print fliers/ brochures Distribute fliers to markets, stores, community centers and other locations with bulletin boards Website development, links to surrounding markets Use of social media to market	Tourism/ Market Manager	3	12
Manage Open the market On a monthly basis, compare projections in business plan to actual expenses and income, to monitor business progress Ongoing training of staff Redirect as needed	Tourism/ Market Manager	4	12

BUDGETS AND FUNDING

The last stage of tourism planning turns to the practical issues, the basics for implementation. Budget projections are necessary to secure resources or to manage existing resources. Strive for a balance of low-cost/higher-cost and short-term/longer-term projects. Starting on a small-scale project such as visitor education may lead to the larger project, such as a tour enterprise. "What will this cost?" is usually the bottom-line question leading to implementation, once desired tourism directions are established in a community.

A carefully planned and accurate budget reflects the way an organization looks after its financial records. In the projections, calculate the funds needed for a comprehensive project, rather than gearing the plan to short-term available funds from one source. With a comprehensive set of projects in mind, combining different sources is useful to fund different sections of the project.

Planning results are invaluable for communicating needs and project ideas. Although avoiding grant dependency is advised in sustainable efforts, using available funding to launch start-ups of enterprises and tourism programs is a step toward long-term sustainability. Small-scale development requires resources for training community members, to build capacity for ongoing expansion of the original idea. Resources form a basis of strength at the starting point.

Sometimes small communities attempt to develop tourism solely with volunteer resources. Although community involvement is the underlying element to developing a tourism program, resources to cover the costs of promotion and some staffing are usually needed. Since promotion, including printing and distribution is expensive, gaining access to resources is a basic step for tourism development.

The process of contacting funders, discovering opportunities, and learning about a funder's goals for assisting communities is strengthened when relationships are formed. Traditional groups usually have good relationship building skills within their cultural knowledge. This becomes a strong point for funding efforts. Funders have internal, agency goals for results with communities and aligning with these goals increases potential for funding.

Example 6.4 SAMPLE BUDGET TO LAUNCH A TOURISM PROGRAM

Line Item*	Start-up Year	Expanded Program
Personnel		
Tourism/Market Manager	$45,000	$46,350
Tourism Assistant @ $14/hr		28,280
Employee Benefits (35%)	15,750	26,121
Travel		
Mileage (@ .45/mile)	2,250	3,150
Long Distance (airfare—tourism conferences, trade shows—2 trips start-up year, 3 trips expanded program)	1,500	2,500
Per Diem (@ $100 per day)	1,200	1,500
Lodging (@ $120 per night)	1,440	1,800
Other travel (parking, etc.)	500	750
Other		
Office Supplies	3,000	3,500
Copying	3,000	3,500
Printing marketing materials (brochures) & placement fees	5,000	7,500
Marketing, advertising placement	7,000	10,000
Postage	1,200	1,500
Website development	3,000	5,000
Consultants (business plan & training)	25,000	10,000
Registration (tourism organizations)	500	750
Equipment & software	3,000	2,000
Telephone	3,600	4,800
Tourism trade shows (marketing)	0	3,000
Construction		
Marketplace booth construction	50,000	20,000
Kiosk updating	3,000	500
Total Operating Budget	**$174,940**	**$182,501**

* Budget projections cover basic administrative costs for a managed tourism program. A business plan is needed for an outdoor market to project income to cover these expenses. Additional funding for the operation of a tourism program would be based upon the implementation of specific projects.

Approaching staff well ahead of the deadline, learning about the agency, networking with other communities that have worked with the agency, and communicating connection with the region—are all strong points for beginning the relationship with a funder.

Once project success develops, a good relationship with the funder may lead to additional grants or contracts in future years. The well-written proposal is a supporting step. Do study the guidelines carefully—page limitations, font specification, and even the required spacing between lines—are frequently indicated.

The well-written tourism plan addresses needs and provides project descriptions, the basics for good proposal design. Securing funding involves linking to expand resources, designing a community-based project, preparing a proposal, locating and approaching funding sources, as well as leveraging resources.

Framing a Project

A common challenge to securing funding for tourism projects is finding the appropriate category fit with funding opportunities. Tourism is rarely a descriptor in funding databases. Structuring a tourism project to fit under economic development, arts, business development, training, transportation, the arts, or youth programs—is a successful way to expand opportunities for tourism funding. Chart 6.1 presents a few examples for "framing" or shaping a tourism project idea.

When a tourism project benefits a community in one or more areas, broader impacts are perceived by the funder—a positive. Balance between broad impacts, yet designing a project focused enough to be considered feasible, relates to successful project design.

To identify funding for tourism projects, look in funding databases under a range of identifiers. USA examples are:

- www.grants.gov
- www.foundationcenter.org
- www.conservationgrants.com

Other databases are available with a basic internet search, useful for linking projects with funders in the plan. Then, approaching local government or using earned income for matches multiplies the total resource for tourism development, taking the plan to action steps.

Chart 6.1 FRAMING A TOURISM PROJECT

FUNDING DESCRIPTOR	TOURISM-RELATED PROJECT
Economic Development	Tourism networks Tourism organizations Tourism plans Marketing
Business Development	Micro-enterprises Enterprises Tours Museum gift shops Art galleries
Training	Entrepreneurial skills Cultural arts Marketing Customer service
Transportation	Visitor/interpretive centers Road improvements Signage Picnic areas Roadside kiosks
Arts	Art classes Business of art classes Cultural preservation Art demonstrations Art shows Festivals
Youth	Tour guide training Cultural arts Youth business club Prevention Language

THE DRAFT PLAN

Data-gathering steps detailed in Chapters 3 through 5 will typically produce a large quantity of information. The skill of producing a plan useful for the implementation phase rests with reducing the amount of information—from the participation stage, market data, project descriptions, timelines and identification of resources—to the most relevant. A plan no longer than 100 pages is a realistic length for review and usefulness in a team effort.

When selecting which data to include, consider the following:

- Balance community input (with brief summaries) and tourism market data—both are important.
- Condense data into easy-to-read charts whenever possible.
- Avoid large plan sections (e.g., maps, charts, graphics, photos) without interpretation.
- Use bullet points to break up text and highlight main points.
- Use text boxes highlighting key findings to condense ideas.
- Identify primary funders and think through the types of data that will support planned project ideas and are required by the funder.
- Condense information that will enable the plan to be used as a tourism management tool (e.g., policy, timelines, job descriptions).
- Create a brief executive summary after the text is finished, highlighting the main findings and directives.

The draft is streamlined, and accuracy improved, if a means of feedback to the planning committee is formalized—based on summaries presented at community meetings along the way.

BRINGING PLAN FINDINGS TO THE COMMUNITY

Sustaining participation depends upon good cultural fit of process, as well as content. A review period of between two to three weeks is productive for revisions, particularly to ensure cultural appropriateness or interpretation. One caution—review periods may expand into a never-ending loop if new ideas or opinions are allowed into the finalizing step. This sometimes occurs when stakeholders who didn't attend earlier meetings attempt to reopen issues or add new projects. Consensus-based cultures are particularly susceptible to these delays. Stating a clear time frame for comments and a clear intention for the review improves the process.

Including all stakeholder groups who participated in the planning sessions is a basic step for avoiding cultural misinterpretations. For example, if religious leaders were included to determine potential cultural privacy impacts relating to religious practices, then these leaders' interpretive reviews of the issues, cultural boundaries, and restrictions on areas appropriate for visitation should be elicited. Several means of communicating plan content are valuable both at the review and at the beginning of the implementation stage, such as:

- A short version distributed to households;
- Summary in local newspaper;
- Executive summary to local or tribal government leaders; or
- Main points on the local radio station.

The review is vital to overall interpretation. Read all of the comments, and if objections to an idea appear repeatedly, only then consider reopening the discussion of projects. Paying particular attention to the omissions mentioned helps to ensure that all relevant cultural issues are addressed.

Finalizing or approving the plan is fundamental to following cultural ways for continued involvement. Whether a consensus process or a vote is the cultural method for moving forward, final approval should also include a procedure for updating the plan. Continuity from plan to action frequently follows a cultural protocol.

A community meeting to begin implementation takes the process full circle. Continuing the discussion on plan findings keeps expanding opportunities for internal teaching, increases cross-cultural understanding, and opens entrepreneurial opportunity.

COMMUNITY-BASED SOLUTION
Eight Northern Indian Pueblos, New Mexico, USA

While tourism provided the primary means of support to the tribal members of the Pueblos of Taos, Picuris, Okhay Owingeh, Santa Clara, Nambe, San Ildefonso, Pojoaque, and Tesuque in the mid 1980s, unemployment remained extremely high—between 40% and 60%—due to economic leakages. Tour companies profited from access to the traditional villages, and visitor purchases occurred largely in the surrounding cities.

A regional tourism planning process conducted by a consortium comprising eight American Indian tribes assessed tourism resources and needs for training, created a directory of businesses, goals for tourism, and strategies for moving forward as a region of tribes. Outcomes of the regional plan included the establishment of a tourism program, training for tribes, creation of visitor etiquettes, the launching of a regional tribal visitor guide, as well as liaison with the tourism industry.

Businesses were surveyed after a ten-year period. Methods of traditional business development, assisted with training in business skills and a promotional guide for cultural tourism, revealed a high level of success. Tourism-related businesses doubled in ten years, from 45 to 91. In other words, the prevalent system in this region of long-term, gradual development with minimal capital investment—coupled with marketing and promotional assistance on a regional basis—resulted in a pattern of increased employment.

Small-scale development, slow growth without loans, linking to entrepreneurs, and extended family cooperation, were the key success factors for business stability and sustainable job creation. Results included accelerated small business development and expenditures drawn directly into the tribal economies to support local employment. The only businesses that "failed" or "closed" were due to deceased owners or people moving out of the area.

Today, tribal economic development includes casinos at several tribal locations. These profits are reinvested into lodging, gas stations, and food service enterprises—creating jobs and extending visitor length-of-stay. (www.indianpueblo.org/19pueblos)

FURTHER READING

Edgell, David, Maria DelMastro Allen, Ginger Smith and Jason R. Swanson. *Tourism Policy and Planning: Yesterday, Today and Tomorrow,* Oxford, UK: Elsevier, 2008.

Bridging the gap between tourism policy and strategic planning, this text integrates the two and examines the future of tourism policy development, with an international perspective on policy through case studies and analysis.

Goeldner, Charles R. and J.R. Brent Ritchie. *Tourism: Principles, Practices, Philosophies.* New York: John Wiley & Sons, 2009.

This comprehensive introduction explains tourism organizations, passenger transportation, hospitality services, organizations, policy, planning, and the essentials of marketing.

Hall, C. Michael. *Tourism Planning: Policies, Processes and Relationships.* Harlow, UK: Prentice Hall, 2008.

As an introduction to tourism planning at global, regional and local levels within the context of sustainability, this text discusses the changing dimensions of tourism planning.

Inskeep, Edward. *Tourism Planning: An Integrated and Sustainable Development Approach.* New York: Van Nostrand Reinhold, 1991.

An overview of the process, principles, and techniques of preparing national and regional tourism plans—and includes surveys and evaluations of the environmental setting, tourist attractions and activities, tourist markets, facilities, services, and infrastructure carrying capacity.

7

MUSEUMS, CULTURAL CENTERS, AND INTERPRETIVE CENTERS

Every day is precious in the process of cultural retention.

Preserving the diversity of traditions, lifeways, and cultural values is a core concern in rural and traditional communities. Although tourism may sometimes be viewed as a threat to the continuation of traditions, a careful planning effort can inspire cultural pride and generate resources for cultural retention. As a community adjusts to changing economic conditions, cultural tourism holds the potential to be one of several options considered for cultural and economic resiliency.

One primary benefit of tourism is the stimulus for developing a museum, interpretive, or cultural center. As a place to provide visitor education, a center may become the focal point for interpreting local history and traditions, as well as a hub supporting cultural revitalization and language retention. With in-depth participation, these centers not only enhance the visitation experience, but also increase direct benefits for a community gathering place—such as jobs and economic support.

Cultural retention, more than an idealistic notion, is a practical necessity for sustainability. This chapter discusses ways of integrating teaching programs and a cultural center into an overall tourism strategy.

> **Framework for Integrating Culture**
>
> - Identify community cultural needs and visitor interests—then, find the best match.
> - Determine community priorities.
> - Honor community members who learn the traditions.
> - Discover how tourism can inspire cultural pride.
> - Identify traditions at risk and begin community teaching programs.
> - Design visitor education on a scale to match community resources.

Mainstream, urban *museums* tend to focus on exhibits, collections, and archives. By determining community needs in a planning process, a museum may serve other community-based uses such as classrooms for cultural teaching and a conference room for gatherings and meetings. Housing a teaching collection—items that are replaceable, yet are excellent examples of traditional art for students to study in classes—is one frequently overlooked component of museum design for traditional communities.

Although the focus of *cultural centers* is often meeting the internal needs of teaching culture, small well-planned exhibits offer valuable information and inspiration to both community members and visitors. A large multi-purpose space for events, such as weddings and large gatherings requiring kitchens, is supportive to traditions when no other space exists in the community. Some cultural centers feature changing exhibits of student work, encouraging community members to participate in learning opportunities.

The focus of *interpretive centers* tends to be visitor education. As a distribution point for media and marketing materials, an interpretive center educates travelers on-location or by website. Smaller exhibits characterize an interpretive center. Although space may be limited, a condensed presentation of information important for understanding the community is possible.

A center may fulfill all three functions—museum, cultural center and interpretive center—when planned well. Careful decisions on the balanced use of space for teaching, exhibits, and collections should include extensive community participation, to clearly define community priorities. If resources are limited, develop a facility in phases—with the first phase concentrating on the top community priority, then addressing other functions over time.

MEETING CULTURAL NEEDS

Immediate action to provide urgent cultural teaching is the primary way to prevent cultural loss. When a tourism planning effort identifies the necessity for a place to interpret and teach culture, the community's needs are served beyond the economic and job focus in tourism. This helps reduce negative impacts upon culture, as such centers become a central point for ongoing community discussion about mitigating negative cultural impacts.

A long-range plan for cultural retention or the development of a center is also an effective step for cultural revitalization. If the community indicates this direction, the following plan outline is recommended.

Plan Outline

    I. Purpose of the plan
   II. Description of participation in the planning process

Internal, community:
   III. Cultural goals
   IV. Intergenerational involvement
   V. Cultural assessment and inventory
   VI. Identification of priorities
  VII. Methods to be used for cultural revitalization
VIII. Storytelling program
   IX. Curriculum for teaching
   X. Facility needs
   XI. Assessment of resources
  XII. Methods identified to protect privacy and sensitivity
 XIII. Specific projects designed to teach and increase involvement
 XIV. Job creation/museum store

External audience (if desired):
  XV. Messages to communicate
 XVI. Exhibit themes

XVII. Collections
XVIII. Curation process
XIX. Policies
XX. Public programs
XXI. Visitor services
XXII. Facility requirements

Overall:
XXIII. Staff training
XXIV. Operating budget
XXV. Action plan—timelines, persons responsible, and resources

The stakes are high for cultural survival—the retention of diversity in traditions is a global issue relating to resilience. Repeatedly, rural communities and tribes echo the same concern: cultural traditions, including the cultural arts, are tied to all aspects of life—food production, earned livelihood, good health practices, and spiritual beliefs. Traditions tied to the land are continually eroded when small farms and ranches are purchased for development and fragile ecosystems are damaged. A community is more likely to become engaged in cultural tourism development when local cultural issues are acknowledged.

Addressing Community Priorities

In most rural and tribal communities, teaching the culture within the community depends upon involvement by the elders, the keepers of the traditions. Regarding the teachings in a respectful way aligns elders to be willing to teach. In relation to tourism—involving elders in defining the types of information appropriate to share and deciding who is allowed to learn certain types of restricted information—is a guiding process.

Yet, there are additional factors to consider in the practice of cultural retention. Youth and parents also need to be involved. When the activities are enjoyable and resonate with the cultural needs expressed by the community, then participation levels will be high. Following tradition is a path seen by most cultures as the best solution for nurturing youth toward positive community involvement, good health, caring for family, caring for the sacred environment, and life away from negative influences. These are contemporary issues basic for cultural retention in rural and reservation areas today.

When connected to a cultural tourism network, a cultural center or museum has the potential to facilitate the integration of cultural retention into different aspects of the tourism system, such as:

- A place for a traditional protocol for welcoming practices, such as greeting songs and dances;
- A visitor information area at the entrance to the museum—a distribution point for brochures and a locator map to direct referrals to local services;
- A place to interpret history from the viewpoint of the community and to tell cultural stories;
- A location to originate tours;
- A connection to buy-local campaigns, promoting the work of cultural entrepreneurs; and
- A place to serve traditional foods or to encourage regional restaurants to serve local foods.

Once a central place is designated to receive visitors, the tourism system connection is strengthened by:

- Producing and distributing cultural interpretations of history, a calendar of events, and information on the arts;
- Encouraging the placement of small art exhibits in restaurants and other public places;
- Sponsoring exhibits of local artists, and receptions to facilitate interaction between visitors and artists—assisting the visitor to understand art beyond an object; and
- Organizing art shows.

A facility designed specifically to practice traditions is pivotal for many reasons. A standard classroom space does not work adequately for teaching most traditional arts. If tourism planning includes documentation of the art-making processes, then this information is applicable to appropriate functional design. Providing a facility for teaching the cultural arts supports a positive cultural future. Rooms with specialized features are often needed for specific arts. Examples are:

- Water faucets and soaking troughs for basket-makers;
- Long tables for hand sewing of traditional dresses, beaded garments, or moccasin-making;
- Traditional pottery firing places (pits and kilns);
- Storage areas for materials (outdoor and indoor);
- Outdoor patio spaces for painters or sculptors;
- Ventilated work stations for silver jewelry makers; and
- An outdoor market area for vending.

If a cultural center is one community-intended benefit from tourism, then a plan must identify activities desired by the community and the spaces needed to practice them. Tailoring the design of a center to the cultural activities and art-making processes in the facility will determine the extent of community use of the spaces. Listening is a basic skill integral to defining culturally appropriate uses and spaces.

Not waiting for the ideal building is important for meeting urgent cultural teaching needs. Small-scale options include: using an existing building, securing a donated house, or even teaching under an outdoor shelter in a temperate climate. Small educational exhibits may be created and housed within these options. Because the preferred scenario of a dedicated building is expensive to maintain, and not always possible, interim solutions may be necessary.

LIVING MUSEUMS

In traditional communities, living museums are learning places for the community, as well as visitors. With a focus on the community in the present, exhibits and educational programs incorporate information about the past, when relevant to understanding a contemporary people and living cultures. This differs from a common mainstream museum focus on objects, their history, and a public-at-large audience. For example, in the Indigenous setting, time may be portrayed as cyclical rather than linear, by showing the link to traditional activities in the seasons.

Museums planned to support cultural continuance are attractive to the general public. A "museum with life," or living museum, shows not only history, but also the learning programs in the present plus an anticipated cultural future for the community. This information need not be detailed with culturally private information, but rather reflects the concept of cultural continuity. Changing exhibits showing student work and interactive exhibits are two features appreciated by the public. In turn, when the public becomes involved, then support to the center is likely to follow.

The concept of living centers and museums involves creating a place that truly serves the community's priorities and needs regarding culture—rather than the model of the urban history museum with exhibits and programs for the general public. Unfortunately, in some communities, these museums do not meet pressing community priorities because of inadequate teaching spaces or collections that are not accessible to the community for learning. Museum consultants who guided these efforts did not understand the cultural needs in these communities.

There is a mainstream concept of "living museum" where live people are the exhibits of a past lifeway, re-enacting traditional activities. A traditional community's living museum may, or may not, incorporate this concept. A different concept of a living museum as a community learning place is suggested here. In this context, cultural revitalization involves increasing the level of practice of a tradition or recovering a tradition, when its practice has declined in recent years.

Cultural revitalization implies making traditions increasingly central to community life.

Living museums in traditional communities focus on teaching and learning culture, giving community members access to traditional materials for the study necessary in the process of cultural renewal. Sometimes people of local cultures serve as greeters, explaining their contemporary community and providing interpretation of the past. As the museum becomes a hub of cultural activity, a place where the community gathers is formed. Creating a vibrant venue where community members are comfortable and feel a sense of ownership will help ensure the museum's success.

Living museums include culturally appropriate spaces for teaching language, cultural arts, and other traditions. Their designs reflect traditional building forms and the kinds of spaces needed to teach the cultural arts. Teaching the public-at-large about cultural revitalization and other messages significant to a community, draws visitors to community-based interpretation.

Cultural learning also occurs in informal interactions connected to events, using teaching studios and gatherings that occur outside of regular classes. When language is taught only in a classroom, worldview is not fully communicated. For this reason, teaching language in everyday context supports all cultural learning. Language teaching integrated with cultural arts classes is an effective example.

Community-based programs with internally determined content are more authentic than "cultural performers" hired by large tourism enterprises. Interpretation is regulated through a cultural process for sharing information, inherent in every culture.

- Internal methods for teaching youth are stimulated by community-based demonstrations.
- Several interpretations of history may exist within a community. Multiple interpretations are difficult to present in profit-motivated industries.
- Cultural understanding and empathy are easier to achieve on a smaller scale.
- Visitor connection to cultural retention efforts are better achieved with small-scale enterprises contributing to the support of teaching programs.

Current successes of community-based cultural centers and museums offer a number of optimistic conclusions:

- The next five to ten years are vital for cultural teaching, due to the rapid rate of cultural loss in traditional communities. Tourism may not only encourage, but also provide support for that teaching.
- It is possible for a traditional community to design a combined cultural center and museum facility that encourages cultural learning on the community's terms and priorities, rather than according to standard museum practice.
- Youth are encouraged through cultural pride when tourism is designed to interface with community centers. Reinforcing

values and cultural identity counters most of the dangers of being diverted into the unwanted values of visiting cultures.

- The most authentic presentation for visitors comes from community-determined priorities, meeting community needs, and then informing the public of current efforts to revitalize culture.
- When several culturally oriented centers or museums link together, they form intriguing itineraries and share successful strategies.

A community-based planning method is effective for reaching these results. Involving the community and discussing values as a foundation for activities is the likely way to design a cultural center or museum successfully serving pressing community needs.

Cultural retention involves increasing the level of practice of a tradition or recovering a tradition when its practice has declined in recent years. The stakes are high for cultural continuance. Creating cultural learning programs, teaching language, and involving both elders and youth are urgent needs—due to the advanced age of the keepers of the traditions in most traditional communities. The following questions are useful for designing teaching programs in a center.

PLANNING PROCESS:
Bringing Back Traditions

- *Identify a tradition that is practiced less frequently.*
- *How many years ago was the tradition last practiced?*
- *What is the cultural meaning or significance of the tradition?*
- *Who in the tribe or in the community still retains knowledge of the tradition?*
- *Who outside of the community (neighboring communities speaking the same language or culturally similar tribes) may have information to share about the tradition?*

> - *What difference will the next five years make to your culture, if action is not taken now to teach?*
> - *What difference will the next 10 years make to your culture, if action is not taken now to teach?*
> - *What difference will the next 20 years make to your culture, if action is not taken now to teach?*
> - *Is there a "skipped" generation in language and culture learning? How will generations become better connected?*
> - *What strategies will you take to create community-wide teaching?*

These questions may be difficult to face, yet are essential for a community to gather the momentum needed to save traditions.

The Need to Redirect Many Museums

For some rural and tribal museums currently guided by the history museum perspective, there is an immediate need to redirect the museum to meet cultural teaching needs. Each cultural center or museum has its own set of strengths and areas in need of improvement. This chapter is useful for strengthening an existing museum concerned with redirecting activities, expanding a facility, and moving forward with a cultural retention program.

The concept of cultural revitalization is frequently referred to as "bringing back" a tradition in Indigenous communities. Returning traditions to a vital practice in the life of a community ensures a cultural future. Unless traditions are preserved and development occurs in a culturally appropriate manner, a cultural way of life tied to a local ecosystem will be eroded. Creating a vision for the future and aligning the community in common goals sets a foundation for balancing new development within the context of cultural continuity.

STEPS FOR MOVING FORWARD

My earlier book, *Planning for Balanced Development*,[1] addresses methods for developing museums and cultural centers. This chapter is intended to make the tie between these centers and tourism.

Step 1. Community-Level Organizing: The Cultural Committee

The most valuable feature of a committee organizing to form a cultural center's link to tourism is representation. Consider age, gender, and knowledge of traditions, as well as representation by governing bodies, arts organizations, galleries, or existing museums. When a cultural committee is formed, this group is a contact point for continuing the connection to future tourism management—and to make certain that cultural exploitation does not occur.

Step 2. Determining Cultural Needs and Ways the Community Will Benefit

A cultural assessment forms the starting place for meeting a diverse range of community needs, from cultural revitalization efforts—to determining traditions that are appropriate to share—to arts that are appropriate to sell. While the assessment is an internal process, consider the appropriateness of needs in relation to tourism. A cultural inventory may generate community participation for the cultural arts plus serve as a reminder of the learning needed.

Step 3. Setting Priorities for Cultural Revitalization

Determining which projects are of the highest priority generally involves looking at their significance to the culture, the number of persons with knowledge of the tradition, and the age of persons who keep knowledge of the traditions. Such an assessment is valuable for determining traditions at risk of becoming lost and setting priorities for teaching.

Messages about cultural continuance are then possible to communicate to the public. When projects important to the internal community are determined, tourism strategies for visitor education and for generating income to benefit the community as a whole are better understood.

Step 4. Identifying Resources

Significant criticisms of tourism relevant to the continuation of traditions include the potential for negative impacts on native plants and materials and culturally significant places. Private access by the community is also an underlying issue. When tourism planning identifies traditions to preserve, then cultural issues concerning resources emerge. One way of minimizing impacts is to restrict access by visitors.

Cultural revitalization gains momentum when the people essential for cultural teaching are identified and involved in the creation or redirection of a center. Teachers, community members willing to learn, and financial resources—plus access to the natural resources necessary to practice traditions—are essential for moving forward. By assessing the financial needs for cultural preservation efforts, information is gathered to keep the process moving along.

Recommendations for starting a cultural center or museum are detailed by Karen Cooper in *Living Homes for Cultural Expression*,[2] a National Museum of the American Indian resource book. This text contains a directory of North American, Native-managed community museums. Linking with other traditional communities is useful for sharing strategies—as they tell their stories to the public.

A PLACE FOR VISITOR EDUCATION

Often, a museum or cultural center is the first visitor stop in a small community. The foyer of a museum may serve an interpretive center function with visitor information. Providing visitor and interpretive information at this location is the ideal point for:

- Locator maps;
- Brochures;
- Visitor guides;
- Information on local businesses, artists and entrepreneurs;
- Interesting educational exhibits;
- Information on traditional arts;
- Explanations of desired visitor etiquette;
- Information on linkages to tourism websites; and
- Booking of guiding services.

In small communities, a museum may be an ideal centralized point from which to manage tourism. Referrals to local businesses, artists, guides, and entrepreneurs further local benefits.

Providing information on local arts and artists—with biographical cards attached to items in museum gift shops, art shows, or outdoor markets—supports cultural entrepreneurs. Information tags increase visitor appreciation of the artist, in turn enhancing the likelihood of appropriate prices for handmade items. Working with other local businesses for visitor education then becomes a unifying function of the cultural center or museum.

An example of a museum advertising project that also educates visitors is the lodging book in motel rooms, bed and breakfasts, or cabins. Content of a lodging book can be customized to a local area by including sections on history, museum exhibits, local culture, cultural arts, information on shops selling locally made items, menus featuring restaurants serving local foods, and a calendar of events. A lodging book project initiated by a museum or cultural center is a service to community businesses.

An effective project for museums is to create placemats for local restaurants, featuring history, locator maps for shops, and a calendar of events. A placemat is a win/win project since visitors have an activity while waiting for food and learn the basics about local culture. Another valuable museum/restaurant interface is a panel or rack card placed in the condiment tray on each table. Again, visitors gain an engaging activity while waiting.

COMMUNICATING CULTURE

As places to share information, museums and interpretive centers communicate culture through messages, exhibit content, and even design of the building. Discussions internal to the community determine information appropriate to share, as well as information intended for private, internal use within the community.

If you are a planner or technical assistance provider from another culture, ask the community to discuss the following issues in private and then identify information appropriate for sharing with the public. By using this technique, cultural privacy will be maintained and the community is likely to feel more comfortable. These considerations are important for sustainable development. An intergenerational planning committee provides a valuable way of giving voice to culture.

208 SUSTAINABLE CULTURAL TOURISM

PLANNING PROCESS:
Representing Culture

- *How does our interpretation of history differ from published accounts?*
- *What are our important stories, appropriate to share, and how will we tell them?*
- *Are there seasonal restrictions to telling stories?*
- *What are our unique lifeways or customs that should be told?*
- *Which are still practiced today?*
- *How will we document stories or viewpoints as told by community members, and use technology to share these?*

Decisions on cultural boundaries, as well as the types of information appropriate to share and not share come from internal discussions. In certain traditional cultures, these decisions are embedded in a religious framework. Avoiding exploitation of the sacred is a commonly held boundary.

Not commodifying or objectifying items with cultural meaning becomes particularly crucial when the traditional arts are of concern. Some communities make adamant statements—"Culture is not to be exploited, not to be sold." New product development is less sensitive to commodification, although symbolic designs used on new products may call for additional community discussion.

Cultural groups telling their own stories fascinate visitors, while extending cultural understanding. Some museums design a storytelling area for school or community groups at scheduled times—then for visitors at other times.

Greeting Traditions

In many traditional cultures, specific forms of hospitality and greetings are a part of welcoming visitors. Particularly in relation to the art-making processes, trade songs, and dance—ritual surrounding hospitality is significant to the richness of culture.

Communicating messages about cultural continuance, such as traditional greetings, presents a positive image of culture to both visitors and the host community. Traditional language use in greetings and songs encourages overall community language learning by enhancing cultural pride. These traditional greetings may be expressed uniquely within a modern context in cultural centers and museums, as well as businesses.

Welcoming within the expression of one's culture heightens the authentic experience. Examples from Native American cultures are the traditional greetings with water in the dry Southwestern United States, or the greeting songs sung by Northwestern tribes. Interviewing elders in a community, documenting hospitality traditions, and renewing these traditions assists a community with cultural retention. Traditional greetings are often extraordinary—from songs to dances, or gifts such as the welcoming lei, given in Hawai'i according to the Native Hawaiian tradition.

When adequate resources are available, traditional greeting songs and dances could be a part of everyday life. This might be possible for the small, focused tourism program. In a cultural center or museum setting, recorded greeting songs and dances are interesting as part of a welcoming exhibit. Demonstrations may be possible for special events.

In the modern context, greetings take the form of personal welcomings, in the language of the visitor, the traditional language, or both—as well as recordings, visuals, brochures, video viewing areas, and larger exhibits. Including a bilingual language greeting enhances the authentic experience. Welcoming tradition, reflecting past and current practice as an exhibit theme, is an engaging topic. Potential to involve the community also increases cultural practice.

Telling a Community Story

Local interpretation of history is a topic that appeals to visitors. *Written historical record* is often documented from the viewpoint of another culture. In traditional cultures, history is frequently passed down *orally,* rather than through written texts. Respecting different points of view in telling stories brings cultural groups together.

An excellent expression of Indigenous methodology and the importance of solutions from within cultural frameworks is presented by Bagele Chilisa,[3] an African educator. In Indigenous cultures, practices and procedures are communicated orally and stored in songs, dances, artistry, cultural taboos, and other traditions. "How do we capture and interpret a reality that takes into account our 'being' relations with the earth, the living, and the non-living; and how can Indigenous knowledge shed light on this reality?" is the pertinent question posed by Chilisa. The answer lies in an interactive way of viewing the aliveness of the entire universe and the traditional ways of passing on the wisdom and teachings, such as ceremonies and teaching circles.

The stories of cultures in conflict (whether contemporary or historical) are often delicate, but possible to tell. Such stories intrigue visitors and lend authenticity to the visitation experience. Almost any story can be told keeping the following in mind.

- Decide a viewpoint for telling significant stories through community participation.
- Avoid anger in telling the story, by staying with the historical facts and describing the impacts on culture.
- Present more than one interpretation—two or three versions of a story by different cultural perspectives. A unifying understanding between cultures may result.
- Balance the positive outcomes with the difficult impacts, showing the persistence of culture over time.
- Include information about traditional arts and foods to enhance the cultural experience and make the link to other community offerings.

Exhibits can be inexpensive yet powerful. For example, photographic exhibits with interpretive guides tell a moving and educational story from an internal point of view. Decisions concerning how to tell the several facets of a story connect to internal cultural communication. The effort is well worth the time for discussion and consensus on presentation. Community involvement is central for defining stories relating to a center's mission, as well as defining details to be kept culturally private. Good interpretation contributes to the uniqueness of the authentic experience offered by the community.

Reinterpretation of history is powerful when expressed from different cultural viewpoints. A guide to steps for exhibition development by Rick Hill[4] explains interpretation for both community and public programs. Visitors like a story well told.

Examples of unique interpretive approaches are:

Quw'utsun Cultural and Conference Center (Vancouver Island, BC, Canada) of the Cowichan Native community offers a powerful storytelling program focusing on origin stories. In the summer months a traditional salmon feast and First Nations contemporary cuisine are served in the Riverwalk Cafe. A hands-on woodcarving shed offers a unique experience for visitors. (www.quwutsun.ca)

Plimoth Plantation (Massachusetts, USA) includes an interpretive exhibit with responses to a set of questions from both the Native American and colonist points of view, illustrating cultural contrasts and differing interpretations of history. The Wampanoag Homesite, a re-created 17th century Native American village offers an experiential visit, with the opportunity for the visitor to sit by a fire in a wigwam and listen to storytelling, in addition to viewing a canoe making demonstration. (www.plimoth.org).

Stereotyping is a basic concern of traditional groups. This emerges as a caution in cultural tourism. Traditional people tend to see themselves in different time periods, such as historical traditional, contemporary traditional, or modern. The historical traditional may be represented with period reconstructions or period performances: for example, in Hawai'i, the hula dance presented in grass skirts vs. post-missionary grass skirts with tops—and in contemporary times, in jeans.

How people want to represent themselves is an important discussion—both internally and then communicated externally to the public—through museum guides, publications, websites and other forms of media. One solution to avoiding the cultural stereotype is to present "re-slices of time" to show the change in traditions over time. The current culture is the cumulative result of all these time periods.[5]

Another consideration for avoiding stereotypes is to communicate that not all individuals are the same within a culture. A New Mexico (USA) Pueblo man was stopped in downtown Santa Fe by tourists who asked him, "Are the Indians going to dance today?" He replied, "They don't dance in this setting." The visitors then asked, "Where can we see the Indians?" He replied, "I'm an Indian." Their response was shock because he was wearing a business suit.

ARTISTS AND ENTREPRENEURS

Linking artists and entrepreneurs to tourism amenities and activities in the tourism system furthers cultural tourism success. The museum or cultural center is an effective place to include learning programs for artists and cultural entrepreneurs, central to successful cultural tourism. The needs of these stakeholders are frequently not included during tourism planning.

Function and aesthetics are often integrated in the traditional arts, reflecting cultural symbolism and values. Mainstream American culture perceives the arts differently than do many culturally diverse groups, separating the arts from other aspects of daily life.

A segmented or hierarchical approach such as that found in Western cultures tends to regard the arts as a separate, higher form of culture. In contrast, traditional cultures and rural communities tend to integrate the arts with all aspects of everyday life. For example, family collaboration in art-making and teaching are predominant in both American Indian and Hispanic cultures. In rural communities, arts such as quilt-making and pottery-making are collaborative—with several people interacting as they make the cultural item. For this reason, intergenerational teaching is a style for learning within cultural context.

> *The meaning of the art-making process, rather than seeing art as a product, is very important to traditional people.*

Planning must take such cultural differences into account. When tourism-related materials interpreting the cultural meaning of the arts accompany the selling of arts, then the art is usually treated with greater respect. A museum or cultural center may become the source of this information. In-depth interviews with artists, as part of a museum project, yield information applicable for use later on biographical cards.

Usually there are restrictions on persons appropriate to include for learning the traditional arts. Symbolism connected to these arts may need to be kept private and other limits to learning and selling are necessary to identify. In some cultures, certain arts are for ceremonial purposes only and are not appropriate to sell. Local fears about tourism may surround these issues in traditional cultures. Teaching in a cultural center or museum context needs to incorporate all of these special considerations.

On a community scale, support for the teaching and continuation of cultural arts usually comes through a museum or cultural center. Both positive and negative influences from tourism must be considered. Positive results coming from visitor attention include reviving arts through increased teaching of those arts at risk of becoming lost. Cultural continuity is then enhanced. One of the dangers of exposure to commercial market demands is an imbalance—focusing on certain arts appealing to tourists. Taking care taken to teach a range of cultural arts maintains a balance between earned livelihood and internal, cultural use.

PLANNING PROCESS:
Honoring the Arts

- *Which locally made arts match well with visitor interests (external market)?*

- *Which arts should not be sold outside of the community (internal market)?*

- *Which arts can be taught in a classroom or cultural center setting?*

- *Who is allowed to learn each art (e.g., internal community or tribal members only)?*

- *How will art teaching involve all generations?*

- *Which materials are defined as authentic for each art?*

- *How will natural material sources be protected from depletion?*

- *How will information on the arts be communicated to the public, to further an understanding of the handmade, authentic process?*

- *How will information about the artists be communicated, to honor the tradition?*

CREATING A DATABASE FOR CULTURAL ARTS

One strategy communities use successfully to begin cultural center or museum planning is identifying cultural artists. In relation to tourism, conducting such assessments requires caution to protect cultural symbolism and meanings that are for the eyes and ears of community members only. A generalized interpretation of the art, if the art is appropriate for the general public to see or purchase, is valuable to document.

Conducting cultural inventories to examine the status of traditions is the most valuable way to organize for cultural renewal. Understanding the extent of knowledge retention is basic to preventing further cultural loss. Opportunities for retention of traditional culture, as well as income generation, are increased through assessments of the status of traditions. Compiling the data from a cultural inventory into a database is useful for finding the traditions that are strong and the traditions at risk of being lost—as well as the number of people with knowledge of particular traditions. The cultural inventory can be viewed as a needs assessment for cultural continuance. One outcome of the cultural inventory is the determination of priorities for teaching and identifying traditions at risk of being lost.

By assessing the age range of the keepers of the traditions and whether or not they are willing to teach, the status of each cultural art and the risk of these cultural arts becoming lost are determined. When these inventories then are given back to the community after they've participated, the priorities for cultural teaching become readily evident. For example, when only one elder has knowledge of a particular tradition, the teaching of this tradition may quickly become a priority.

The basic cultural inventory generates community participation for learning the arts, for organizing teaching, and serves as a reminder of steps ahead to meet cultural retention needs. A database may include the following variables (Example 7.1):

- Name, contact information;
- Age grouping;
- Specific art known;
- Arts wanting to learn;
- Whether willing to teach; and
- Whether willing to demonstrate.

Example 7.1 CULTURAL ARTS INVENTORY

Date: _____
Community: _____
Person completing: _____

Age Codes:
1= 1-19 years
2= 30-39 years
3= 40-59 years
4= 60 or over

Name Address Phone E-mail	Art(s)	Age	Demo? (yes/no)	Teach? (yes/no)	Arts want to learn
Artisan A (contact info)	Pottery	2	yes	yes	Sculpture
Artisan B (contact info)	Stone Sculpture	2	no	no	Basketry
Artisan C (contact info)	Beadwork, earrings	4	no	no	Moccasins
Artisan D (contact info)	Beadwork, Shawls	3	yes	yes	Moccasins
Artisan E (contact info)	Basketry	4	yes	yes	none
Artisan F (contact info)	Tanning Hides Moccasins	3	yes	yes	Sculpture
Artisan G (contact info)	Silver Jewelry	3	no	no	Moccasins
Artisan H (contact info)	Dancing Regalia-making	2	no	no	Sculpture

Participation and momentum tend to follow this extent of community involvement. In relation to public programs, demonstration programs generate visitor interest and assist local artists with sales. The arts inventory is also useful documentation for demonstrating need to a funding agency or organization. This discussion of assessment and database method is expanded in the next chapter, with additional marketing variables to address earned livelihood for cultural entrepreneurs.

THE VIRTUAL MUSEUM

Using the internet for a virtual museum is one way of furthering cultural understanding, interpreting historical events, and presenting the cultural arts. The virtual museum on a website may be a starting place in the sequential development of a cultural center, or may serve the community well on its own.

Frequently the first intent of a virtual museum is the creation of a cultural information base for the community. Positive benefits of a virtual cultural center include: increasing cultural pride within the community, making information readily available, enhancing the traditional economy, and stimulating language learning. Including history, historic photos, and photographs of those collection items curated in other museums is supportive for improving traditional community members' access to their own cultural resources for learning purposes.

Visitor education through a virtual museum minimizes environmental and privacy impacts of widespread visitation—instructing the visitor on history, arts, events, and visitation protocols before the physical visit. This increases respect for community and culture in advance of the visit.

Effective visitor education and a draw to remote locations is enhanced economically by developing a virtual museum. Although common for a community to consider developing a cultural center with a building, costs of maintaining and staffing a center may be prohibitive. For this reason, the first phase of a cultural center may be a virtual information center, serving several purposes.

Visitor education prepares tourists coming to traditional communities for a culturally-based vacation. A virtual cultural center site is useful for: 1) visitor education at the pre-visit stage, 2) on-site visitor education with access at museums or cultural centers, and 3) use at visitor centers and locations of tourism partners—both on websites and physical locations. The virtual cultural center or museum provides an orientation to visitors that understaffed centers do not have the capacity to fulfill.

If the story reaches across cultures and communicates to a range of ages, stories of cultural history and revitalization set the context for visitation. Storytelling, a traditional way of passing down an interpretation of history, is possible through audio clips on a virtual museum. Merging traditional sources of learning with digital sources enhances the youth participation in cultural activities, as well as language learning. Traditional youth may not fully understand the accounts of history from different viewpoints and such a resource is valuable to realizing local cultural identity. In contemporary traditional cultures with internet access, this is an additional way of supporting cultural retention.

Cultural privacy is maintained by limiting public access.

Not all traditional cultures approve of storytelling on the internet. Culturally private information may be protected with a password. This may have limited applicability, both in content and depth of the story. A short message may be allowed rather than the entire story. Placing a computer terminal in the museum facilitates visitor access to a broad range of interpretive topics, providing cultural understanding at on-site locations.

Cultural artists are encouraged to engage in cultural art-making when authenticity is widely understood through digital cultural exhibits and video interviews with artists. When community members practice and earn a living through the cultural arts, they may not leave rural or tribal lands as young adults—but stay and earn a living and teach other community members. This factor is basic to cultural continuance.

Additionally, researchers and scholars gain ready access to materials difficult to locate by other means. Travel expenses are reduced, as well as repeated permission needed for access. Collections at urban locations are frequently without interpretation from the culture of origin. By including photographs and interpretive statements from cultural artists, cultural history and material culture become better understood.

Assessing materials readily available for a virtual cultural museum is a foundational step. Community input into preliminary planning holds the potential to indicate the messages to convey. In summary, recommendations for topics to be addressed on a virtual museum website include:

- Traditional welcoming;
- Traditional history;
- Stories, if appropriate;
- Photographic collections;
- Artifact and cultural collections;
- Documentation and interpretation for collections;
- Virtual exhibits;
- Event listings;
- Video interviews with artists;
- Local efforts to further cultural knowledge retention;
- Directory of artists;
- Connections between regional communities and offerings;
- Membership information;
- E-newsletter (with member password);
- Donor names (to honor); and
- Links to other websites, organizations, and museums with culturally related collections.

Cross-links to the websites of other museums and organizations guide potential visitors to rural and Indigenous people for greater participation and cultural understanding. A tribal virtual museum website example, the House of Seven Generations at the Jamestown S'Klallam site, features history, photographs and artifacts. (www.tribalmuseum.jamestowntribe.org)

ENCOURAGING SUPPORT OF LOCAL INITIATIVES

Diversifying support for cultural centers and museums creates a "security net" in times of economic uncertainty. In some countries, support has come largely from grants or government funds. While some support is still available, tapping a broad range of support sources not only generates income, but also broadens the function of a center to meet a diverse set of community needs. Income for operations and programs can be generated from: admissions, tours, special events, grants, membership programs, donors, earned income (e.g., museum store, food service, tours), and a local government or tribal tax.

Earned income is a source of museum support that also creates earned livelihood for community members. Sources include a museum store or art gallery, tours (museum, nature, historical), traditional meals, or offering training to other communities. Micro-loans are sometimes available to entrepreneurs for start-up and feed into the gift shop or art gallery enterprise. Suggestions for different ways of framing projects to broaden funding applicability are given in Chapter 10, under sustainability. Grant support is a source for securing start-up capital for a business. Chapter 9 on creating an enterprise gives guidelines for developing a business plan, the necessary step for improving business success.

Charging an admission fee is sometimes an option, yet usually generates less than 10% of operating expense. Appropriate pricing—carefully based on admissions fees of culturally similar and regional museums—is fundamental to the tourism draw. Packaging an admission plus a tour at a discount is a strategy used successfully by many museums.

Donations and Other Sources

Donations are a central way to benefit from tourism. Visitors interested in cultural diversity tend to support local cultural retention efforts. If local stories of cultural preservation efforts are made known to visitors through small exhibits, a brochure or a website, visitors will be moved to assist with donations.

Fundraising for cultural centers and museums should be planned in a diversified manner to maximize leveraging potential. Membership programs are valuable for visitor education, as well as to secure funds for furthering cultural programs. A donation structure is a tool to establish an endowment for long-term earnings on investments.

These can fund general operations or support specific projects, such as construction or classes. Short-term funding may support classes to address cultural retention, or for preparing artists in the business skills necessary to be a part of job creation through a museum store, or an outdoor market.

Networking with potential donors in the region and donors who visit from national and international locations is part of a diversified support strategy. When these individuals gain an awareness of the local history and particularly local cultures, a relationship is formed. By launching a "Friends of ___" organization and distributing an e-newsletter, a cultural center or museum is capable of informing members locally, nationally, and internationally. Messages on the importance of preserving and restoring traditions, creating employment, supporting local conservation efforts, and progress of cultural revitalization efforts, create interest.

Fundraisers, such as traditional feast meals, frequently are planned to involve the "Friends" organization. A schedule of memberships should be identified on the center's program materials. A sample membership scale is:

Annual membership

Individual	$35
Family	$50
Patron	$250
Contributing	$750

Life membership $1,000

Donor over $1,000

A "Friends" membership program created in conjunction with a virtual museum generates connection—particularly when a special "page" is created for use with a member code. By heightening awareness of the role of traditional culture and arts and history, a cultural center or museum provides a meaningful cultural education experience for the public. Members become part of a living history process, through their support of cultural retention programs.

Many types of available funding, such as construction, operational, and teaching grants, require matching funds. Donations are flexible funds, ideal for use in matching fund requirements. Benefits to the community increase by involving visitors.

Special events for donors may be low cost, yet informative. For example, in a Native American community, a trip to see the buffalo herd, a hike on an historic trail, or an outdoor camp in a tipi and eating a traditional meal—are precious experiences for friends of the tribe and heritage-oriented visitors.

For large donors, a museum may consider the idea of small, special events to not only keep these donations coming in, but also to inspire large donors to tell their friends about ongoing work in teaching the cultural traditions. These may include pre-opening receptions, talks by local artists or historians, gifts, classes, or recognition plaques.

Ongoing community participation via an electronic newsletter, outlining progress on teaching and cultural revitalization efforts, is the usual incentive for keeping members involved year after year. This may be brief, with photos showing classes or events. By developing a list of member email addresses, it is possible to keep in touch and send out notices when new membership fees are due each year.

Small offerings of thanks—such as a special place on the website—appeal to donors and create the connection of relationship. Providing a letter of thanks, along with the amount donated and the museum or cultural center's IRS 501(c)(3) number, is a must to ensure continued donations. The majority of donors need this documentation for tax deduction purposes. A form letter with the amount filled in at events, or a letter sent afterward is sufficient.

MOVING FORWARD WITH AN EYE TO THE PAST

In summary, a cultural center or museum can serve several functions—from welcoming, providing visitor information, telling stories from the community's viewpoint—to interpreting history and communicating worldview. As a gathering place, cultural centers involving generations for teaching tend to succeed. Linking cultural entrepreneurs to visitors is another significant opportunity.

While benefits of linking include a strong referral network for tourism, the advantages of multi-community collaborations also accrue to the individual community. Tourism is a likely rallying point for other types of collaborative action. Frequently, linkages stemming from tourism result in knowledge collaborations between communities of similar traditions, resulting in success at "bringing back" traditions nearly lost.

Within a referral network, use of a similar theme, a unifying concept, or a brand adopted by all participating communities for both internet and hardcopy marketing, is effective. If cultural centers or museum locations in each community use a large brochure rack and distribute the brochures of all communities and entrepreneurial businesses, a unified regional concept is created. Reciprocation, rather than paying a steep distribution fee, makes marketing possible for small communities. Flat screen representations and internet-linked computer terminals are other levels of presenting information for reciprocation in a tourism network.

As cultures worldwide move into an era of adaptation to challenging economic and ecological conditions, opportunities to present culturally-based solutions will increase in importance. Community-determined messages to share in relation to sustainability can stimulate innovative intercultural solutions. Global resilience in the future depends upon the cumulative, bio-cultural knowledge base developed over the past thousands of years. For this reason, retaining cultural diversity is of far-reaching importance.

COMMUNITY-BASED SOLUTION

Sister Indigenous Cultural Centers: The Poeh Cultural Center at Pojoaque Pueblo, New Mexico, USA and Guaraní Paraty, Brazil

The Poeh Cultural Center and Museum located at the Pueblo of Pojoaque trains over 100 Native cultural artists each year through a curriculum merging the cultural arts with business skills. By identifying the arts at risk of being lost, the initial phase of the cultural center focused on teaching those arts, intergenerational involvement, and use of Native languages. Uniqueness of this model of cultural revitalization is reflected in a living museum concept, with changing exhibits featuring the ongoing progress in renewing Native artistic traditions.

Integrating value-based business skills into the arts curriculum and assisting cultural entrepreneurs with employment linkages, are other unique features of the cultural center. My book *Planning for Balanced Development* documents this successful cultural revitalization effort.

Many American Indian tribes and Indigenous people internationally are learning from the Poeh Center. In one collaborative interchange, the Guaraní Paraty Indians (Indigenous Association of AWA Ropedju) in the State of Rio Janeiro, Brazil, visited the Poeh Center. The renowned Pueblo potter Roxanne Swentzl traveled to Brazil and taught pottery-making methods to Guaraní tribal members, assisting to revitalize the tradition. Renewing the weaving traditions is a focus of the center, as well.

The Center provides for the preservation of the Guaraní culture through workshops, traditional crafts, music and dance, legends, medicinal herbs and stories—inspiring quality-of-life through the expansion of international markets.

Subsequent volunteer coaching on cultural center development by Poeh Center staff traveling to Brazil, and through internet communications, as well as assistance from the National Museum of the American Indian (Washington, DC, USA)—supported the Guaraní to develop their cultural center. Exhibits explain the revitalized Indigenous basket and pottery traditions, as well as an exhibit on the Poeh Center as a "sister" cultural center.

FURTHER READING

Chilisa, Bagele. *Indigenous Research Methodologies*. Los Angeles, CA: Sage, 2012.

   This innovative text presents an overview and synthesis of Indigenous research methodologies and the relationship between data gathering, analysis, and policy making from a cultural viewpoint.

Cooper, Karen Coody and Nicolasa Sandoval, editors. *Living Homes for Cultural Expression: North American Native Perspectives on Creating Community Museums*. Washington, DC: Smithsonian Institution, 2006, (www.nmai.si.edu).

   A development text from the indigenous viewpoint, addressing exhibition planning, teaching programs, public programming and tribal collections—written from the direct experience of several Native museums and cultural centers.

George, Gerald. *Starting Right: A Basic Guide to Museum Planning*. Nashville, TN: American Association for State and Local History, 2004.

   Economic and cultural issues are integrated into a framework for museum planning—including pros and cons of establishing a museum, up-to-date resource lists, and basic advice on all aspects of museums from the choice of a building through collections care, registration, exhibitions, conservation, staffing, financial management, and fund raising.

Kovach, Margaret. *Indigenous Methodologies: Characteristics, Conversations, and Contexts.* Toronto: University of Toronto Press, 2009.

Indigenous methodologies flow from tribal knowledge, story as method, cultural protocol, and ethical responsibility. This book integrates the stories and perspectives of six Indigenous researchers.

McKercher, Bob and Hilary du Cros. *Cultural Tourism: The Partnership Between Tourism and Cultural Heritage Management.* New York, NY: Routledge, 2002.

In relation to achieving sustainable cultural tourism, topics explore issues of collaboration and competition, several possible relationships between tourism and cultural heritage management, tangible and intangible heritage, cultural tourism products, commodification issues, assessments, management of resources, marketing, and presentation.

8

CREATING JOBS

*Visitors appreciate authenticity
when they feel a connection to local culture.*

Employment is high on the list of desired community outcomes for tourism. Why is this outcome so important? The future of a rural or traditional community often depends on local options for earned livelihood. If jobs are lacking, community members may move away to urban areas for employment and young people tend to not return after their education is completed. Populations of numerous rural communities are decreasing with each decade—and these locales carry deep concern for their survival as a community. To stay connected to place, while creating a means of livelihood compatible with culture, supports sustainability.

This chapter encourages community discussions about local skills and small enterprise development, prior to considering larger-scale ideas. When smaller, entrepreneurial businesses create products and services to feed into larger community businesses—rather than importing services and products from outside of the community—then tourism generates local jobs and becomes compatible with the culture.

A primary advantage of small-scale, linked enterprises over a large scale tourism business is the potential for authentic expression of local culture. Training to develop the skills of cultural entrepreneurs is basic to the success of small-scale enterprises.

> **Framework for Integrating Culture**
>
> - Identify household means of employment and whether there are several income streams.
> - Determine which forms of employment support culture, quality-of-life, and environmental integrity.
> - Discover ways employment can encourage cultural learning.
> - Create a database or directory of cultural entrepreneurs.
> - Identify selling issues of cultural entrepreneurs.
> - Deliver training in entrepreneurial skills.
> - Assist entrepreneurs to develop a mini-business plan.
> - Protect cultural designs and information as determined by the community.
> - Raise awareness among community members for needed environmental protections.

EMPLOYMENT AND CULTURAL SURVIVAL

Cultural survival often depends upon staying in the traditional geographic location, with access to traditional plants, animals, sacred sites, and sense of place. For this reason, sustaining a cultural future based on tradition may depend upon generating cash flow to supplement subsistence activities. When culturally-based business ideas emerge, a unique network of businesses is created—far more exciting to visitors than the larger-scale enterprise convenient for travel agents to book.

The notion of full-time, large-enterprise employment in relation to quality-of-life is dissected in this chapter. A frequent measure of success generally used in tourism, in addition to revenue, is the number of jobs created. Yet a large number of immediate jobs does not necessarily translate to a long-term means of sustainable earned livelihood. For rural and traditional communities, there is an expanded range of employment options that also sustains culture, family, community, and environment—while maximizing job creation. Local community needs may include employment options that offer freedom of schedule to participate in the annual cycle of cultural activities critical to cultural survival.

Cultural tourists look for authentic food, cultural arts, and regional-style lodging. They enjoy demonstrations, interpretation, and tours offering contact with local people for an authentic experience. Heritage tourists look for opportunities to learn history and educational experiences. Ecotourists tend to seek out unique geographic areas, wildlife, and a natural setting to stay. Local people telling their own stories pique visitor interest in community, history, and ecosystems.

> *The experiential dimension to a visitation experience is enhanced with local management.*

EXPANDING JOBS

Primary employment consists of full-time or part-time jobs provided through businesses, cultural centers, museums or local organizations related to tourism, usually with employee benefits. *Secondary employment* includes entrepreneurs that provide services or products to local businesses and organizations, or to businesses outside of the region. Sometimes these concepts are called "direct" and "indirect" forms of employment.

Addressing rural needs usually implies creating many jobs. Offering support services to provide secondary employment is a significant way of addressing these employment needs. To obtain an accurate way of counting actual impacts on earned livelihood—calculate primary employment plus secondary employment to document the widespread, actual benefits of an enterprise or assistance project.

Gaining a true count of employment in an informal economy, or where an industrial economy of "eight to five" jobs is not prevalent, creates baseline data for measuring progress. Funders often use definitions of employment that do not fit in rural areas where *multiple income streams* are the norm. Defining measures of employment and educating funders is a way of representing the community successfully and increasing accuracy in documenting need. Additionally, secondary employment generated by entrepreneurs provides the local supplier end to tourism, thus enhancing the local tourism concept.

Small business development loans, business training, and internet promotion can support the expansion of secondary employment, thereby reducing the unemployment rate. Developing a curriculum for small business skills tailored to cultural values increases entrepreneurial involvement.

QUALITY OF EMPLOYMENT

Community input to determine locally defined, appealing ideas for job creation—combined with an inventory of local skills—increases long-term means of livelihood. Training developed for a realistic scenario of enterprise and product development is based on both market potential and cultural boundaries. When asked to think about integrating values and culture into the creation of enterprises, entrepreneurs will see ways to connect their own culture.

Benefits of small-scale local employment developed from within communities include the potential for extended family interaction through earned livelihood. Much of culture and language is taught through everyday activities, in context.

PLANNING PROCESS:
Quality of Jobs

- *What are the current sources of earned livelihood in the community?*
- *Are items sold made within the family context?*
- *Which traditional arts are appropriate to sell?*
- *Are there restrictions on the use of traditional designs?*
- *What other products, such as agricultural, are sold?*
- *Are there seasonal restrictions upon gathering from nature, making art, or selling items?*
- *Is there locally produced food that could be sold to visitors?*
- *What new items could be made specifically for visitor purchase?*
- *Is lodging locally appropriate and if "no," how could lodging be provided and be less intrusive, locally owned and managed?*
- *What level and quality of jobs does the community see in the future?*

Tourism frequently encourages the learning of traditional arts. A good example is the pottery revival in the Pueblos of New Mexico (USA), stimulated by an increase in tourism in the 1930s. American Indian tribes sold pottery to visitors on train stops. These sales encouraged the renewal and practice of this tradition. Today, a renaissance in pottery-making translates to a solid entrepreneurial living.

Respecting the wisdom of the community to define cultural boundaries concerning appropriate items to sell in tourism settings, and to consider impacts of market demand upon traditional art forms, supports the culture. Cultural groups usually have an internal means for discussing issues and keeping art forms evolving in a culturally allowable way.

Periodic roundtable discussions or gatherings regarding the teaching and selling of the arts are recommended to resolve such issues. Policy may then follow on who is allowed to learn techniques and cultural meaning of the arts. Within their own internal processes regarding authenticity, cultural groups discuss the appropriateness or non-appropriateness of selling items, as well as changes allowed in materials or art form.

The role of a planner—either from outside or inside the community—can be to bring up authenticity in relation to tourism, to stimulate discussion, or even to help organize a community forum where artists discuss these issues and others pertinent to their culture. "Planting a seed" is the start. How that germinating idea evolves is the community's cultural responsibility.

Within the community context, there is sometimes a continuum of traditional arts, from those not to be altered, to others that are less sensitive. Guiding a community to define those arts and the possible impacts of market pressure is useful to a community. For some arts—particularly those used ceremonially—the details may not be appropriate for someone outside of the community to hear. For culturally sensitive topics, consider not documenting the details, but rather the larger categories of items appropriate or inappropriate for sale.

The need for artist education in business skills and marketing is useful to document. For example, even if the arts are not at the core of the local economy, the opening of an art gallery or gift shop at a cultural center or museum will provide the door of opportunity for employment and supplemental income—while supporting cultural renewal efforts. For this sector of the traditional economy to grow, artists and other cultural entrepreneurs need business skills.

Tiered levels of training for artists and service personnel are necessary for different entrepreneurial stages. Limited success of business training occurs when different skill levels are not taken into account.

THE SKILLS DATABASE

Identifying and tracking local skills for tourism development creates a foundation for generating employment. In addition to considering planning participation from a broad range of business, management, and local government expertise—securing intergenerational involvement provides cultural insight on priorities.

Recording the results of a skills inventory into a database is extremely useful for training and supporting local entrepreneurs after the planning phase.

- Use the level of technology available in the community. Database software or the common spreadsheet software EXCEL provides a good means of organizing, documenting and passing information on to others. If this type of software isn't available, create a chart in a word processing program.

- A handwritten record is valuable, if computer technology isn't available. Using a set format enables the same type of data to be collected for all persons. Make certain that copies are distributed to several people in the community, since one handwritten database is easy to misplace.

- Update the database annually at minimum, and encourage community participation in ongoing training opportunities.

Then, analyze the skills available and the gaps in skills. The essential factor involves knowing what skills will be needed. A planner or tourism industry personnel assisting the project may provide valuable input on the skills needed—from development through management stages. An artist and entrepreneur database with marketing information is valuable to create, if maximum opportunity for earned livelihood is to occur.

Summarize the key findings on strengths and needs for expanding internal expertise to present baseline data in the plan. This information will be useful for measuring progress later. The skills database is valuable as an appendix to the tourism plan as a reference point for training and marketing. Identifying matching topics and resources for training, business development, marketing, evaluation, and management encourages implementation. The database format in Chart 8.1 expands the teaching formats presented in the last chapter and includes marketing information needed to assist entrepreneurs.

PRODUCT DEVELOPMENT

As mentioned previously, the concept of a "product" tends to be a culturally sensitive issue. The tourism industry widely refers to a product as a tour to book, or as an object to be sold. In traditional communities, there are many cultural boundaries concerning both items and information about the use of these items. Ultimately, each community must make its own decisions based on tradition, values, and the need for livelihood.

Cultural arts evolve over time. Some evolve more slowly than others due to the symbolism connected with those arts. If the art form is used for cultural reasons, the form and materials have cultural significance. Also, demand through tourism holds the potential to impact traditional arts by depleting natural resources needed for traditional uses. Protecting these resources is vital to cultural survival.

When local groups participate, consider "Who benefits and who pays?" A well-structured tourism plan will direct benefits to local groups rather than to tour companies owned by large corporations. In some geographic regions, large tour companies also own the shops selling souvenirs and art, garnering the entire benefit of the tourist dollar.

A smaller-scale option is a network of local entrepreneurial services and activities, with support services in marketing and business training. Often a local organization, museum or cultural center will coordinate entrepreneurial activity, conduct marketing, and book tours as a service. Guiding the benefit to community entrepreneurial activity produces the local gain.

Focused Sense of Product

Economic multipliers increase in a locale as additional products are made within the region, rather than imported. The challenge is finding the intersection between a cultural fit with the community that also meshes well with the broader industry. Referrals to a community's businesses are directly related to income and jobs.

Chart 8.1 CULTURAL ARTS TEACHING AND MARKETING ASSESSMENT

Date: _____

Community: _____

Person completing: _____

Name Address Phone E-mail	Art(s) know	Age Group	Demo? (yes/no)	Teach? (yes/no)	Arts want to learn
Artisan A (contact info)	Pottery	2	yes	yes	Sculpture
Artisan B (contact info)	Stone Sculpture	2	yes	no	Basketry
Artisan C (contact info)	Beadwork, earrings	4	no	no	Moccasins
Artisan D (contact info)	Beadwork, Shawls	3	yes	yes	Moccasins
Artisan E (contact info)	Basketry	4	yes	yes	none
Artisan F (contact info)	Tanning Hides Moccasins	3	yes	yes	Sculpture
Artisan G (contact info)	Silver Jewery	3	no	no	Moccasins
Artisan H (contact info)	Dancing Regalia making	2	no	no	Sculpture

Age Codes:
1= 1-19 years
2= 30-39 years
3= 40-59 years
4= 60 or over

Want business skills training? (yes/no)	Want to market at Cultural Center (yes/no)	Number of items could market per year	Price range (retail) items want to market
yes	yes	10	$100-$150
yes	yes	5	$300-$600
no	yes	25	$25-$40
yes	no	n/a	n/a
yes	yes	3	$300-$600
no	no	n/a	n/a
yes	yes	20	$125-$250
no	no	n/a	n/a

A basic interpretation of the tour package concept is a self-guided tour. How does the visitor learn about a self-guided tour? Visitors find local interests by picking up a brochure in an urban area, through a website, social media, or in a visitor guide—in addition to the word-of-mouth referral visitors.

In the small-scale sense, there is another concept of product, significant in a cultural way—selling cultural items with respect so as not to commodify cultural meaning. Opportunities for entrepreneurs include the cultural arts: jewelry, baskets, pottery, textiles, beadwork, carvings, and food products as well as smaller scale tours and guide services.

Targeting a market or several markets increases the potential for sales in several ways. Admissions, lodging, and food service comprise a segment of potential sales. Art items, souvenirs, and packaged local foods are all opportunity niches. Food service offering regional specialties ranks high in visitor appeal.

To understand differences in urban and rural tastes, ask visitors about their food preferences. This is the best way to tailor a menu to the visitor profile, either through a visitor survey or customer comments. A range of options, from traditional foods for the adventurous to mainstream food choices, will best match visitor preferences. Most cultural travelers are from urban areas, have disposable income, and seek a new experience.

> *Cultural tourists are seeking information about the artist, as well as authenticity of materials and the art-making process.*

By providing training and advertising support to local entrepreneurs, the amount of earned livelihood created through entrepreneurial activities is multiplied many times beyond the basic tourism amenities. Both are complementary and draw visitors for the culturally-based vacation. The handmade item and traditionally based service draws visitors initially, building a market for the larger amenity businesses. As internal community capacity and the range of amenities grows—then a complete vacation concept develops and length-of-stay increases. Additional expenditures and jobs reflect the potential for an upward spiral supporting local livelihood.

Product development suitable for entrepreneurs, interpreted as a range of services and cultural items, includes:

1) Art items;
2) Souvenir lines;
3) Food products;
4) Guide services;
5) Specific tours—cultural, agricultural, ecological, hunting & fishing;
6) Entrepreneurial food services; and
7) Small-scale lodging, such as bed and breakfasts, cabins and campgrounds.

Maintaining a variety of products and representing a range in pricing, attracts visitors. The souvenir line generates the majority of sales and is generally considered to be items costing $25 (USA) or less. The mid-price and upper-end relate primarily to the cultural arts and depend upon the local region and culture. Examples are reflected in Chart 8.2.

Gift boxes combining products, such as a coffee mug and local agricultural products, are a valuable way of increasing sales. This strategy works best if shipping services are provided for large or difficult to carry items.

Repeat orders from long distance are an additional source of income for entrepreneurs, when contact information is given through a business card or a bio-card—even if handwritten—at the time of the sale. Setting a bio-card in a piece of pottery or a basket, or attaching the card to an item, ensures that the information will stay with the piece. When visitors make notes, these usually become lost by the end of the trip.

Product development is more likely to match local offerings with visitor preferences through training by a consultant familiar with the preferences of the market. Targeting a market or several markets increases the focus for sales in several ways. Lodging, food service, shopping, and admissions comprise the largest segment of potential sales. These essential services keep visitors in the area longer, resulting in increased entrepreneurial sales.

Chart 8.2 PRODUCT LINES WITH HIGH POTENTIAL

• Tote bags
• T-shirts and sweat shirts
• Scarves with traditional designs
• Key chains
• Handmade cards
• Value-added agricultural products
• DVDs/CDs
• Posters
• Photographs
• Children's toys
• Books
  • Recipe books
  • History, with local interpretation
  • Novels set in the region
  • Children's books
	• Jewelry
	• Pottery
	• Coffee mugs with designs
	• Candles
	• Local Foods
	  • Honey
	  • Jams
	  • Dried stew mix
	  • Dried meat or fish jerky
	  • Dried fruit
	  • Trail mix
	  • Fresh produce

TRAINING PROGRAMS

Effective training and mentoring of local people in business skills is essential to small-scale tourism. Training tailored to the local cultural and environmental setting is frequently difficult to find. To change the scenario of management from outside the community, with community members holding lower-level positions, a local community must begin training programs prior to business development. This develops local skills before business start-up occurs.

    Not everyone is well suited to being an entrepreneur. Essential traits for this type of business are: vision, initiative, creativity, persistence, tolerance for risk, and the ability to grow from mistakes and failures. Assisting entrepreneurs to see their abilities in terms of these skills, plus needed additional skills, combines for potential success.

Often cultural entrepreneurs do not perceive themselves as being in business. By not planning income and expenses, marketing or managing finances, the entrepreneur loses possible sales. Personal financial management training called "financial literacy"—adapted to the entrepreneur—expands community resources. Being in business is a state of mind, as well as a process of generating and managing resources.

Two types of employee training needs are important to distinguish: the storefront enterprise and the small entrepreneur enterprise or cottage industry. Training for entrepreneurs and cottage industries is usually not readily available but may be developed from collaborations. Combining the skills of knowledgeable business people with those of successful local entrepreneurs gives a tailored cultural perspective. For example, many talented artists in rural and reservation areas have art skills but few business skills. Therefore, finding people in the community who have success at entering the arts and crafts market is a necessary step for developing a training program to meet local needs.

Quality of the training relies heavily on an interface between the community (value-based), the training topic, and the correct entrepreneurial level. Aim for a training tailored to the local community or culture, not a pre-prepared "canned" approach.

> *Training offered for small business is often designed for a larger scale than the scale needed to benefit the entrepreneur.*

The benefits of training include increased awareness of potential market pressure. Consequently, questions may arise: Is the traditional method of producing items changing, and is change negatively affecting the meaning of the cultural art? What measures will be taken to protect traditional items and cultural meanings? To determine answers to these questions, the community may decide to hold periodic meetings to discuss the relationship between business and culture.

Available business trainings frequently assume a retail approach to business. When the training is not tailored to a specific level, the instructor ends up with participants who are at different levels. The trainer has to adjust to a medium level, therefore not providing the depth of information essential for the experienced entrepreneur, while oftentimes losing the non-experienced entrepreneur. For these reasons, courses need to be carefully designed and the appropriate level of entrepreneur attracted to them. Promotion for a course needs to be clear about the topics and about the level.

Entrepreneurial Topics to Include

This section suggests a place to start with business training, as well as curriculum content. Courses effectively begin at the entrepreneurial level and then build to the storefront business, from the home cottage industry to a formal business setting. Avoiding "canned" training packages geared to large scale tourism businesses and not tailored to local culture helps avoid a cultural skew.

Unfortunately, most textbooks on the subject are intended for the profit-motive cultural orientation, rather than a broad range of community values. Local college staff may be a training resource, offering course credit as well—if local businesses collaborate on the design of the training to ensure inclusion of cultural values and in-depth experience with the local market.

In my experience working with traditional artists, there are several different levels of entrepreneurial capabilities. For example, at least five tracks for artist business training are possible.

1) A workshop for artists enrolled in traditional arts training, who desire business skills to earn supplemental income;

2) An artist intensive for those students taking several courses in one or more arts with the intention of earning a full-time living;

3) Workshops for artists with selling experience who desire to upgrade their business skills;

4) Topics for the experienced businessperson who may conduct sales for the family; and

5) A workshop series for the storefront gallery business.

Significant training topics for an *artist entrepreneurial* program include: focusing the business idea; assessing the market; identifying qualifications; the mini-business plan; creating the bio-card with artist information; financial record keeping; taxes; vending, art shows; evaluating success and redirecting efforts.

Topics effective for a *food service training* cover: general food preparation; traditional food preparation and interpretation; food handling and storage; the work environment; safety practices (lifting and carrying); welcoming customers; taking orders at tables; appropriate clothing; opening/closing; cash register procedures and operation.

Topics for a *tour guide training*[1] include: cultural history; natural history; cultural considerations for privacy; code of ethics for guides and travelers; customer service; leadership and conflict resolution skills; equipment operation; safety and survival techniques; first aid; and business skills for managers.

Since entrepreneurs tend to listen first to other entrepreneurs, guest speakers with visible success contribute to a thriving entrepreneurial program. Organizing field trips to nearby places that sell to tourists is a valuable way for cultural entrepreneurs to learn which items are selling well, how displays are created, and ways of delivering customer service in a local manner. Observing and then critiquing in class assists students in making decisions regarding their products and livelihood.

Consistency in the delivery of a service or product is essential to training for the tourism market. For example, if store hours are advertised, then provide coverage during those hours. Otherwise, a frustrated tourist will not return. In contrast, a satisfied customer will rapidly spread the word about a good business or product. An entrepreneur operating from the home must be consistent in answering messages or filling orders to maintain that most economical referral means of marketing. Being friendly and interactive toward customers creates mutual satisfaction in business.

Mentoring Programs

Pairing experienced entrepreneurs through mentoring, with those beginning to learn skills, is an excellent way to provide practical experience. Although sharing information within a particular culture may be the traditional way of learning, participation in a cash economy through tourism sometimes skews traditional ways of learning, particularly if competition for sales is sensed. Or, the experienced entrepreneur may not be willing to commit the time required to be a mentor.

There are several ways to work with culture if this happens. Offering perks—or benefits for the experienced entrepreneur—such as assistance with marketing or participation in a booth at an outdoor market or art show, encourages mentoring. Including booth space for family members encourages an intergenerational incentive.

Some cultures discuss a spiritual obligation to teach and continue traditions. Looking within cultural ways of teaching fosters traditional ways of mentoring.

AUTHENTICITY ISSUES

What is the boundary between sharing culture and over-commercialization of tradition? This question is at the root of authenticity issues. To not exploit culture, yet to share; to sell, yet not change tradition; to give some information, yet respect cultural boundaries—these are the challenges of maintaining authenticity of both cultural arts and experience. Cultural arts are constantly evolving. Past, present and future are considerations for traditional cultures, as a circle of continuity.

Cultural sharing, in an ideal world, would not involve a monetary exchange. Yet the reality of community and family needs, where some movement into cash economies is complemented with subsistence activities and barter, indicates the necessity for balance in sustainable development. A proactive approach toward tourism and increased awareness of alternatives in communities enables options for engaging in tourism in a way that an agrarian lifestyle or traditional economic activities—such as hunting, fishing, and gathering—are still practiced. Using the concept of multiple income streams leads to flexibility.

Factors basic to the authenticity of cultural arts are: ethnicity, materials, techniques, cultural accuracy, quality, and heritage connections. Visitors are seeking the work of local artists, traditional methods, the stories connected to the arts, as well as traditional materials and designs—the authentic. There is an ongoing debate in the field of tourism on the meaning of authenticity. Does tourism impact, negatively or positively, the authenticity of a culture?

One astounding feature of this debate is the discussion occurring primarily outside of communities, based on external observation—rather than asking the communities directly about their perceptions on authenticity. An observer approach rarely captures the internal cultural discussions and awareness of cultures evolving.

In *Issues in Cultural Tourism Studies*[2] Melanie Smith presents a balanced view of tourism as influential for cultural revival, but potentially forcing a shift in traditional artistic expression as a response to the demands of tourism. A productive and realistic view is to shift the focus to community response, encouraging internal discussions on authenticity decisions, and increasing access to community-based training implemented according to these decisions. What is needed from technical assistance providers is a highly developed capacity to listen, the primary way of communicating information in traditional cultures.

Conserving cultural values central for an economy based on quality rather than quantity and natural resource protection rather than extraction—focuses on the effects of cultural retention and ecosystem ties, over immediate economic gain. Critics of the viability of the "authentic" tourism experience see culture as static, whereas culture is always in a state of flux, incorporating new ideas into time-honored traditions. Yet, uniqueness disappears when others copy, affecting cultural sustainability.

For this reason, many cultures are hesitant to engage in "hands on" demonstrations and are not allowed to talk to outsiders about the prayers and customs that are part of cultural creative practice. External pressures may skew this process, by introducing new development ideas without understanding internal practices.

Maintaining authenticity requires careful consideration by a community. For example, plant knowledge shared in detail sometimes results in the stripping of forest resources—severely impacting art-making, healing, and food-gathering practices. Clay resources for pottery or trees for basketry may likewise be depleted. Environmentally sound gathering practices involve an insightful knowledge of the plant and how to harvest without depletion or damage, and even how to harvest with stewardship, contributing to the thriving of the plant.

In some cultures, an art item takes on an animate or living quality through the traditional art-making process. "Talking with the clay" with respect and prayer during pottery-making brings the pottery to life—an example from Pueblo cultures in the Southwest USA.[3] However, when people from outside the culture learn the detailed specifics of a traditional art-making process, they may replicate and sell the item without imparting the "life giving" property to the cultural item. This form of cultural imitation tends to be considered by many disrespectful to the environment and to tradition.

In addition, the erosion of the market for the authentic piece negatively impacts traditional artists. Such potential negative impacts need to be considered by the community when drawing the cultural boundaries appropriate for sharing knowledge. These boundaries are unique to every culture, highlighting the need for an internal planning discussion.

For the experience to be authentic, the local community takes the initiative in communicating culture. Not idealizing the past—but rather moving forward with an eye to the past—is the desire of many traditional cultures. Effectiveness of the cultural tourism experience from the standpoint of community lies not only in the quality of information provided, but also in the mode of communication. Storytelling is most often the traditional way of transmitting knowledge in traditional communities.

To not impose cultural bias in the perception of authenticity is not simple, for any culture. The true meaning of a special event to the hosting culture is a factor relevant to authenticity. For example, several Native Alaskan dances on stage involve youth encouraged to learn in classes, increasing overall cultural participation. The story behind the story creates a fulfilling visitation experience. Cultural boundaries and public access limitations to cultural information are openly discussed in the process of deciding how to present.

An effective logo representing authenticity is the Silver Hand emblem, used to identify arts and crafts produced by Alaska Natives since 1972. The emblem provides a "guarantee of authenticity," that the article is "made in Alaska, handcrafted and finished by an Alaska Native artist or craftsman." Any Alaska Native of 1/4 or more Native blood is eligible to register for the state-sponsored program.[4]

Fliers describing the art-making techniques (even if simply xeroxed) or the cultural revitalization efforts taking place through community learning programs—greatly enhance the buyer's understanding of the time and materials taken to produce an authentic cultural art item. Educating the buyer that the item is more than an object (without revealing sacred or traditional meanings), but rather a part of history, will increase the willingness to pay a fair price in exchange for the privilege of owning an authentic piece.

Protection from Cultural Appropriation

As termed from within Indigenous communities, the "stealing of culture" refers to people copying symbolic designs and methods of making cultural items, and selling items as if they were made by the people whose culture is represented. This situation can be very serious—both culturally and financially—to a local culture. Particularly when symbolic interpretations also carry sacred meaning, fear of the practice of appropriating culture may be sufficient reason to prevent participation in cultural tourism.

Awareness of intellectual property rights is now coming to the forefront in regard to Indigenous symbolism and stories. The cultural difference lies with the concept of "ownership," which is not perceived the same way as in Western/European cultures. In Indigenous cultures, ownership is often not with an individual, but rather information and designs are held by a group culture or community. Or, ownership may not be a cultural concept.

> *The message from traditional cultures is clear: observe and learn about others, don't copy. This is the ethical credence of cultural visitation.*

For example, in most Southwestern (USA) American Indian tribes, a pottery design belongs to the "tribal community" as a whole and should not be used on items made outside of that community. In many Northwest Coastal Indian Tribes, designs belong to individual tribal members or families and are not to be copied beyond that individual or family.

Protecting images placed on the internet is fast becoming a concern. Authenticity issues and cultural boundaries addressed early in tourism planning define how culture is presented and what is reserved as a private internal practice. Communicating clearly that an image is not to be copied, and whether it is culturally rather than individually owned, may protect to some degree.

There are some possible measures to protect cultural property rights. One of the most effective is generalized education to the visitor about traditional materials and techniques, and what constitutes the authentic piece or cultural experience. Copyright and trademark are two widespread means of protecting information and designs, yet carry limited protective value between countries or internationally.

The cultural tourist of the next several decades will be more aware of cultural differences and will be looking for the authentic experience. Therefore, local groups must plan a means of educating visitors. This may be accomplished through the development of locally owned visitors guides or educational pieces where traditional communities present an explanation of the methods used to make authentic cultural meaning.

In evaluating new product ideas for tourists, one must consider the difference between seeing the item as an object only and understanding that some products hold meaning. In other words, in cultures where the worldview is animate, cultural items may be perceived as alive. After they are purchased, they must be cared for in a special way. A replicated item not made through the cultural process that brings this item alive loses cultural value as an authentic item. Some communities develop policies around the production of cultural items for use internally in the culture, versus those allowed to be sold in the tourist trade.

These are delicate questions and must be decided by each community, for their community. There is no one direction that these policies would take. Therefore, caution is advised in not adopting other communities' policies, but rather taking the time to develop one's own policy regarding cultural arts and crafts.

Biographical cards attached to items lend personal context to marketing, which is respectful and more culturally acceptable for some traditional communities. For example, information about the artist, the art process, and the materials is then imparted. This "value added" approach increases the perceived worth of the authentic to collectors.

Information conveyed to the tourist sparks an interest in learning about the culture and being appreciative of the work. In other words, it is educational for the cultural tourist to understand when the visitation experience is not an imitation of culture, but rather is authentic culture.

Increasing Ways of Selling

Diversifying ways of selling encourages cultural participation and family cohesion while reducing a sense of competitiveness. In traditional and rural communities, gift shops or art galleries are frequently located adjacent to, or in the home (when local laws allow)—lending flexibility to business structure.

Outdoor or indoor marketplaces are cost-effective ways of linking entrepreneurs together. These vending opportunities are effective when an educational component such as demonstrations or educational fliers are provided, meeting the learning choices of cultural tourists.

Santa Fe Indian Market is an outstanding example of supporting earned income through the cultural arts. This weekend outdoor market in Santa Fe, New Mexico (USA), draws an estimated 100,000 people, supporting sales for over a thousand Native American artists—with an economic impact of over $19 million.[5] The market features pottery, jewelry, textile weavings, painting, sculpture, beadwork, basketry, and other traditional as well as contemporary work. It is the oldest and largest juried Native American art show in the world.

With the pattern of generations working together, participating families earn the majority of their annual income through this one weekend show. Started in 1922 as Indian Fair and sponsored by the Museum of New Mexico, Indian Market is now organized by SWAIA, the Southwest Association for Indian Arts. (www.swaia.com)

Another means of increasing opportunities for selling is developing a business incubator—with reduced costs for a period of two or three years—to provide office space, training, and sometimes access to computers and copiers. Artist studio space in a cultural center is another way of providing needed resources for local entrepreneurs.

Cooperatives are another form for possible collaboration. The true meaning of a cooperative, ownership shared by the members, does not work well in all cultures. Whether group ownership or ownership by an entity such as a community development corporation would work effectively should be explored. Following the track record of cooperative formation in similar cultures, as well as examining how well consensus works in a particular culture, are useful ways of guiding decisions.

Lodging is another niche for entrepreneurial development. Bed and breakfast concepts are less expensive to develop than larger-scale lodging. This type of lodging does not necessarily need to be in the owner's home, which may be culturally intrusive, but rather in a constructed dwelling with a traditional breakfast delivered to the site.

A thorough analysis of the tourism system in the planning process will identify niches for services and entrepreneurial opportunities. Constant linking and referrals expand entrepreneurial potential.

CUSTOMER SERVICE

Tourism-related customer service is the skill of taking care of visitors. In traditional cultures, this involves a culturally-based way of connecting with people and is not a scripted response. When provided in a spontaneous, authentic manner by the cultural entrepreneur, customer service draws upon traditional ways of caring for people.

Training in customer service is pivotal—and will make or break a tourism effort. Visitors feel secure and taken care of, and therefore more comfortable about visiting another culture. Well-delivered customer service provides an outstanding draw to visitation. Marketing costs are reduced if personal referrals are continual.

Telling a story, offering a native tea, and explaining local history are examples of added value to an authentic experience. Small, subtle, attentive actions form the core of good service. Bridging cultural differences is a challenging, yet a basic part of developing customer service tailored to a region or culture. When entrepreneurs and larger businesses take time to notice visitor needs and come together to design solutions, quality and consistency of the overall tourism network is vastly improved.

Skillfully avoiding culturally invasive questions rather than becoming personally offended by the asking—is the successful strategy to encourage repeat visitation. Most visitors are unaware when they are crossing cultural boundaries. If visitor education pieces communicate the information desired to share, the majority of visitors will be satisfied with the learning experience.

Part of the authentic experience is the learning of different styles of interaction. Hesitancy to interact with visitors is sometimes attributed to "cultural shyness" and the fear of making a mistake. In real situations, most visitors are forgiving and eager to engage.

Friendliness, as defined in the local cultural style, is an essential part of customer service. Some cultures may hesitate in friendliness from fear of inviting culturally invasive questions. This hesitation may be overcome by recognizing the degree of information appropriate to share. Successful entrepreneurs are friendly and take the time to "chat" with customers, learning about their preferences. These conversations enable them to customize their inventory or services over time.

There exists a fine line between the amount of time appropriate to spend with one customer, yet not ignoring other customers waiting to speak to the entrepreneur. Cultural differences in appropriate time length are useful to understand; customers will go away if they perceive the entrepreneur is too busy for them. Vendors must avoid getting caught up in conversations with each other, cell phone use, or texting during business hours.

Limiting conversations with customers during busy times keeps waiting visitors from becoming frustrated and leaving. This is basic attentiveness for gaining sales. If visitors require follow-up information or the filling of orders, keeping excellent documentation on contact and order information supports a good track record and willingness to trust a whole community or a specific event.

In relation to sustainability, the culturally appropriate form and timing of business development are basic to finding a good "cultural fit" in customer service. The degree of comfort felt by both visitor and the community determines the quality of the experience.

PRICING

One of the barriers to entrepreneurial success is lacking a thorough understanding of pricing and positioning in the market. Beginning entrepreneurs sometimes expect to receive retail prices (the price sold to the public) when trying to sell wholesale (the price to the entrepreneur, before retail markup). After markup, overpriced items will not sell. Learning local pricing structures is basic for setting retail prices competitive in the marketplace.

When purchasing an item wholesale, a storefront shop typically pays the artist between 40% to 50% of retail — which is the price the store expects to receive from the customer. In other words, for an item selling at $100 in a retail store, the artist would receive $50 at 50%, or $40 at 40%. On consignment items, a retail store generally pays 60% of retail price to the entrepreneur, and takes 40% of the retail price for the store. A cultural center or museum may pay up to 70% of retail to the artist, depending on the setting.

In some regions, the entrepreneur does not receive a fair percentage of the selling price gained. For example, sometimes a markup of four to ten times is seen. This is not fair to the local producer or artist. Assessing the pricing structure locally for cultural arts and food products is advisable for the start-up entrepreneurial business. Consistency will not only connect directly to sales, but also to community collaborations in the tourism network. While this may be seen as competitiveness in the mainstream business concept—pricing according to local levels creates harmony within the community.

VENDING

Selling outside of a storefront business or in a marketplace is known as "vending." Artists or persons selling other handmade items create a business opportunity reflecting local culture. Some families engage in vending for supplemental income. In a traditional economy, most families have several income streams, or different ways of producing parts of their income. Jobs or part-time jobs are supplemented with sales at art shows, fairs, feast days, pow-wows, cultural events, festivals, concerts, cultural events, and conferences or at tables outside of museums. Identifying local art shows in the region, or other opportunities to sell, creates additional income streams for families. In vending, family members usually work together, reinforcing extended family cohesion.

THE MINI-BUSINESS PLAN

A brief mini-business plan, a short summary for the small entrepreneurial business owner, is a good starting place to focus the business concept. A summary of approximately five pages is sufficient to describe the business, identify the market, and project potential income and expenses. This tool is useful for guiding sustainable development at the entrepreneurial level.

In egalitarian cultures, business success is often defined in terms of family and community, rather than individual gain. When cultural, family, and community requirements are anticipated, the outcome is more likely to be positive.

Cultural values affect business decisions on a daily basis. Entrepreneurs tend to enter into business activity not being aware of the degree to which they have to make cultural decisions in every aspect of their business development and management.

CHART 8.3 MINI-BUSINESS PLAN OUTLINE

VALUES IN BUSINESS:

- Which cultural values do you want reflected in your business?
- How will you communicate these in managing your business?
- How will you connect to, and contribute to, community resources?
- How will environmental conservation be addressed?

BUSINESS DESCRIPTION:

- What will you sell or which service will you provide?
- Is this a wholesale or retail business?
- How will cultural significance be communicated to your customers?

BUSINESS LOCATION:

- Will the business be storefront or cottage industry, from the home?
- How will you describe your location, or give directions?
- Will you be able to reach a market sufficient to operate the business, from this location?
- Is your location optimal for the business type?

BUSINESS GOALS:

- What is your target level of support?
- Does this level include family and community responsibilities?
- How does your business contribute to cultural continuity?

QUALIFICATIONS AND STAFFING:

- What is your training or experience for this business type?
- Will you need additional training?
- What resources are available for training?
- Is your business intended for one person, a family, or will you need to hire additional people?

TARGET MARKET AND STRATEGIES:

- What is the age range and gender (male/female) of your intended customers?
- Where does your intended customer live?
- Who is also selling a similar item or product?
- How do their prices compare to yours?
- What will your business initiate to attract sales?
- What is your budget for marketing to reach customers?

INCOME AND EXPENSE PROJECTIONS:

- Are there several sources of income? Identify and list them.
- How many items or services (tours, meals, etc.) do you expect to sell in a year? At what price?
- What expenses do you expect to operate for a year? Will travel be required?
- Will you make a profit or a loss in that year?
- Will you need a loan to reach the break-even point (at which income equals expenses)?
- How will you support yourself during the business start-up?
- Is there enough profit to sustain you?

    The business plan for a small entrepreneurial enterprise is useful for anticipating costs for start-up (e.g. training, equipment, supplies, furniture, website, other initial marketing) and operations (e.g. rental space or booth costs, utilities, telephone, charge card service, banking, transportation, ongoing marketing materials, insurance, postage, website maintenance, tax preparation, taxes).

    An important consideration is a salary for the entrepreneur. Even though the exact salary amount is difficult to know in advance, setting a target salary is useful for gauging success. Keeping track of actual expenses is valuable for comparison to the original projections and redirecting the business as needed.

The purpose of a culturally-based business plan is: 1) to bring awareness of values that are always present, 2) reflect how these values affect daily business decisions, and 3) to decide whether or not to enhance these values in the course of business decisions.

Sometimes business ideas combine well to form a unique concept and at other times the business idea becomes too broad to target a specific market effectively. Focusing the business idea or purpose is related to success, since thinking through the relationship between values and business development is likely to encourage entrepreneurs to participate fully in the local economy.

The following example income and expense projection form is intended for an artist in the one-year time frame. Calculations for three years are preferable, yet if this time frame is difficult for the entrepreneur, a one-year operating budget and estimated income is useful for managing income and expenses (cash flow) to reach the goals for the year (Chart 8.4).

Entrepreneurs frequently transition successfully from a full-time job with self-employment in the evenings, building a clientele until the business provides substantial support. A mini-business plan is an excellent way to project the **break-even** (income equals expenses) or "sustainable point."

The Difference Between Gross and Net Income

Entrepreneurial businesses tend to run into difficulty by not clearly tracking the difference between overall income to the business, or ***gross business income,*** and ***net business income***—or the amount of business income after expenses are deducted. ***Expenses*** are the cost of conducting business (e.g., rent, supplies, phone, business cards, advertising, taxes).

Personal income is the amount available to pay a salary, leaving a cushion in the business for cash flow to be held in the bank to cover months when bills must be paid, but income might be less. ***Personal income after taxes*** is the amount of income actually in hand, available to spend for personal expenses after personal income taxes are paid.

Chart 8.4 ENTREPRENEURIAL INCOME AND EXPENSE FORM

	Jan	Feb	Mar	Apr	May
BEGINNING BALANCE					
INCOME					
Sales - Jewelry					
Sales - Pottery					
Sales - Baskets					
TOTAL INCOME					
EXPENSES					
Personnel					
Your Salary					
Additional Assistance					
Health Insurance					
Travel (mileage)/gas					
Website					
Business/Bio-Cards					
Credit Card Services					
Insurance					
Postage & Shipping					
Training					
Telephone					
Office Equipment					
Office Supplies					
TOTAL EXPENSES					
INCOME-EXPENSES					
ENDING BALANCE					

Jun	Jul	Aug	Sep	Oct	Nov	Dec	TOTAL

KEY REASONS FOR ENTREPRENEURIAL SUCCESS

There are many success factors unique to entrepreneurial businesses—different from the small business with several employees. Entrepreneurs tend to be self-motivating, goal oriented, and good managers if they are to be successful. Ask community participants to assess how they could improve their business after reviewing the entrepreneurial characteristics of businesses that fail and succeed. This step helps the entrepreneur contemplating a business startup, and the entrepreneur who needs to manage more effectively or expand a business.

Chart 8.5 FACTORS IN ENTREPRENEURIAL SUCCESS

- Seeing oneself as a business owner
- Thinking ahead and being strategic about managing the business
- Being clear and focused with a business concept
- Becoming knowledgeable of current and potential markets
- Having strong family links to help in the business
- Marketing well and consistently
- Searching for training opportunities and participating fully
- Linking to other businesses for referrals or becoming part of a tribal economic development network
- Avoiding financial losses through interest payments
- Keeping accurate records on income and actual expenses
- Paying taxes on time to avoid penalties
- Maintaining a good credit rating
- Integrating culture to enhance satisfaction with being in business
- Carrying business cards
- Using the internet and business directories
- Belonging to a Chamber of Commerce for training and marketing assistance
- Maintaining friendships but keeping business transactions formal (avoid giving away products at no cost, low cost or on credit)

Often the entrepreneur wants to stay small-scale to have more time with family or to participate in community or cultural and religious activities. Others want to expand their business and services. Assist entrepreneurs to evaluate these alternative intentions, in relation to culture and sustainability.

KEY REASONS FOR ENTREPRENEURIAL FAILURE

Trouble spots in entrepreneurial success are valuable to understand. Not paying attention to business management practices leads to financial difficulties quite quickly in the entrepreneurial business. This section contains a checklist of business management characteristics that most frequently contribute to businesses running into debt or failing completely. Generally, entrepreneurial businesses fail due to lack of business planning and management.

Chart 8.6   REASONS FOR ENTREPRENEURIAL FAILURE

- Not clearly defining a market
- Offerings and products not matching market preferences
- Not conducting marketing or allocating funds for marketing
- Operating in isolation, not linking to other businesses who could potentially provide referrals
- Not scheduling enough work time
- Family obligations consuming work time
- Business start-up on a credit card with high interest
- Not keeping detailed records of income and expenses, to calculate actual income
- Not keeping savings to cover essential expenses when income is low
- Burn out—working excessive hours without time off
- Time for tasks not currently estimated or scheduled
- Not enough training for the multiple skills needed to run a small business
- Not finding a reasonable source for health insurance or quitting business to get health insurance
- Not paying bills on time

- Not pricing products or services correctly
- Product not unique enough to fare well in competition

Understanding the common pitfalls of entrepreneurial businesses is a great aid in starting up a business successfully, or for redirecting business management practices. Marketing, financial record keeping, and time management tend to be the weak spots for entrepreneurs. Entrepreneurs, who tend to work in isolation, often view themselves as the only ones experiencing these difficulties. Communication with other entrepreneurs and participation in training workshops is useful to overcome isolation.

AN INCLUSIVE PROCESS

The role of planning assistance is to suggest a process for community possibilities. Gradual change over time happens to a culture and the cultural arts in traditional cultures. Whether this change constitutes a threat to the community is an internal discussion point. Sudden changes to meet market demand may alter culture in impactful ways, from family interaction to ecosystem interrelationships. This contrasts to Western culture, where sudden changes in art styles may become *avant-garde* and the way to sudden success.

Including entrepreneurs and artists in both the planning and development stages fosters a better cultural fit for tourism business ideas. The entrepreneurial segment of the local economy is frequently neglected—yet essential—for tourism success. The greater the fit to cultural values while satisfying community needs for jobs and additional services, the more sustainable the tourism development scenario.

As people retain the ability to live and work in their small communities and the local environment is protected, a sense of place is reinforced for future generations. Creating the authentic cultural experience is relevant for maintaining traditions internally, as well as for market considerations.

COMMUNITY-BASED SOLUTION
The Huichol Center, Jalisco, Mexico

The Huichol Center for Cultural Survival and the Traditional Arts is located in the desert region of San Luis Potosi in Jalisco, Mexico—an area designated as a world biodiversity reserve. The Huichol Center is helping to preserve a unique Indigenous culture deeply rooted in pre-Columbian spirituality, healing arts, and mysticism.

The goal of the Huichol Center is to create enduring lifelines between Huichol traditions and the future. This allows traditional wisdom to thrive in the 21st century by empowering the people who carry its spirit and substance. Protecting the ancient heritage maintains traditional lifeways—now threatened by mining companies and business polluters. The Center teaches the arts and encourages children to value their culture as well as to read and write in their Native language. Economic self-sufficiency is promoted by enhancing the skills of Huichol artists in the creation and marketing of their artwork.

The Huichol people are known for their beaded wood sculptures, beaded jewelry, and yarn art. Visions seen during spiritual rituals are transcribed as images onto carvings, yarn art, t-shirts, note cards, framed arts, and shamanic vision cards. The idea of balance—central to the Huichol religion—is reflected in the culture's integrative relationship to the seasons.

Success factors include use of the internet to tell the Huichol story and sell in support of efforts to preserve biodiversity, as well as utilizing sales outlets in the United States, such as the Centro Indigena Huichol outlet in New Mexico (USA) and a gallery near Puerto Vallarta (Mexico). Messages are also conveyed to the public by furthering visitor education efforts through museum exhibits in other countries, such as the "Huichol Art and Culture: Balancing the World" exhibit at the Museum of Indian Art and Culture in Santa Fe, New Mexico. (www.thehuicholcenter.org)

FURTHER READING

Comaroff, John L. and Jean. *Ethnicity, Inc.* Chicago, IL: University of Chicago Press, 2009.

With a focus on issues concerning commodification, this text exposes the ways in which corporations co-opt ethnic practices to open up new markets and stimuli to consumption—within the interrelationships of culture, capitalism, and identity.

Indian Arts and Crafts Board. *Introduction to Intellectual Property: for American Indian and Alaskan Native Artists.* 2010 (www.doi.gov/iacb)

This brief guide describes ways of generating income through intellectual property, trademark, copyright, design patent, trade secrets and internet concerns.

Indian Arts and Crafts Board. *Forming an Arts and Crafts Cooperative.* n.d. (www.culturalentrepreneur.org or www.iacb.doi.gov).

The principles of cooperatives are explained in relation to ownership, control, and benefits. Steps to form a cooperative are described.

MindTools. *Entrepreneurial Skills: The Skills You Need to Build a Great Business.* 2012 (www.mindtools.com).

An overview is given of entrepreneurial characteristics, interpersonal skills, critical and creative thinking skills, and practical skills useful for training.

Northwest Area Foundation. *Native Entrepreneurship: Challenges and Opportunities for Rural Communities.* Washington, DC: Corporation for Enterprise Development, 2004.

Entrepreneurship policy, education, business training and technical assistance, access to capital, and networks are discussed in relation to fostering entrepreneurship in Native communities.

Rossouw, Dirk, Jo Zeelie, Darelle Groenewald, and Andreas de Beer. *Entrepreneurial Skills.* Johannesburg, ZA: Double Storey Books. 2009.

The entrepreneurial skills covered in this book include: creativity and innovation; self-confidence and a positive attitude; goal-setting; assertiveness; time management; networking; leadership and teamwork; creative problem-solving; and, strategies for dealing with conflict and confrontation.

9

THE TOURISM ENTERPRISE

*Value-based enterprises support family
and community—as well as cultural retention.*

What is the purpose of business? The depth of this question is rarely considered outside of the mainstream sense of business-for-profit. Decisions shaping a business concept might look different in a traditional community—such as working to keep traditional culture alive and strong. Small-scale business development for cultural tourism requires careful consideration of cultural values. Will there be a community climate of competition or cooperation? Will business profits be reinvested back into the community? The business with the good "cultural fit" reinforces cultural values and provides financial support.

Business development styles may differ markedly in a rural, reservation or urban setting. Success may be defined from varying cultural viewpoints, value positions, and practices. By recognizing these differences, strengths can be increased and weaknesses overcome. Cultural styles and business forms are discussed in this chapter. Each community must define strengths and measures of sustainable success from within the culture. In the ideal scenario of planning cultural tourism, a strategic tourism plan would be completed before enterprise development begins—first weighing the impacts, both positive and negative, of several business ideas.

> **Framework for Integrating Culture**
>
> - Determine business niches that complement each other, to foster community cooperation.
> - Define a business concept compatible with cultural values.
> - Identify a scale for business that matches management skills.
> - Consider extended family and community cooperation.
> - Identify products that will encourage cultural learning.
> - Use a business style that fits culturally, yet one that meets basic visitor needs.
> - Identify a community-based approach for product development.

These enterprises may include a range from individually owned, to community owned, cooperatives, or corporate owned. Then, the feasibility of different businesses is evaluated, guided by input from the community. Several questions guide the inquiry.

- Are the businesses complementary in a referral network?
- Do the businesses work together to keep visitors in the local area, thus extending visitor length of stay?
- Are there any business niches missing to form a cohesive vacation itinerary?
- Is there a business directory to guide visitors directly to entrepreneurial services and small businesses?
- Is the directory readily available online and in paper format at visible community locations?

After the business environment is well understood from market assessment, then the business plan for an individual business focuses the business idea and assesses feasibility within a total business network. Although monitoring expenses and profit is essential for the business to survive—creating small-scale alternatives for family livelihood, retaining culture and maintaining local ties to the land may be the criteria for defining business success.

CULTURE AND BUSINESS STYLE

Entrepreneurs, artists, and tour guides providing the draw for tourism comprise the largest percentage of business offerings—yet most are without the support services needed to succeed. As alternatives to the larger-scale, businesses can be small, family owned, and operated from the home. In regions where traditional culture is retained—extended family businesses in rural areas and reservations or reserves link family members together in a barter system meeting some of their needs. Ranches and small farms often operate on this level of business form. Cash tends to be supplemental income when several income streams are pieced together for a livelihood, reinforcing family and community inter-dependence.

The next scale of business includes small storefront businesses trading with local and nearby markets. Still larger businesses include locally owned service stations, restaurants, lodging, RV parks, cultural centers, or casino operations. On Native lands, these may be tribally operated or managed by an outside contractor.

Larger-scale businesses owned by corporations and part of a chain are the non-local business form. These operations are often characterized by frequent turnover in personnel and reliance on non-local management. Larger businesses lose tourism customers when they fail to include links to entrepreneurial activity. These connections can be accomplished by providing brochure rack space, web links, space for demonstrator or artist booths, and word-of-mouth referrals. Being generous with referrals in a small community actually creates a "hub" effect, drawing business and customers.

Culturally diverse groups tend to see the Western mainstream way of developing business as high risk and want to pursue a slower, gradual way of developing business. These communities are correct in their caution about the amount of risk in the Western style of developing business. In the United States, over 60% of small businesses fail—usually due to capital intensive start-ups, poor customer service, lack of marketing, and lack of monitoring profit and expenses.

Assistance and Business Style

What must be done to reverse the current trends in business development assistance—or to expand the understanding of what must be offered to effectively assist the small scale enterprise within a cultural context? Addressing a new approach for small business development, in a cultural context, is central to a shift.

- ➢ Determine the nature of small-scale. How small is small, according to a particular community and culture?

- ➢ Expanding the time frame over which assistance must be delivered to one client increases effectiveness. Small business development programs have targets set up by their funders to show a high number of short-term business startups. This extent of business startup is not a true reflection of success in business or long-term employment created, when the business failure rate is high.

- ➢ Instead, the emphasis needs to be shifted to long-term success measurements and the creation of stable, sustainable employment in communities. Otherwise, the vicious circle of business failure, bankruptcy, and unemployment prevails.

- ➢ While small business development providers see the long-term, gradual method as expensive—communities may be able to break through this notion by documenting business success and furthering the facts of enterprise sustainability. Long-term, stable business development is, therefore, a gradual, sound and successful way to proceed.

- ➢ The small-scale gradual way of developing business does not work for every industry, particularly when large capital investments for equipment must be made. A restaurant doesn't gradually acquire its equipment, but might start with used equipment and a plan to gradually upgrade. In relation to cultural tourism, however, the small-scale approach is overall a viable alternative and one that holds the potential for involving whole communities.

- ➢ Developing new, value-based curricula or training approaches in small business skills supports culturally aligned development, as well as sustainability.

- ➢ Sustaining contact through follow-up with small or microenterprises is necessary for long-term success. There are different levels of small business to be considered in a region and resource providers must acknowledge these levels that are desired by local people and learn to work within their framework.

- Community-based assistance involves conducting local surveys to see what type of training, promotion and marketing assistance local people want, and structuring a program that has a good cultural fit for the region. Generic, nationally determined, technical assistance and training often do not address local sustainability criteria.

- Value-based, micro-enterprises need different types of assistance at different stages or levels of expertise. Unless sustained support is offered, the nature of those different types of assistance will be missed. For example, the first year of assistance may tap the local market, whereas the third or fifth year might tap a regional market or an international market. As local capacity grows, new curricula or means of training are needed. Training topics identified in the previous chapter are relevant to include.

Achieving sustainable results requires restructuring the forms of technical assistance offered. A "trainer-of-trainers" approach is often the most productive when an introductory training is adaptable to local needs and cultural ways of conducting business.

Business Formation

How businesses form and grow differs according to scale. Owners of the small-scale family business generally do not choose to borrow money from outside sources or to incur long-term or even short-term debt. Community members may not find it necessary or desirable to expand their businesses and in some cases are content to live on their existing profits. When viewed in a cultural perspective—extended family interaction, long-term stability, benefit to the community, and the maintenance of culture may become more aligning than constantly increasing profits. Matching the appropriate type of assistance needed and keeping the solutions in cultural context are valuable steps for sustainability.

Effective linking between urban Chambers of Commerce and rural areas creates a strong region. Utilizing business resources from outside of the community to continually network and train local people involves two-way learning. Continued planning, networking, strengthening of management skills, and reinvestment of profits—all provide the foundation for building an economy and sound businesses within that economy. Furthermore, building upon cultural strengths increases long-term ability to provide within the community.

In many cultures, the reason to own a business is to support the extended family and the community. Whether family is defined as the "nuclear" family (husband, wife and children) or the extended family (grandparents, aunts, uncles, cousins) is largely a cultural consideration. Traditional and small communities' tendency to buy from family first supports the cultural vision of being in business. The "commons," or the benefit of all in the community, is the "net worth."

A different system of earning income for family members still exists in some traditional communities, particularly egalitarian cultures. Several family members participate in making and selling items, pool the inventory, and then divide the profits among the participating family members. This style of business encourages family cohesion and incentive for family members based on traditional values.

A caution—putting quality and price first is critical for sales. Giving attention to wholesale versus retail pricing when buying from family or friends is essential, since buying at retail prices to markup and resell at retail, raises the retail price to an unrealistic, and not saleable level. Pricing at retail competitively in the market is central to making sales. This is of particular concern in small communities.

Loans

A standard procedure in corporate business development is securing capital by means of a loan. This way of developing a business is not always applicable cross-culturally or in the rural setting. In small communities, the idea of evolving a business slowly as capital is saved from profits may reflect a more acceptable way of developing the business.

Benchmark targets for business success—such as the "break-even point" or seeing profits within three years—are geared to the idea of securing a loan and then paying back the loan at the end of three years. Business development resource providers commonly require a business plan to secure a loan. Emphasis is seldom placed on long-term technical assistance, such as five-year technical assistance for the gradual evolving of a business.

Recognize the local strengths already existing in business styles, to avoid disrupting traditional economic lifeways. The new paradigm demands a shift from the short-term and the larger "small business" corporate approach, to the recognition of the different levels of small business as defined in a specific cultural setting. A business may evolve through several of these levels over time.

To make an economy grow, long-term sustained follow-through must occur as the targets set by assistance providers shift to long-term stability of business and long-term employment—rather than the current mainstream short-term approach. Discovering the appropriate level of business development involves respecting local views and not pushing a larger-scale agenda. By finding out what local people want and structuring a business development program around their views, respect is communicated and leads to participation once the program is developed.

FOCUSING THE BUSINESS CONCEPT

The carefully planned enterprise concept is more likely to spark visitor awareness when authenticity is central to the business idea. Several questions that might "shape" the business concept are suggested.

PLANNING PROCESS:
The Business Concept

- *How will the business reflect your cultural values?*
- *How will local/cultural values be reinforced by the enterprise?*
- *How might local values be affected negatively?*
- *How might time with family be integrated into the business concept?*
- *How will natural resources be protected by the business concept?*
- *What amount of income is "enough" income, to balance retention of values with income needed to pay for basic needs and adequate savings?*

- *Can the business be started on a small scale and expanded at a later date, if necessary?*
- *What influences might market or profit pressure have on changing traditional art forms?*
- *How will the community take action to relieve those pressures by developing new product ideas, such as souvenir lines?*
- *How can a discussion internal to the community lead to complementary enterprises being developed?*
- *How will one business connect to others to support a business network with referrals, training, and collaborative marketing?*

Phasing a business reduces financial, personal, and environmental risk. One personal risk important to traditional cultures is the family time sacrifice made to push for large profits. Small-scale businesses tend to better accommodate personal and family needs, as well as anticipate environmental impacts and evaluate needed changes over time.

THE TOURISM-RELATED BUSINESS PLAN

Business plans guide enterprise development. Projections of expected income and expected expenditures enable monthly monitoring of business income, to determine adequate availability of funds for business operations. One frequent business start-up error lies in spending profits rather than keeping adequate profits for reinvestment, expansion, promotion, and other needs.

For these reasons, a business plan as an initial calculation is a valuable management step. For some small business concepts the standard 50-page business plan developed for the purpose of securing a loan may seem like a monumental task. This chapter demystifies the business planning process.

The purpose of a business plan is to focus the concept, as well as to project income and expenses. If applying for a loan or a grant, the larger business plan may be necessary. For an entrepreneurial business, such as the individual artist, a mini-business plan may be adequate. In either case, the mini-business plan outlined in the previous chapter is a great way to shape the enterprise idea and get started.

The well-written business plan serves not only as a document to plan a business, but also as an effective management tool. Central to business success is the quality of the market analysis to target marketing efforts and redirect those efforts as needed. Comparing a monthly budget report against monthly projections is useful to determine whether a business is on track.

In the conventional business planning process, those projections are completed for the purposes of securing a loan, and tend to contain the biased intention of a favorable outcome. The thorough market analysis is often missing. Obtaining customer and community feedback, effective marketing, evaluating financial statements periodically, and redirecting, are the factors relating to business sustainability. When businesses in a community work together well, an economic system thrives and is more resilient in times of economic fluctuation.

Outline for a Business Plan

The following business plan outline for a small-scale tourism enterprise introduces the cultural element and takes into account community benefit—particularly in a culture where business goals are culturally-based and extend beyond profit motivation. Such an enterprise may be community owned, for example, a non-profit or a cooperative. Community organizations sometimes launch businesses to support their non-profit services. When the issue of profits is discussed in the beginning and adequate time is taken with plans, the community is likely to reach agreement on how profits will be spent, preventing disagreements down the road.

Examples in this chapter are shortened descriptions. Actual business plans would require additional detail. Although community benefits are rarely mentioned in a business plan, consideration of them leads to sustainable development. This approach requires a delicate balance in business planning, because financial viability still remains the most critical factor in making business decisions.

Business Plan Outline
    I. Introduction
    II. Community and Cultural Benefits
    III. Location

IV. Products/Services
V. Market
VI. Marketing Strategy
VII. Market Share
VIII. Market Penetration Assumptions
IX. Organizational Structure
X. Key Personnel
XI. Financial Analysis and Pro-Forma Operating Statements
XII. Community Reinvestment Plan
XIII. Appendices:
Résumés of Key Personnel
Supporting Documents

Introduction: The introduction serves as a foundation for the business concept and reflects cultural values. Although this section comes first in the business plan, the business summary should be completed as a last step in the process. The one- or two-page summary of a business planning outcome is often used for a preliminary funding decision.

Whether the owner is funding the business, preparing a loan application, or applying for a grant, a concise overview section is invaluable to include as a summary. A short description of the business includes the nature of the business, product or service, when it was first formed (if an expansion), and the special or unique qualities about the business, the anticipated market, profit projected, and the community benefits expected. Relating the tourism business to the regional economy furthers context and linkage, demonstrating the place of the business in a supportive network. Short examples follow for an Indigenous tour enterprise.

Brief Example 9.1: NATIVE TOURS INTRODUCTION

For thousands of years, the Desert Mountain Tribe's sense of place as a trade center has been a part of cultural identity and heritage. The majority of tribal members gain their income from a broad range of jobs relating to the arts and tourism. The Native Tours Enterprise is envisioned as a hub for tourism activities to enhance the existing benefits from tourism, while containing visitors and protecting privacy. Cultural values of hospitality, generosity, and extended family cooperation are central to the business.

This business concept emphasizes substantial potential through a central intake point at the museum—for tourism to educate visitors in the rich traditions of the Tribe, both artistic and agricultural. Through a coordinated effort, the Tribe will increase sales and increase jobs through tourism without necessarily increasing the number of visitors to the community. With a population that is growing rapidly, strategies relating to managing tourism are valuable for reinforcing quality-of-life.

There are strong possibilities for creating multipliers in the local economy. The larger the share of tourism dollars captured, businesses will develop to provide basic services for purchase by tribal members—thus increasing the number of times a dollar is recirculated in the local economy. By looking at ways in which the tourism market sector and local economic sectors can interact efficiently, true economic development stimulating the creation of multipliers is likely to occur.

This plan addresses both operations and financial feasibility of a tour enterprise. The enterprise will provide services for managing visitors, creating income multipliers, and directing visitors to other tribal businesses. Overall goals of the enterprise are to create a safe, educational, and healthy environment, in addition to generating profits. Special considerations are given to tribal entrepreneur referrals, creating a cooperative community win/win situation for tourism development.

Community and Cultural Benefits: Cultural tourism, when designed thoughtfully, benefits a community in several ways. These include contributions to community development in terms of needed services and income. Economic benefits include the number of jobs generated plus the purchase of goods and services from local entrepreneurs, thus increasing the economic multiplier effect.

Cultural values reinforced by the business create a culturally-based approach, relating business activities to the teaching of cultural knowledge, such as: businesses relating to the arts, new technical skills, and management training. All contribute to culturally-based development within the community. This section describes ongoing community contributions resulting from business earnings.

Multiplier effects create community employment. A multiplier effect (see Chapter 2) is the total change in spending in the business network that results when new spending creates greater levels of income—which in turn is reinvested within an economy, rather than leaving the economy as economic leakages. The more income created in the chain reaction, additional jobs are likely to result and local resources to increase.

Brief Example 9.2 COMMUNITY AND CULTURAL BENEFITS

The community vision reflected in the enterprise is to offer traditional hospitality, promote an understanding of authentic arts, share scenic beauty, and interpret our unique heritage to visitors. For the long-term, developing the Native Tours Enterprise will protect community closure for religious purposes.

It is clear from the experience of other Native communities succeeding in tourism that tours are a means of containing visitors as well as securing the profits needed to manage tourism and provide visitor services. Stopping visitors before they enter the community and then providing orientation and visitor education would increase the likelihood of respectful visitors. Moreover, the museum is seen as a hub, referring visitors to appropriate locations—such as businesses, entrepreneurs, and interpretive programs providing education to the public.

Products and Services: Tourism products range from tours to artwork, to food service or lodging, or any other service designed to meet the needs of visitors. Clearly defining the product is important in order to calculate projections. A description should detail the products or services to be sold. Photographs may be useful to illustrate the unique product or tour. In the case of products, a discussion of any intellectual property rights, patents, or proprietary features protects the business. Potential for expansion of a product line is a valuable topic to include.

The valid fear in cultural tourism is that artistic designs or other forms of cultural property will be copied by entrepreneurs outside of the community. Measures that can be taken to protect authenticity—or to prevent the replication of culturally specific designs—are visitor education concerning authenticity, quality, and cultural boundaries.

Characteristics of the available labor pool, such as educational level of the populations and special training to be offered—are valuable to detail in this section of the business plan. Training resources available to increase the capability of the labor pool to produce a quality product are important to identify. Whether sufficient product will be available to produce the desired business result underscores business success.

Brief Example 9.3 NATIVE TOURS SERVICES

Guided tours target several objectives for managing tourism. The most severe tourism impacts occur when visitors wander through the community intruding upon cultural privacy, taking unwanted pictures, and damaging a fragile ecosystem. By containing visitors to designated areas, impacts will be reduced, visitor education enhanced, and jobs created. Native Tours will distribute the Native Experience Guide *and emphasize the importance of buying from local businesses—75% of families earn a living through the arts, resulting in approximately 200 households available for participation.*

Three tours are outlined below. The Village Tour is seen as the introductory tour to the culture and the community location, thus preparing visitors for the advanced and longer tours. Visitors will be encouraged to take this tour first as an orientation to history and visitor etiquette.

The following fee overview addresses the full range of rates for each tour. Groups of over 10 persons will be able to negotiate a group rate.

Fee Summary

	Adult	Child	Senior
Village Tours	$17	$8	$12
Artist Studio Tours	20	10	15
Historic Site	22	11	16

Market: An effective market reach must consider existing potential customers, as well as the broader range of prospective visitors. Who is the community attracting now? Who could be attracted with additional marketing efforts? How does a strong tourism referral network increase length-of-stay within the region? Defining the potential market is an initial step in business planning.

First, describe the total market. For example, the dollars of annual expenditure in a specific business category can be determined by examining tax records. Next, the target market needs to be defined—whether it is the county, the region, the state, the nation, or international. Market segments are identified for each of the categories of products to be sold.

If tax reports do not list a specific category, another way to obtain market data is to inquire about gross sales of similar businesses in the region. Interviewing potential purchasers (visitor survey is best) is a way to determine what their projections for expenditures could be for local products.

Market trends are crucial to understand. What is the potential annual growth of the total market and of the market segments? Major factors affecting market growth, such as industry trends and population shifts, must be addressed. For example, is there out-migration from the region, and is this likely to affect a balance of local buyers and visitors? Is there a projected influx into the region? A profile of customers and their preferences is basic. A good business fit is the match between customer preferences and an innovative, authentic idea.

Brief Example 9.4 NATIVE TOURS MARKET ANALYSIS

Although the cultural tourism market holds great potential for the Tribe, the provision of services must match the expectations of the experienced visitor. Many segments of the community do not want an increase in the total number of visitors, but rather seek a way to manage and educate visitors, while increasing sales directly from local artists.

Specifically targeting cultural tourists who are likely to purchase tours and quality arts will be a central strategy. The different levels of tour pricing will address a range of income levels represented by tourists. The overall intention is increased cultural understanding and supporting the community's families in the most beneficial and cost-effective way.

Feasibility and high impact already established by studies conducted by the State Office of Tourism (2010) illustrate the opportunity existing for increased income to the Tribe through tourism.

- *Scenic beauty, historical sites, Indian culture, and outdoor recreation (in that order) were the highest ranking reasons for visiting the State. The Tribe offers all four top reasons for visiting. Emphasizing these assets and linking them together in the visitor guide will produce a strong draw for tourism.*

- *The most popular activities were led by sightseeing (92.6%), visiting historical places and museums (77.0%), visiting national parks (59.2%), shopping (39.8%), and outdoor recreation (35.7%).*

- *Of all visitors to the State, 54.6% visited Indian lands, up from 42.3% in 2009. This upward trend indicates potential to capture visitation with a managed program.*
- *The primary reasons for choosing to visit Indian lands were for Indian arts and crafts and to visit tribal museums/interpretive centers. The Tribe offers a wide variety of Indian arts and crafts for sale in shops and the tribal museum.*
- *Statewide, average spending per travel party was $1,303.30, up from $895.07 in 2009. This increase in dollars spent indicates potential for arts and crafts purchases, as well as food and lodging.*
- *A majority of visitors traveled to the State by private vehicle (70.5%), up from 66.8% in 2009. According to local business owners, visitors traveling in private vehicles tend to spend more on tribal arts than those on tour buses.*
- *The average length of stay was 7.3 days in 2010 compared to 6.05 days in 2009. This trend indicates the market niche for increased lodging at the tribal community.*
- *Visitors spent an average of 13.0 weeks planning their trips (up from 11.9 weeks in 2009). Since the tourism season starts to rise dramatically in April, the* Native Experience Guide *should be ready for distribution no later than early January, to reach visitors as they plan their vacations. Distribution through the State Office of Tourism's fulfillment program would reach visitors during that time period.*

Marketing Strategy: Creating the tourism draw is the central result desired from marketing. The market strategy developed in this section interprets the market analysis in relation to a specific business idea. In a changing economy, staying informed on trends not only supports the initial stages of the business concept, but helps to fine-tune the business annually—to keep up with market trends.

Assessing the competition is the first step in forming an effective marketing strategy. Knowing the competitive products and services and assessing their strengths and weaknesses forms a realistic basis for evaluating the strength of the competition. How are other businesses similar? How are they different? What is a unique point about the business that could provide a good tourism draw? In the sections of a business plan leading up to the marketing strategy, specific data sources and statistics need to be presented to back up the market analysis.

Price, reliability, authenticity, and services available are all variables for assessing the competition. Strengths and weaknesses of competing companies should be assessed in terms of management capability, capital available, plans for expansion, and any other product-specific variables. What strategies will be used to compete? What strategies will be used to collaborate with other local businesses for a win/win situation? The following example addresses these concerns.

Brief Example 9.5   NATIVE TOURS MARKET STRATEGY

A valuable estimate of tourism impact on tribal lands and for Native arts and crafts was calculated for the first time in 2009 (State Office of Tourism) by utilizing data from a statewide visitor survey. These are the most recent data available. The average spending, including admissions, arts and crafts, food and beverages, etc., while visiting reservations or Native communities was $252.80 per travel party.

Given the percentage of visitors that actually visit tribal reservations and the high level of their spending on arts and crafts, the Office of Tourism roughly estimated 2009 traveler expenditures in the amount of $160,163,000 in total on Native lands. Several strategies are recommended for the process of increasing market share to our community:

- *Coordinating tourism services to enhance visitor understanding of total vacation and educational offerings available at the community location;*
- *Providing direct referrals to tribal government and tribal-member-owned businesses;*
- *Working cooperatively with surrounding tribes in promotional efforts;*
- *Working with the tourism industry on international, national, regional, and local level itineraries;*
- *Linking to Native art shows, to promote a "loop" or Native vacation concept;*

- *Extending length of stay by developing a motel or a campground;*
- *Targeting the cultural tourism market, visitors who tend to appreciate handmade items and spend more on vacations;*
- *Increasing promotional efforts, such as advertising in vacation guides, as well as producing and distributing brochures and the Native Experience Guide; and*
- *Launching a "Buy Native" campaign for both locals and visitors, to encourage a turnover in dollars to stimulate economic growth.*

Market Share: A comparison between the total market and the business gain expected in that market is an estimate of market share. To calculate this, identify potential customers for the first year and the dollar amount in sales. Correctly focusing the potential market is the basic step in estimating market share. Local tax records at government offices are often utilized to calculate the total market in a business category. A visitor survey with specific questions is one way to target activities and purchases desired plus an intended dollar amount of purchase. The more local the data, the greater potential for estimating a specific market share. Generally, a three-year period is calculated for market share, with the first year being the most specific.

A business plan should indicate the strength of customer preferences and why these customers are likely to continue at the same or a different rate for subsequent years. Market share is used to project business expenses and income later in the pro-forma analysis. A caution—market share is an estimate, a point for comparison to actual income as the business develops. "Is the market being missed?" or "Was the estimate of the size of the market off?" are important questions to ask if earnings are not as high as the original projections. Also look closely at management and marketing practices.

Market share would increase from the first to the third year, in a developing business. A useful step in estimating market share is an explanation of how an ongoing assessment of market potential will be determined as a business progresses.

Is the concept unique enough to attract a market share? The emphasis is on an estimate, derived from examining other tourism-related businesses to see how the business concept fits into a network.

Brief Example 9.6 NATIVE TOURS MARKET SHARE

Tour operations in the county are estimated at a total income of $3,237,000. Based on these data, market share is estimated at 12.2% of the total, or $450,000 annually by the end of the third year of operation.

Market Penetration Assumptions: How is the business different from others in the local area and the region? How is the business similar? Effectively entering the market requires a strategy for capturing an estimated share of the total market. Determining effective pricing is part of entering the tourism market successfully. Overall considerations in pricing include: 1) acceptable rates to attract buyers, 2) increasing market share over time, and 3) potential profits. Targeted tourism markets are summarized in brief. The market level—such as local, regional, or national, should be addressed—as well as plans for expansion to other markets.

Critical risks and assumptions are identified in the planning stage of a business. Identify any potential problems or risks and the actions anticipated to solve these problems if they arise. In addressing them now, any investors or boards approving the enterprise will see that assumptions are recognized and risks are assessed.

Brief Example 9. 7 MARKET PENETRATION ASSUMPTIONS

Several variables underlie the potential success of the Native Tour Enterprise. Penetrating the market effectively will depend on the following assumptions.

Assumption #1: The Tourism Market Will Maintain a High Level

National strategies now demonstrate a "bounce back" in tourism from the 2009 downturn, although visitors are choosing carefully the value for their trip dollar. By keeping prices reasonable and focusing on an educational experience for the cultural tourism market, the Tribe is likely to find visitors willing to spend on tours. A high quality, educational tourism experience will be necessary to maintain a good draw from the market.

Assumption #2: The Community Will Support Tourism Management Efforts

Work with the community must be continued to define cultural boundaries and levels of comfort with ongoing efforts to manage tourism. If promotional efforts of the enterprise expand the market for all community businesses, employment for tribal members will be greatly increased. This continual interaction with the community contributes to sustainable tourism development, for the community determines the extent of visitation allowed.

Assumption #3: Promotional Efforts Will Be Effective

The allocation of adequate funds for promotion is necessary for business success, along with excellent management. Where marketing funds are spent to effectively target the market is vital to the result—reaching potential visitors as they plan vacations has the largest impact on increased expenditures. Effective use of the internet, to inform the public of tribal offerings and to book tours, will be a way of maximizing tourism dollars.

Assumption # 4: Tours Will Be Consistent, Reliable and of High Quality

Native Tours is planning a high quality, educational experience for visitors. The tourism industry places emphasis on reliability of the product. If a product is of high quality plus reliable in availability and consistency, industry personnel are quick to provide referrals. Likewise, if the product is inconsistent or unreliable, word will spread rapidly and the product becomes "un-recommended." For this reason, reliability of the product will be an underlying factor for success of the enterprise.

Analysis of Competition: Identifying factors significant to success, as well as determining effective pricing involves examining similar businesses both regionally and in other locales. Their brochures and websites give pricing and main features of the business. Talking with these businesses casually may reveal the difficulties they encounter, as well as found solutions.

Brief Example 9. 8   ANALYSIS OF COMPETITION

Competition will come primarily from the total of Native cultural centers and tribal tour operations in the region. Although private tour companies include reservation stops on their tours, the product of most is not as authentic. For comparative purposes, this document assesses the fees of tribally owned tours in the region, the main sources of competition. Visitors looking for an authentic experience are the target market.

The closest and most comparable site is the Lone Pine Tribe, since a tour is offered with a full range of visitor amenities. Tour fees are $12 for adults, $10 for senior citizens, $7 for children and youth, and $10 for still cameras. Group rates are available.

Several non-Native tours are promoted in the region. Deer Canyon Tours in Holbrook, Arizona offers a one-and-a-half hour sightseeing tour of Deer Canyon at $27 for adults, children 7 to 12 years of age at $16, and children under 6 are free. Totem Tours in Red Valley, Utah offers jeep tours. Charges are $20 per adult (13 years and over) for an hour and a half, with children at half price; two-and-a-half hour tours are $25 per adult, with children under 13 at half price. Garcia's Tours in Red Valley, Utah charges $375 for two nights of lodging, half-day tour for two persons, and a western style cookout for two persons.

Also, Indian Country Tours offers eight- and ten-day tours, with an average rate of $1,650 to $1,950 per person. Desert Tours offers three- to seven-hour tours priced from $75 to $95. A rate and itinerary sheet follows.

In relation to these competing tours, Native Tours will offer a high value per fee, experiential visit. Keeping fees reasonable and increasing referrals to community entrepreneurs are anticipated outcomes of the business.

Organizational Structure: A description of the organizational structure should address the chain of command or supervision and the number of personnel under each position type. A graphic representation or chart is usually preferred, along with an explanatory overview. Prior experience of the team in working together is useful information. At the community or regional level, an economic development corporation may be sponsoring or managing a business oriented toward community good. In the case of a tribal enterprise, the structural relationship to a tribal council or to an enterprise board may determine success. The following example illustrates such a structure.

Brief Example 9.9   ORGANIZATIONAL STRUCTURE

To create an efficient business management structure, the Desert Mountain Tribal Business Development Corporation was established in 2005. The function of the corporation is to create a structure with business expertise, separate from political decision making. The corporation supervises the business manager, who is responsible for monitoring daily activities of businesses. Tribal government retains ultimate control of the business operation by forming policy and approving the Board of Directors. A balance of business skills is represented on the enterprise board (e.g., cultural knowledge, banking, accounting, business management). The enterprise will prepare monthly financial reports for the Desert Mountain Tribal Business Development Corporation. Then, the Development Corporation reports back to the Tribal Council on a quarterly basis to keep members adequately informed for policy level decision making.

A list of the first seven Desert Mountain Tribal Business Development Corporation's Directors is included in Appendix A. The organizational chart on the following page shows a parallel structure between tribal government and the Enterprise Corporation.

Key Personnel: The hiring of experienced management personnel supports business success. Customer service is a necessary area of experience for tourism. An overview of the expertise and accomplishment of the principals on the management team should be highlighted in this section. The team must reflect the range of skills necessary to manage a particular business. Specific job descriptions and résumés are useful to include in this section or in the appendices.

Brief Example 9.10   PERSONNEL

One strength of this enterprise start-up is the highly qualified team available to manage the business. A tribal employee with experience managing tourism and tours in particular is available for the Tour Manager position. Additionally, the tribe has a well-established relationship with highly experienced consultants. The qualifications of managerial-level staff are described below, with résumés given in Appendix B.

John Gomez is available to fill the Tour Coordinator position. The Tour Coordinator is experienced in tour scheduling and guide training, as well as in all aspects of office management and administrative support. Familiarity with tribal tourism issues and experience interacting with visitors are significant qualifications also. Mr. Gomez is uniquely qualified for the position as a tribal member, a graduate of a Hospitality degree program, and experienced as the prior coordinator of Eco-tours, Inc. This unique combination of business management skills and familiarity with tribal culture are excellent for the position of daily scheduling, training, and managing tour operators for the Native Tours Enterprise.

Financial Analysis and Pro-Forma Operating Statements: Experience in business is essential for completing solid financial estimates. A business developer or entrepreneur presents the most informed estimate of enterprise operations. The short-term operational costs and profits for cash flow are examined. A financial analysis is an operating plan for management, or a blueprint for success of the business. Estimating inventories, capital expenditures (equipment, buildings, etc.), and debt incurred is necessary for accurate projections. Sources of capital are outlined to present the financial capability and viability of the business.

Using a format that will be easy for the enterprise owner or employees to follow later is critical to creating an effective management tool with the business plan. The objective of a pro-forma income and expense statement is the monthly planning of cash flow. As a guide in forecasting the timing of earnings and anticipated cash flow needs, the pro-forma is a tool for managing the business after the planning stage.

Brief Example 9.11   PRO-FORMA OPERATING STATEMENT

Pro-forma operating statements on the following pages detail projected income and expenses for the three-year start-up period of the Native Tours Enterprise. Management costs will be kept to a minimum by cost-sharing staffing with the Desert Mountain Tribal Museum. Additional business expertise is secured through management oversight by the Desert Mountain Tribe's Business Development Corporation.

Costs are calculated for a Tour Manager, an Administrative Assistant to book tours, and a three-person tour guide crew. Employee benefits are calculated at a standard rate for the Tribe.

To summarize the three-year projections, an initial injection of funds through grants and tribal resources is needed primarily for promotion and start-up costs. Given the initial expense of staffing, promotion and training of tour guides, the business shows a favorable ending balance at the end of years two and three. The true break-even point, once grant funds are considered, occurs in year three.

A total of five full-time jobs will be created for tribal members, in addition to secondary employment for 40 entrepreneurs, through referrals. This employment generation result is meaningful to the community, due to an isolated location and lack of nearby employment other than the arts. Community and cultural benefits of the enterprise are not quantifiable, yet are crucial to reducing cultural loss and the loss of sales. Launching this enterprise will restore significant cultural benefits, such as access to spaces to teach the arts and marketing venues for the cultural arts. These cultural benefits are equally important as profit to the Tribe.

The following example pro-forma statement for a tour enterprise illustrates the first year of three-year calculations. A break-even point occurs in the third year and designates the percentage of profit to be reinvested in the business, as well as the percentage allocated to supporting a cultural center, at the end of the third year.

Reinvestment Plan: A clear statement of the percentage of profits to be reinvested in maintenance and expansion of the business—as well as the percentage available for investment into community programs—is a main part of the community-oriented business plan. Examples of community reinvestments are training, referrals to other businesses, and forming a Chamber of Commerce to foster all businesses in a tourism network. These are examples of using business profits to further community goals. A lead business might pay more than an equal share to launch a collaborative marketing effort, realizing the importance of promoting a vacation itinerary to create a tourism draw.

Reinvestment into the business includes such line items as: training, additional facility space, advice of a consultant, time and travel to attend conferences, vacation time, networking activities, or expanded

Chart 9.1 NATIVE TOURS FIRST YEAR OPERATING PRO-FORMA

	Jan	Feb	Mar	Apr	May	Jun
BEGINNING BALANCE	0	37512	19024	3036	59047	39558
REVENUE						
Sales	0	0	8000	10000	12000	20000
Grants	75000	5000	0	75000	0	0
Photography Permits	0	0	2000	2000	2500	4450
Advertising Donations	0	5000	5000	0	1000	1000
Total Revenue	75000	10000	15000	87000	15500	25450
COST OF OPERATING	37488	28488	30988	30989	34989	32989
ENDING BALANCE	37512	19024	3036	59047	39558	32019
EXPENSES						
Personnel						
Tour Manager	2800	2800	2800	2800	2800	2800
Tour Guides	0	0	4500	4500	4500	4500
Administrative Assistant	2080	2080	2080	2080	2080	2080
Employee Benefits	1750	1750	1750	1750	1750	1750
Travel (staff)	480	480	480	480	480	480
Transportation	0	0	5000	5000	6000	7000
Marketing	2500	2500	2500	2500	2500	2500
Point-of-Sale Software	6000	0	0	0	0	0
Employee Training	0	0	0	0	0	0
Insurance	0	0	3000	3000	3000	3000
Postage & Shipping	150	150	150	150	150	150
Development/Contract	5000	0	0	0	3000	0
Rental Space	500	500	500	500	500	500
Utilities	100	100	100	100	100	100
Telephone	350	350	350	350	350	350
Surveillance System	3000	0	0	0	0	0
Visitor Education	0	0	0	0	0	0
Office Equip/Furniture	3000	10000	0	0	0	0
Office Supplies	350	350	350	350	350	350
Registration	2000	0	0	0	0	0
Website	7428	7428	7428	7429	7429	7429
COST OF OPERATING	37488	28488	30988	30989	34989	32989

Jul	Aug	Sept	Oct	Nov	Dec	Totals
32019	89480	90370	56310	61250	50690	39130
25000	26000	11000	10000	9000	8000	139000
65000	0	0	16500	0	0	236500
4450	4450	2500	2000	2000	1000	27350
1000	1000	1000	0	0	0	15000
95450	31450	14500	28500	11000	9000	417850
37989	30560	48560	23560	21560	20560	378720
89480	90370	56310	61250	50690	39130	39130
2800	2800	2800	2800	2800	2800	33600
4500	4500	4500	4500	4500	4500	45000
2080	2080	2080	2080	2080	2080	24960
1750	1750	1750	1750	1750	1750	21000
480	480	480	480	480	480	5760
7000	7000	5000	5000	3000	2000	52000
2500	2500	2500	2500	2500	2500	30000
0	0	0	0	0	0	6000
0	0	0	0	0	0	0
3000	3000	3000	3000	3000	3000	30000
150	150	150	150	150	150	1800
0	0	0	0	0	0	8000
500	500	500	500	500	500	6000
100	100	100	100	100	100	1200
350	350	350	350	350	350	4200
0	0	0	0	0	0	3000
5000	5000	25000	0	0	0	35000
0	0	0	0	0	0	13000
350	350	350	350	350	350	4200
0	0	0	0	0	0	2000
7429	0	0	0	0	0	52000
37989	30560	48560	23560	21560	20560	378720

marketing. Include these additions in the pro-forma line items for the next year, if the pro-forma determines that profits will accommodate the expenditures.

A clear reinvestment plan prevents two common errors in business development: 1) exhausting the profits, leaving too little working capital for the business to succeed, and 2) leaving the distribution of profits to the discretion of one person, when the business is owned by the community. Gaining community opinion during business planning prevents later conflict over reinvestment policy.

Brief Example 9.12   REINVESTMENT PLAN

The Native Tours community-based business will reserve 40% of annual profits after year 3 to fund arts training at the Desert Mountain Tribal Museum, with 60% of annual profits retained to maintain business operations.

Appendices: Include only the essential. Appendices are not "filler" and are easily detected when not relevant to the potential success of the business. Supporting documents should be included in the appendices. As in any plan or report, important charts or pieces of information should be placed in the text. Résumés are critical supporting documents in a business plan, since the experience of managers is a defining element in business success and should represent the persons mentioned under the "key personnel" section.

Other supporting documents may include detail on capital requirements, documents supporting the financing of the enterprise, such as matching funds secured thus far, or additional detail on management expertise. Letters of commitment for financing and equipment or volunteer assistance are also extremely useful. For example, a local Small Business Development Center or SCORE (retired business expertise) may commit an amount of time for business coaching. All of these supporting documents should be clearly labeled, paginated, and mentioned in the text.

STARTING A TOUR ENTERPRISE

This section describes an example of how to start a tourism-related business, the guided tour enterprise. Integrating cultural content into a tour concept—while maintaining awareness of cultural boundaries—

enhances cultural tours, heritage tours, ecotours, and outdoor adventure tours. Visitors seeking a learning experience enjoy information about cultural viewpoints—to include the arts, history, foods, animals, and ecosystems. How this information and local stories are tied together forms the unique cultural interpretation.

Beyond developing and delivering educational or cultural programs, the effective tour guide adapts to different learning styles and participant needs, as well as develops expertise in cross-cultural communication. Other useful skills include operating presentation equipment, and knowing local concerns regarding the protection of resources. Being knowledgeable about natural and cultural heritage sites is also useful, along with experience working with groups.

The following steps are recommended for a culturally relevant approach:

1) **Focus the tour concept.** Decide on a general area, then a specific theme. For example, a cultural arts tour might focus on pottery-making or weaving. If several tour ideas emerge, consider phasing-in additional tours after experience is gained.

2) **Choose a company name and a tour name.** Find a name generating attention, yet clear in relation to the business theme. The easier the name is to remember, the greater the effectiveness of referrals for attracting customs. Although names in a traditional language may seem appealing to the host community, they are likely to be difficult to remember for customers.

3) **Be clear about messages to convey.** Cultural travelers are fascinated with learning. Short, culturally specific messages focus the learning experience.

4) **Assess local resources.** Identify and include people with cultural knowledge (e.g., storytellers) and entrepreneurs (e.g., artists, food products). Maintain close liaison with the community to improve overall financial benefits and job creation (e.g., referrals to other community entrepreneurs).

5) **Ensure an accurate and consistent interpretation.** Interpretation provides uniqueness to the experience. Following an outline for the narrative, presented informally (not memorized), focuses the information while interacting in a natural

way. Information on history is used to present multiple viewpoints. Avoid anger in presentations.

6) **Be clear on cultural boundaries.** A visitor etiquette or protocol welcomes and guides the visitor to culturally sensitive interaction and creates a comfort zone.

7) **Decide on an experience outcome.** Content and direct interactions with community members determine the learning experience. Examples include gaining an understanding of authentic materials, handmade art-making technique, or historical context of the art for a cultural arts tour—or gaining a sense of being connected in nature for an ecotour.

8) **Link to local events and sites.** Offering tours at the same time, or on days adjacent to festivals and events in the region encourages visitors to extend length-of-stay and include a tour, particularly when local interpretation is provided.

9) **Develop a pricing system.** Carefully research the price of other tours in the region, comparing tour length and whether transportation is provided. Explore possible linkages for lodging and food service, and if extremely reliable, consider collaboration for a package price.

10) **Complete a business plan for the specific enterprise.** Project income and expenses for three years, on a month-by-month basis. If utilizing small business assistance, make certain that the projections are clear, for use later as a business management tool.

11) **Participate in available training.** Skills in organizing, leading, and marketing tours are relevant for launching the enterprise, as well as financial management and understanding taxes. Seek out culturally-based approaches when ever possible.

12) **Finance/insurance.** Secure finances needed for start-up, if needed. Locate small grants and micro-loans. Insurance coverage for tour operations is essential.

13) **Market the enterprise.** Communicate clearly the learning experience, value for the price, the pricing system, authenticity, the means of booking, and the schedule. Attend tourism trade shows. Consider no-cost and low-cost marketing, becoming part of a referral network for inclusion in visitor guides, use of the internet and social media—as well as possible collaborations for cost-sharing of marketing expenses. Highlight authenticity, the learning experience, and uniqueness of the business.

14) **Manage well.** Customer service requires patience, attentiveness to participant needs, constant follow-up, and a commitment to long working hours during the tourism season.

15) **Evaluate and redirect.** Secure feedback from customers and from the tourism industry network to improve services. Compare actual income projections and expenses with business plan projections, to assess progress and redirect as needed. Seasonal fluctuations in income and expenses are particularly relevant for adapting schedules.

FROM PLAN TO ACTION

Success factors for small business emphasize: quality of the market analysis to base the projections, adequacy of start-up capital, reaching the potential market adequately, management skills, comparing actual monthly income to income projections, and redirecting the business as needed. Primary reasons for business failure include—not completing a business plan, misjudging the market, not marketing, insufficient start-up capital (particularly to survive the off-season), lack of management and customer service skills, not enough linking with other businesses for referrals, and not paying attention to actual income and expenses—or redirecting as necessary.

With business planning complete, obtaining financing or funding is usually the next step in business development. Leveraging is a basic step for generating larger amounts of capital needed to support a business. An example of leveraging for a non-profit organization or tribal business is securing a small foundation grant, a federal grant, or a local economic development corporation commitment for funding—to offer as a match for a larger loan or grant. The following sources of capital are valuable sources: 1) grants, 2) loans, 3) commitments from reinvestment of other community business earnings, 4) a local tax share, and 5) community or tribal contributions.

If the business is being managed by a non-profit organization, training in understanding the pro-formas and monthly budget reports is necessary for monitoring business profit. "Non-profit" doesn't equate to business losses, or the business will no longer be in existence. The goal of a non-profit organization is to generate income to support services, or to provide jobs. In order to reach those goals, the business needs to generate a profit.

Securing adequate capital, marketing ahead of the tourism season, launching the business in the opportune tourism season, and staying connected to an effective tourism network, are factors underlying success beyond the business planning. The well-designed business plan is an excellent tool for managing the business, if the tourism season and characteristics of potential customers are understood and effective marketing is in place.

Using the monthly projections to compare actual sales enables the savvy entrepreneur to fine-tune the business and redirect when necessary. For example, if additional marketing is necessary to reach broader markets, other expenses may need to be reduced, or more working capital secured. Or, low-cost and no-cost marketing strategies may be emphasized.

Another area of evaluation is tracking business progress according to the definition of success projected in the business plan. Pro-formas calculating expenses and income on a monthly basis are useful for monitoring cash flow and tracking business income as well as expenses month-to-month. Using the business plan monthly as a management tool is necessary for long-range success. When progress is tracked monthly, the business can be redirected before income targets fall behind.

In the larger community context, businesses are considered in relation to an overall economic development plan, outlining reinvestment strategies that leverage matching funds to generate a larger pool of capital. Reinvestment by the community increases the multiplier effect for tourism, as well as related businesses. Culturally-based customer service—and working with small-scale entrepreneurial activity to create multiple earned livelihood opportunities—are factors for widespread community success in cultural tourism.

COMMUNITY-BASED SOLUTION
Sky City Tours, Acoma Pueblo (USA)

The Sky City Cultural Center at Acoma Pueblo offers a full range of culturally-based activities to visitors, while managing tourism in a way that protects the ancient Pueblo village. Located atop a 367 foot sandstone bluff, Acoma Pueblo is one of the oldest continuously inhabited dwellings in North America—since 1150 AD.

The Haak'u Museum serves as an education and research institute focusing on the preservation of Acoma history, with exhibits interpreting history and present-day lifeways for the public. Activities for revitalizing art forms at risk of being lost and the retention of traditional language are also a focus of the museum. Food service at the Y'aak'a Café focuses on traditional foods and the Gaits'i Gift Shop features handmade Pueblo arts, such as pottery and jewelry, as well as books on Indigenous culture.

Access to the ancient village is by tour only, with bus transportation and village interpretation provided by step-on-guides. Managing access protects the road to the mesa and reduces impacts to the ancient dwellings still used for traditional activities.

Success factors include: a strong management structure, financial monitoring, effective marketing, unifying tribal offerings, linking past and present, visitor education fostering appreciation of the cultural arts, an informative website, annual events keeping visitor interest to return, posting a clear schedule of tours, and visitor etiquette available in six languages. (www.acomaskycity.org)

FURTHER READING

Adams, Barbara Berst. *The New Agritourism: Hosting Community and Tourists on Your Farm,* Auburn, CA: New World Publishing, 2008.

    This practical guide explores foundational topics—developing the business plan, and promtotion, rules, regulations, and liability as well as options for educational tours, B&Bs, food service, dairies, and seasonal agritourism events are featured.

Hall, Derek, Irene Kirkpatrick, and Morag Mitchell. *Rural Tourism and Sustainable Business.* Tonawanda, NY: 2005.

    Strategic considerations include policy, effective marketing, cooperative marketing structures, regional cooperation, globalization, and quality in sustainable business. Global examples illustrate issues and solutions.

Mitchell, G.E., *How to Start a Tour Guiding Business.* Charleston, SC: Gem Group Ltd., 2005.

    A practical, step-by-step process is presented for starting a tour guide business, conducting market research, pricing and marketing, as well as managing tours.

Patterson, Carol. *The Business of Ecotourism: The Complete Guide for Nature and Culture-based Tourism Operators.* Victoria, BC: Trafford Publishing, 2007.

    Business planning steps addressed include: defining the product, marketing, building partnerships, financial management, customer service, managing business risk, and the ecotourism difference, as well as industry standards and associations.

Whelan, Tensie, ed. *Nature Tourism: Managing for the Environment.* Washington, DC: Island Press, 1991.

    Linking natural resource conservation with local economic development—the topics of planning, economic evaluation, local participation, and marketing outline specific steps for maximizing benefits and minimizing potential damage.

10
INCREASING SUSTAINABILITY

*Sustainability only occurs from a cyclical worldview,
rather than a linear perspective, through constant
evaluation and redirection.*

Sustainability, in essence, is about interdependence. Balance in cultural, economic, and ecological relationships is central for maintaining harmony. And hospitality—sharing food, appropriate information, and cultural arts—coming from a genuine respect for tradition, indicates the wise use of resources.

Up to this point in the sustainable development process, planning has involved the community, visitors or potential visitors, and local government, to create a direction and a general guideline for tourism. After the planning, a culturally and socially harmonious tourism approach involves continually increasing internal capacity, marketing, developing local businesses, and evaluating success.

Methodologies developed from within a cultural framework and grounded in nature are likely to be sustainable in the longer time frame. This chapter gives parameters for assessing sustainability from a cultural viewpoint, with sustainability seen as more than a matter of doing no harm, but rather as restorative action.

> **Framework for Integrating Culture**
>
> - See ways in which culture affects actions on both the local economy and ecosystem stewardship.
> - Design criteria to periodically evaluate impacts on traditions and cultural privacy to practice traditions.
> - Ensure a cyclical feedback loop with the community to assess community satisfaction and needs for redirection.
> - Measure local long-term job creation based on culturally supportive industries.
> - Periodically assess impacts on natural resource depletion.
> - Communicate protection and privacy needs to visitors.
> - Create a local tourism program to guide visitors, implement policy, and lessen environmental impacts.
> - Create a donation structure for visitors to contribute.

SUSTAINABILITY FACTORS

As a concept related to tourism, sustainability is frequently used in reference to reduced environmental impacts. Although this view of sustainability is meaningful to rural and traditional communities, cultural criteria are also intertwined and integral.

Guiding principles for sustainability reflecting the "Three Es"—ecology, economy and equity—outlined by Andres Edwards[1] are valuable for integrating cultural and social concerns.

1) **Stewardship**—Maintain integrity and biodiversity.

2) **Respect for limits**—Live within nature's means.

3) **Interdependence**—Respect ecological relationships as well as economic and cultural ties at the local, regional, and international levels.

4) **Economic restructuring**—Expand employment opportunities while safeguarding ecosystems.

5) **Fair distribution**—Integrate social justice and equity in areas such as employment, education, and healthcare.

6) **Intergenerational perspective**—Use a long-term rather than a short-term view to guide the critical choices facing society.

7) **Nature as a model and teacher**—Acknowledge the 3.5 billion years of evolution of living systems and the rights of all species.

Cultural values regarding people as being a part of nature underlie actions and care of the environment, whether on the part of visitors or the host community. Sense of place, with a cultural basis, connects communities in nature.

> *Contemporary discussions of sustainability focus on ecosystems and often overlook the importance of culture as a basis for all actions.*

For example, the need for access by Native Americans to wilderness areas for tending wild plants and harvesting plants or cultural art-making materials comes from a view of being in, rather than with or connected to, nature. In many instances, protection of privacy for activities such as the gathering of medicinal plants or pottery clays is seen as a necessity to protect traditional practice.

Why the secrecy? Experience has taught these communities that most other cultures do not understand the concept of "take only what you need" for personal use. These resources become depleted when accessible to the public. Also, resources are to be used with respect and ceremony, and not merely as objects. Respect to plants, animals, rivers, clay, and even stones is extended in an internal, all-encompassing and related way.

In Chart 10.1 indicators of sustainable tourism developed by the World Tourism Organization [2] are expanded in relation to the cultural factors emphasized in this text.

Following local and cultural traditions for land stewardship is one aspect of maintaining eco-cultural sustainability through the long-term. As stewards of their ecosystems, traditional and Indigenous cultures hold ecological knowledge and caring for their environments. Additionally, their methods hold promise for educating other cultures.

Chart 10.1 WTO INDICATORS OF SUSTAINABLE TOURISM

WTO Indicator	WTO Specific Measures	Additional Cultural Factors
1. Site protection	Category of site protection	Sacredness of site, boundaries needed for cultural privacy
2. Stress	Tourist numbers visiting site	Interference with cultural activities, culturally perceived crowding
3. Use intensity	Intensity of use in peak period	Needs for community closing or limiting visitation for cultural practice
4. Social impact	Ratio of tourists to locals	Equity in benefits, continuance of traditional earned livelihood
5. Development control	Existence of an environmental review procedure	Equity in benefits, continuance of traditional earned livelihood
6. Waste management	Percentage of sewage from site receiving treatment	Costs to community absorbed by those who profit
7. Planning process	Existence of an organized regional plan	Traditional planning processes considered, intergenerational interaction
8. Critical ecosystems	Number of rare/endangered species	Access to plants and animals protected for traditional subsistence and sacred practice
9. Consumer satisfaction	Level of satisfaction by visitors (questionnaire-based)	Verbal interaction with visitors to elicit suggestions/use of traditional hospitality methods
10. Local satisfaction	Level of satisfaction by locals (questionnaire-based)	Community talking circles to assess satisfaction and gather suggestions for improvement/consensus building
11. Tourism contribution to local economy	Proportion of total economic activity generated by tourism only	Equitable return for participation in tourism/retention of traditional economy/increase in retention of cultural practice

Many cultures have internal methods for mediating decisions regarding sustainability. When planners and technical assistance providers appreciate and foster these internal discussions, then offer information on potential consequences of alternatives—forward movement is generated from within a community. In the Indigenous worldview, value judgments inherent in the concept "primitive economy" come from inaccurate opinion about complexity in these cultures and are considered offensive. Listening carefully to cultural interpretations of progress is useful for guiding planning in relation to form, scale, and timing.

The power of actions that have worked well over time and come from wisdom passed down for several generations, sits at the core of sustainability. In Indigenous cultures these are called the "Original Instructions."[3] How to live on Earth in a way that lasts over time, conserving resources, is central to these teachings.

Small, traditional communities perceive the destruction of the past fifty years in terms of environmental impacts, cultural loss, and the need for immediate action. Protecting community access to sacred areas is essential. The very practice of culture, spirituality, and seasonal rituals depends upon access to these sacred sites. If a lifeway embedded with the wisdom of connectedness and conservation is to continue, these issues must be addressed. Fortunately, the potential match of conscious travelers seeking to learn about diverse ways of relating to ecosystems, agriculture, land stewardship, family cooperation, and community support networks, is growing.

Moving the community along in all areas helps prevent uneven development leading to gaps in services. These gaps in turn cause impacts on community, environment, and guests. Keeping the sustainable development factors of form, scale, and timing at the forefront paces protection, as well as new innovations.

The role of culture in sustainability of small-scale tourism is often not seen, yet is pivotal. Not putting people into the sustainability equation is sometimes an oversight in discussions focused on ecological inputs and outputs. When analyses overlook the importance of factors motivating behavior, insight on sustainable solutions may be lost. Culture guides actions, whether related to following traditional land stewardship practices or the formation of tourism policy—and even the decisions of whether to participate in tourism or not to participate. The first question is not "How many visitors before environmental impacts are seen?" but rather "Does an intrusion affect both cultural practice and ecological integrity?"

When cultural appropriateness and connections underlie motivation in a community, then tourism may become a stimulus for teaching and retaining culture through recognition of cultural arts and practices. Including the entire community by providing entrepreneurial opportunities, training, and access to resources sustains a community-supportive effort.

Chart 10.2 WAYS OF INCREASING SUSTAINABILITY

ENVIRONMENTAL/ECOSYSTEM:
- Target a specific market, culturally oriented (cultural tourists, heritage tourists) and environmentally oriented (geotourists, ecotourists, recreational tourists)
- Less people = fewer potential impacts
- Use visitor education to reduce impacts
- Manage the flow of visitors and carry out periodic assessment of environmental impacts
- Keep visitors away from environmentally sensitive areas

CULTURAL:
- Teach cultural history and arts intergenerationally
- Integrate traditional language use
- Encourage learning of the arts by youth
- Increase family activities
- Share successes and challenges with other communities

ECONOMIC:
- Integrate business skills into art classes
- Develop locally owned small businesses
- Encourage a broad range of services
- Create the maximum number of jobs
- Direct employment
- Indirect employment

- Increase marketing linkages to a respectful customer base
- Assist entrepreneurs with marketing
- Encourage multiple income streams

EVALUATING IMPACTS AND REDIRECTING AS NECESSARY:
- Conduct community surveys
- Update visitor surveys to determine trends
- Hold public meetings
- Increase cultural retention
- Implement environmental indicators
- Track job creation
- Increase the number of people trained
- Reduce unemployment rates through locally owned businesses

THE MANAGED TOURISM PROGRAM

Continuity of an idea by managing tourism takes people, time, and some resources. Benefits to the managed tourism approach include increased community gains and minimized cultural, economic, and ecological negative impacts. Tourism produces optimal benefits when a management structure coordinates or oversees all aspects of tourism—businesses, services, transportation, and activities.

Managing tourism is a process that considers the suitable carrying capacity. Several types of carrying capacity, as defined by John Swarbrooke,[4] affect cultural, economic, and ecological impacts:

- **Physical capacity,** or the number of tourists a place can physically accommodate;
- **Environmental or ecological capacity**, or the number of tourists that can be accommodated before damage is caused to the ecosystem;
- **Economic capacity,** or the number of tourists that can be welcomed before the local community starts to suffer economic problems, such as inflated land prices;
- **Social capacity,** or the number of people a place can welcome, beyond which social disruption or irrevocable cultural damage will occur;

- **Perceptual capacity,** or the number of people a place can welcome before the quality of the tourist experience begins to be adversely affected; and
- **Infrastructure capacity,** or the number of tourists that can be accommodated by local infrastructure.

One frequent mistake made in rural tourism development is lack of cohesion to the tourism network. Chambers of Commerce, Convention and Visitor Bureaus, and governments commonly create these networks in cities when tax revenues are available. Rural and tribal communities may not readily perceive the benefits of management and promotion or have the resources. In these communities, promotion frequently focuses on one or just a few larger businesses, not realizing that promotion inclusive of both small and larger-scale businesses creates a more cohesive vacation concept.

As tourism profits begin to be seen, a small share set aside to manage and promote tourism increases momentum. Some small villages, where monitoring entry is possible, designate a charge or a permit for entering into the community and fund tourism management with this income.

Another strategy is to reinvest a percentage of tax revenues for visitor surveys, assessing visitor satisfaction, promotion, visitor education, and future planning. This investment is a worthy outlay not only to grow the tourism market, but also to prevent negative impacts and increase community satisfaction with tourism.

Organizing for Increased Sustainability

The concept of linking smaller-scale enterprises and activities together into a larger, connected tourism itinerary relates well to sustainability. In review, organizing for tourism is a critical activity for:

- Assessing all services and activities potentially available to the visiting party;
- Creating a vacation concept;
- Protecting the regional environment;
- Designing itineraries, therefore extending length of stay;
- Projecting infrastructure needs, such as road improvements, water, solid waste (garbage) and sewage;

- Assuring the availability of food service, lodging, fuel, and adequate restrooms;
- Creating collaborative maps to guide visitors through a vacation;
- Collaborating for marketing to purchase advertising in publications with broader distribution; and
- Creating a welcoming atmosphere.

Regional organizing is useful for bringing a cohesive effort to tourism planning, management, impact assessment, and redirection. Otherwise, individual businesses tend to move forward alone, without forming an effective tourism network. The starting point is collaboration and defining a tourism strategy. Options include a tourism committee, tourism board, tourism association, or a Chamber of Commerce (limited to businesses and non-profits).

A gap in tourism services commonly occurs between the functions of planning and promotion. What occurs in between—business development, training in business management skills, assessment of success, and redirection—are the factors that sometimes fall between the cracks in a smaller community. Organizing to provide these services creates a support structure for businesses and entrepreneurs to thrive.

Whether bringing one community or several small communities together in a region, a managed vacation concept provides the comfortable experience for both community and visitor. Because tourism depends upon linkages, or creating enough services and activities to constitute a stop on the traveler's route, a coordinated network is essential.

Small communities vary in their structure. In some, such as Native American tribes, government tends to own most of the businesses. Within this structure, coordination through a community tourism program is then more feasible than in communities where business ownership is primarily through the individual. For other communities, informal collaborations or Chambers of Commerce offer the capacity to provide promotion and training. One of the most effective ways of coordinating tourism is through a staffed position in a local government.

Chart 10.3 presents a sustainable tourism management assessment.

Chart 10.3 SUSTAINABLE TOURISM MANAGEMENT ASSESSMENT

Development	Low				High
Tourism plan completed Clear vision/goals/assessment resources	1	2	3	4	5
Visible point/intake center for entering the community	1	2	3	4	5
Community welcome visible	1	2	3	4	5
Provide information/cultural history	1	2	3	4	5
Signage clear	1	2	3	4	5
Environmental impacts assessed	1	2	3	4	5
Consistent with land use plan	1	2	3	4	5
Transportation plan in place	1	2	3	4	5
Micro-loans available	1	2	3	4	5
Product development assistance	1	2	3	4	5
Assistance with tourism business plans	1	2	3	4	5
Management	**Low**				**High**
Staff time allocated for managing tourism	1	2	3	4	5
Visitor etiquette readily available	1	2	3	4	5
Visitor's survey conducted (know interests)	1	2	3	4	5
Method for counting visitors	1	2	3	4	5
Restrooms adequate and clean	1	2	3	4	5
Food service interesting and efficient	1	2	3	4	5
Lodging interesting and reliable	1	2	3	4	5
Community members trained to give directions	1	2	3	4	5
Training available for businesses	1	2	3	4	5

Training available for entrepreneurs	1	2	3	4	5
Tours available	1	2	3	4	5
Community satisfaction assessed annually	1	2	3	4	5
Visitor satisfaction assessed annually	1	2	3	4	5
Adequate water & sewage	1	2	3	4	5
Regular trash collection	1	2	3	4	5
Ecosystem restoration	1	2	3	4	5
Improvements made annually/redirect	1	2	3	4	5
Promotion	**Low**				**High**
Maps available of community and businesses	1	2	3	4	5
Vacation itineraries developed, detailing local offerings	1	2	3	4	5
All scales of business - small, entrepreneurial, larger included	1	2	3	4	5
Partnering with other communities for an effective referral network	1	2	3	4	5
Linkages established to surrounding communities	1	2	3	4	5

As an approximate guideline, scores below a 2.5 average indicate a tourism effort in need of redirection, between 2.5 and 3.5 need improvement and re-examination of sustainable strategy; from 3.6 to 4.5 are on the sustainable path and need to keep improving; and above 4.5 are excellent in sustainable implementation. By assessing, evaluating, and redirecting, negative impacts are likely to be reduced and positive benefits increased.

IMPROVING CUSTOMER SERVICE

Good customer service reduces impacts by welcoming and caring for people through guidance. Community discussion opens the possibility for integrating unique cultural practices into a customer service training tailored to the community. While a unique experience is sought by the cultural tourist, comfort on both sides is the most satisfying interchange.

The most common mistake made in customer service is to assume that all visitors are from the same culture and have the same preferences. Is the visitor satisfied and comfortable while in the community? This question is important to customer service and not easy to answer by formula. The outcome of customer service depends not only on basic principles of service, but also upon the expectations of visitors and the comfort level of the host community. Tailoring a customer service training to local culture is the most effective route.

Differences in visitor preferences usually stem from: regions or country of origin, languages spoken, interests, income levels, age grouping, or ethnic group. Understanding cross-cultural differences and providing an interpreter when necessary is useful for the host community of every culture. When different cultures are in the visitor/host setting, the situation becomes more complex. "This is just the way we do things here," is the common reaction. Let the visitor adjust.

Yes, visitors must adjust and frequently enjoy the sense of adventure in adjusting. And, there is also a delicate balance point between adjustment and inconvenience or fatigue at adapting to a new culture. A sense of meeting part-way creates a friendly business interaction, rather than leading customers to the "take-it-or-leave-it" option.

> *The best customer service for cultural tourism feels genuine to the community, yet comfortable enough to the visitor for a restful vacation.*

The appropriate cultural fit also determines the form of customer service, when values underlie interactions with visitors. While customer service training is available to communities through Chambers of Commerce and small business development centers, as well as universities and colleges—the critical question to ask is whether these sources use a standard, profit-oriented business model. Customer service based on the principal of intense monetary profit may not have a good cultural fit. An alternative model encouraging family and community support, as well as value-based and sustainable development—with less emphasis on monetary accumulation—may have a better cultural fit. Here are a few examples.

Situation 1: Cultural differences in the perception of time frequently leave visitors frustrated as they wait for food, if service at a local restaurant is slower than the average in an urban setting.

Solution: Give visitors an interesting activity. Examples are a placemat printed with cultural history, a coloring sheet for children, a visitor guide, or a panel card placed on the condiment tray. Time will pass quickly for the visitor and the local business won't feel rushed by the different time perceptions.

Situation 2: Failure to meet expectations in the level of basic service provided to visitors is likely to cause a decrease in the desire to return—due to a perception of lack of attentiveness. For example, in some regions business owners will deny visitors access to restrooms in their stores. This policy is particularly difficult for families with small children and retirees. Once the visitor has the need, the timing is not opportune to say no. Visitors then leave.

Solution: If visitors are able to find information on basic services, such as restrooms, food service, lodging or campgrounds, trash receptacles, pay phones (in case cell reception doesn't work), ATMs, and locator maps to businesses as they enter the community—sales will be abundant and visitors will be satisfied.

Situation 3: Friendly behavior is another aspect of the visitor/host interaction where interpretation varies widely across cultures. In some regions, residents are reluctant to speak very much to "newcomers," while in other regions, the initial reaction is warmth.

Solution: Urge employees to respond with a degree of friendliness, yet encourage them to protect their personal and cultural privacy. This can be rehearsed in a training format. Again, knowing where visitors come from helps form business policy and the training of employees. Educating employees about regional, national, and cultural differences, as well as providing ample information on where services are located, are two effective solutions to cross-cultural differences in perception.

FEEDBACK FROM THE COMMUNITY

Creating a feedback loop from community to local government and tourism management personnel is valuable for improvement of the tourism system. Although some tourism challenges may be difficult to resolve, feedback is necessary for moving ahead. Community patience is likely to increase when problems are recognized and solutions are sought.

PLANNING PROCESS:
Reducing Negative Impacts and Increasing Positive Gains

- *Are privacy and traffic impacts occurring in residential areas?*
- *Are there concerns about visitors entering environmentally fragile areas?*
- *Are there observations on occurring environmental impacts?*
- *Are areas where privacy is needed for cultural practice entered by visitors?*
- *Is traffic impacting community life and work?*
- *Are local community members succeeding with small businesses?*
- *Are additional training, marketing, or capital opportunities needed?*
- *Are small businesses linking together effectively?*
- *How could businesses form a more powerful referral network?*
- *Are there services to visitors in need of improvement?*
- *Are there other community needs not being met?*
- *What suggestions do community members have for improving tourism?*

Feedback generates information for community understanding of the tourism development process and fine-tuning. Review the original intentions for tourism—as defined in the planning process. A few formats for continuing community discussion to redirect tourism outcomes include the following:

- Talking circles and feedback sessions (with food served);
- Tourism committee meetings;
- Interviews and comments (certain community members understand the local environment better than others); and
- Discussions with businesses, visitor center, and museum personnel.

Community businesses are the "front line" personnel with the most visitor contact and give valuable community ideas for resolving negative impacts. In leading the feedback process, be certain to include community suggestions for improvement to each issue raised. This structure will prevent the meeting from turning into a "complaint session."

Chart 10.4 IMPROVING THE TOURISM PROCESS

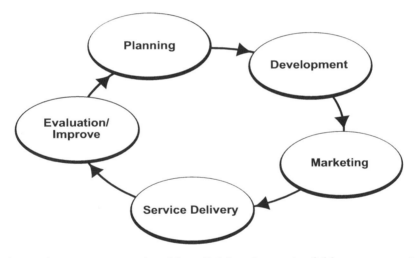

When a direction is considered beneficial and meaningful by a community, it will be continued.

EVALUATING VISITOR SATISFACTION

The premise is basic. Ask visitors what they want and they will indicate preferences. Why is this most effective way of obtaining the information needed for business improvement usually avoided? Fear of criticism (or seeing feedback as criticism) is a factor keeping communities from discovering whether the right match between services and visitor interest is occurring. Constant improvement of the business to meet customer satisfaction improves business success as well as sustainability. Yet, this is a frequently neglected step and the cause of both business failure and negative impacts.

Verbal customer feedback and evaluation using customer satisfaction cards or internet tools enables managers to fine-tune services and inventory. This continually refines the correct fit between the business and customer preferences. Keeping up with changing trends requires this fine-tuning process.

Given the opportunity for feedback, customers will indicate what they liked the most—or offer constructive suggestions. This enables the community to do more of what is working well, and improve what isn't working. Understanding the new services or food they would like strengthens improvement of a business, by meeting market needs.

Evaluation also directs management in ways to improve employee performance through additional training or replacement. Without customer feedback, managers are working with educated guesses, and may be overlooking potential market niches. Customer feedback or comment cards are basic for evaluating the quality of service, as well as matching the business concept to customer interests. Visitors tend to be experienced travelers, know what they want, are able to pinpoint weak spots, and give good constructive comments. The asking is well worth the effort. And the negative, "off the wall" comment is rare.

Formats for evaluation should cover topics including: level of service, quality of products, inventory, artist bios, and other information provided—as well as space for comments or desired items to purchase, service improvement, or food items. Rating scales are frequently used for evaluation cards. While rating scales are convenient for tabulating scores, open-ended questions are invaluable to include for assessing specific details that are "off" in service and items or service levels desired by visitors. The sample evaluation card below illustrates these effective card features:

- Keep the card brief—visitors are busy;
- Be friendly;
- Keep the language easy to understand; and
- Thank the visitor.

Making an evaluation card readily available to customers is a basic part of the process. Frequently staff and mangers are fearful of the impact comments will have on their jobs and either do not keep the cards out—nor do they encourage visitors to complete them. The card kept under the counter is useless. Look for opportunities in locations where visitors have time to spend filling out a card. The condiment rack on restaurant tables and in lodging rooms are two successful locations with a high return rate. An email follow-up to the customer is another way to elicit evaluation data. However, the return rate will be lower than the in-person effort. Offering a discount upon the return is another way of encouraging visitor feedback.

❖ ❖ ❖ ❖ ❖

Chart 10.5   SAMPLE EVALUATION CARD

VISITOR SATISFACTION SURVEY

("hello" in local language)

Please rank your satisfaction with this visit and give us your comments.
Your feedback assists us in our efforts to improve services.

	High	Med	Low
Were the activities interesting?	O	O	O
Is the signage clear for you to find your way?	O	O	O
Was the visitor etiquette presented to you?	O	O	O
Was the customer service friendly?	O	O	O
Overall, how would you rank the customer service?	O	O	O
Did you find the products you were looking for?	O	O	O
Quality of the food?	O	O	O
Type of food available?	O	O	O
Lodging quality?	O	O	O
Pricing on lodging?	O	O	O
Restrooms clean and easy to find?	O	O	O
Did you gain a satisfying learning experience?	O	O	O

Are there additional items besides what you found that you would like to purchase?

Did you gain a sense of our history and an appreciation of our culture?

What is your favorite part of the visit?

Any other suggestions?

Your business assists us to maintain a traditional lifestyle in our community and sustain our culture. Visit our website, www.community.com to find updates on our cultural retention efforts and the membership program at our museum.

Please return this card to the museum desk. Thank you (also in the local language) for your participation and come to visit us again!

Another effective means of evaluation is verbal interaction with the customer. The successful manager frequently monitors interactions with customers and asks for feedback. Friendly, interactive service is rare to find. Customers respond enthusiastically to friendliness and are more likely to return beyond the first visit when asked about their visit. If service was less than perfect—yet the effort in trying to improve is visible—then visitors will tend to try a second time.

Central to wise use of visitor feedback is not viewing comments as complaints. Rather, feedback guides improvement and sustainability. Emphasize this strategy to employees and in entrepreneurial training. When customer service leads to visitor frustration, invaluable feedback will be obtained—if the employee remains calm and asks reasons for the discontent. Cultural differences can be explained and a learning experience is perceived.

Tracking changes in customer preferences, assessing and fine-tuning, is a process that adapts to changing trends in customer interest. Employees should be trained to be flexible, allowing substitutions and documenting customer requests.

Awareness of *green tourism* preferences among travelers is increasing every year. The health-oriented and environmentally aware markets are looking for natural fabrics, filtered water, organic food, natural insect control, and ecosystem learning experiences.

Travelers today frequently have allergies, especially those who come from urban areas. Lodging must accommodate their needs, often with pet-free and smoke-free rooms, and air filters to remove allergens and chemicals. Overnight visitors with chemical sensitivities need to avoid pesticides, strong cleaning chemicals, and fragrances in their rooms. For the "green" customer, less of these "extras" is better—as well as sound practice for nature.

By following customer recommendations, the business will remain flexible and capable of adapting to a changing customer base. Awareness of how to bridge cultural differences comes from community-based expertise, more valuable than the advice of experts from outside of the community.

Visitors sometimes cause discomfort. For example, visitors to Native American communities who insist on direct eye contact, vigorous handshakes, or ask many questions often create a level of discomfort. By communicating cultural preferences to travelers through a visitor etiquette, most visitors will not only be intrigued, but also respectful.

Cross-cultural differences deeply affect the success of tourism services. Products and tours appealing to one culture may not be appealing to another. Knowing the visitor clientele group and their preferences in the marketplace is essential. Learn and refine through interaction.

Achieving Balance in Sustainability

The pull between access and preservation may cause friction in communities. Scenic beauty usually ranks #1 in visitor surveys. Yet, paradoxically, how easy it is to destroy the beauty with visitor impacts. Achieving the delicate balance between access and protection is possible with policies or restrictions, visitor management, community education, visitor education, evaluation, and redirection as needed. Long-range community satisfaction with small-scale tourism has the potential to reinforce significant aspects of culture and restore interrelationships in the natural world.

PLANNING PROCESS:
Sustainability, Continuity, and Innovation

- *How will values be supported and serve as a foundation to enterprise development, connecting deeply to culture and community?*
- *How will traditional economic forms be strengthened?*
- *How will resources be sustained and protected for the long-term?*
- *How will visitor education continue to support respectful visitation?*
- *How will benefits continue to spread, encouraging mentor exchange?*
- *How will environmental impacts be prevented? And beyond, ecosystems restored?*
- *How will traditions foster being a part of nature, and beliefs that tie to the environment be integrated, rather than separated from culture?*

A strong evaluation process is necessary for realizing sustainability. For traditional communities, evaluation poses a dilemma. Although qualitative factors may be of the greatest importance to traditional communities, sources of funding and other resources usually require quantitative measures.

Evaluation improves business success and is useful for providing feedback to the community. In a cyclical rather than linear concept of progress, conducting an annual evaluation of tourism benefits and impacts measures the extent to which each objective is achieved. Additionally, evaluation aimed at sustainability considers the effectiveness of the community participation process toward long-term improvement.

SUSTAINABLE EVALUATION CRITERIA

Determining the success of tourism projects is a topic subject to cultural bias. Since cultures and communities are different, a predetermined definition of success by a funder or other resource provider rarely fits a community's definition of success. For this reason, the most effective tourism program includes a culturally-based measure of progress.

A formative evaluation, aimed at "forming" a tourism program to maximize the use of resources and improve results, is conducted by program staff at the six month interval. This intermediate evaluation is not only used to monitor progress on objectives, but also the degree of community member participation on an ongoing basis.

Summative evaluation at the end of the year or project examines community feedback, visitor satisfaction, jobs created, business support, encouragement of cultural activities and retention, as well as ecological integrity or restoration. Assessing results not only assists the community to redirect as necessary, but also to document achievements in a format desired by funders.

Even if an evaluation plan is not required by a funder, providing one in a funding proposal expresses the willingness to be accountable and to set targets. Funders need quantitative numbers to respond to their organizational goals. The next chart presents some examples of balancing both qualitative and quantitative criteria in relation to sustainability.

Qualitative measures of success are termed intangible, or not readily measurable benefits. Instilling cultural pride is an example, basic to cultural continuance. Increasing intergenerational interaction and promoting cultural understanding are other examples of intangible benefits. Qualitative criteria tend to be expressed as questions to explore, whereas quantitative criteria are numerical targets to measure.

Chart 10.6 SAMPLE EVALUATION CRITERIA

CULTURAL/SOCIAL:

Qualitative:
- Is the learning of cultural arts increasing?
- Are community resources for cultural practice increasing?
- Is language use increasing?
- Is cultural privacy impacted negatively?
- Are measures to protect cultural privacy in place?
- Are protocols for visitation in place?
- Are basic needs for health care and housing increased?
- Is access to sacred places protected?
- Are welcoming songs and dance traditions documented?
- Is intergenerational interaction increasing?
- Is cultural pride enhanced?

Quantitative:
- Develop five goals and objectives for tourism and museum/interpretive center.
- Develop a tourism policy, protocols, and a visitor etiquette.
- Develop an interpretive guide to history and the museum collection, and distribute 500 copies.
- Pilot a storytelling program for visitor education, with 30 participants.
- Establish a formalized donation structure for ongoing support to entrepreneurial programs, with a target goal of $50,000.
- Increase income to the museum/interpretive center, by 48%.

ECONOMIC:

Qualitative:
- Are entrepreneurs and small-scale businesses benefitting?
- Are traditional forms of economy, such as barter, family cooperation in businesses, and multiple income streams, surviving?

- Is training cultural-value based?
- Is high-nutrition food available for the community?
- Are traditional foods being grown for meeting future needs?
- Are basic community transportation needs being met?

Quantitative:
- Create a database of 80 entrepreneurs.
- Pilot workshops in entrepreneurial skills with 50 participants.
- Establish contact with six tourism partners for commitments.
- Produce tourism and revised museum brochures and distribute 6,000 copies.
- Work with 10 tourism partners for inclusion in promotion.
- Planning progress on tourism market trends, earned livelihood vision, six market niches for entrepreneurs.
- Reduce the unemployment rate by 6.4% (from 42.5% to 36.1%, over three years).
- Increase income to 40 entrepreneurs, at 15% of baseline.
- Increase community member participation in art shows, to 45 people.
- Youth entrepreneurial program participation, with 45 youth.
- Complete a written directory of entrepreneurs for promotional purposes, with a minimum of 50 entries.
- Develop a tourism website landing page (history, cultural arts, events, entrepreneurs, maps, trail itineraries).

ECOLOGICAL:

Qualitative:
- Is ecological restoration taking place?
- Is visitation contained to a specific area?
- Are visitors respectful of fragile areas? Are these identified and protected?
- Are gathering and hunting areas for community protected?
- Is traditional stewardship being taught?
- Is trash being collected and contained?

Quantitative:

- Community implementation of a visitor intake point.
- Establish kiosk to distribute 1,000 copies of tourism materials.
- Implement a trail concept to contain visitors from restricted areas.
- Educate visitors on Indigenous views toward being respectful in the environment, especially in relation to plants and animals, through 150 tours.
- Provide a picnic area for visitors with seating for 12 people and 2 trash cans.
- Develop a unified signage system for 5 locations.

WHEN TOURISM RESULTS ARE NOT OPTIMAL

Tourism may not always create the anticipated results for a community. By following the improvement circle—planning, developing small-scale, evaluating and improving—a community is able to determine effectiveness. Other forms of economic development may be more appropriate for providing jobs, or tourism may be redirected to avoid negative impacts.

Frequent reasons for lack of community satisfaction with tourism are:

- Development without planning on an appropriate scale, or without community involvement;
- Not providing a welcoming atmosphere;
- Lack of visitor information;
- Not protecting needs for cultural privacy;
- Authenticity of cultural arts compromised;
- Leadership not put into place for moving forward;
- Community capacity, or "bringing the community along" not adequately developed to manage tourism;
- Lack of business plans and adequate capital;
- Lack of ownership from within the community;
- Not providing basic services such as restrooms and food service;
- Not defining areas to restrict visitors;

- Community not aligned with project ideas;
- Projects designed on too large a scale for available skills and funding;
- Lack of environmental protection, causing negative impacts;
- Not resolving a love/hate relationship with tourism;
- Not promoting by assuming "open it and they will come;"
- Not targeting specific markets;
- Community enterprises see themselves in competition, rather than cooperating for referrals;
- Liaison work with local resource providers not strengthened;
- No evaluation of weaknesses, success factors; and
- Lack of problem correction.

One increasing danger to sustainability is the trend of technology exhaustion in techno-based countries. While appropriate use of technology in tourism may be beneficial (for marketing tourism, measuring quantitative economic benefits, or measuring ecosystem impacts), visitors could increasingly introduce new technology to communities. A caution should be heeded to avoid adopting the overuse of technology, a pattern so prevalent in Western cultures.

REDIRECTION AND SUSTAINABILITY

Culture—always adapting to change—balances the dilemmas of innovation and preservation. Retaining time-honored traditions that work well and incorporating them into new technologies requires rethinking how we deal with change, culture by culture.

Most redirection addresses problems encountered in tourism, and small-scale approaches are by far the easiest to redirect. In summary, several solutions exist for changing a less than optimal result from tourism.

> **Adjusting the scale of tourism**, or expanding the effort to support and link entrepreneurial businesses to larger community businesses, increases the visitor draw and creates a place for everyone wanting to engage in tourism. Small-scale lessens risk, provides access to community members, and has the better potential for local management capability.

> **Managing tourism** reduces negative impacts by building upon strengths, recognizing weaknesses, and redirecting tourism efforts. When community allocation of funds for tourism development, assessment, evaluation, and improvement is perceived as an economic investment—valuable cultural benefits may result. Marketing and infrastructure improvements are the most neglected in a tourism scenario.

> **The development of a visitor center** or an interpretive center provides an intake point and staffing to manage tourism. A museum or cultural center can serve that function, as well as provide in-depth interpretive functions and cultural teaching, thus continuing the creation of both attractive visitor activities and cultural retention.

> **A dynamic cultural learning program** keeps the interest for community participation at a high level, given the urgency of cultural teaching needs in communities. This, in turn, will interest and draw visitors, if they are kept informed through a website or e-newsletter.

> **Partnerships for tourism development** must continue to be formed for tourism projections to become a reality—including local governments, cultural entrepreneurs, non-profits, artists, teaching programs, and other organizations. Such collaborations are critical for tourism success—in terms of innovation, development, marketing, training, evaluation of success on cultural terms, and redirecting. When the local tourism market accelerates slowly—in tandem with community capacity—a vacation concept is developed that creates a large enough draw to bring visitors, yet increases the capacity to be managed on the small-scale. This step creates the maximum employment.

> **Land use plans** are sometimes completed after tourism has occurred initially. The need to manage access and the flow of visitors becomes increasingly apparent in order to reduce environmental impacts.

> **Planning after the initial development phase**—to revise tourism strategy—is better than no planning at all. Once public

awareness is established from visitation, local residents then begin to realize the potential of tourism. Visitation by large tour buses is sometimes curtailed, as communities understand the environmental impacts being created and develop their own, locally owned enterprises. Or, access by tour buses is clearly defined and communicated.

> **Limiting environmental access** by visitors addresses the potential loss of fragile ecosystems. Loss of the cultural knowledge about plants and animals indicates an urgency to engage in protective measures before negative impacts occur.

Rather than retreating from tourism altogether, there are possible alternatives. Developing tourism in a location away from the community, to avoid impacts to both privacy and to local ecosystems, is an alternative way to benefit from tourism markets.

SUSTAINING THE CULTURALLY MEANINGFUL

All aspects of sustainability increase long-term cultural renewal and preservation efforts. Although financial capital is one factor contributing to starting a project or an enterprise, community capital focusing on—a welcoming atmosphere, unique concepts, sustained practice in tradition, authenticity, development of internal capacity, maintenance of ecological integrity, and new as well as continued forms of earned livelihood—establishes the basis for long-term success. Gaps in learning result in "skipped generations," leading to the loss of cultural knowledge. Addressing learning needs along the way prevents cultural loss.

For this reason, thinking through sustainability within a specific community context is effective at the beginning stages. A small start, delivering constant benefits to a community, is more likely to grow over time than an effort that starts too large with too few resources. Locally originated concepts are culturally meaningful and likely to be invested with community dedication or community capital, and continue into the future.

COMMUNITY-BASED SOLUTION
Saxman Native Village Tours, Alaska (USA)

The Saxman Native Village Tour in Southeast Alaska (USA), educates visitors on Tlingit Native culture while generating extensive earned income through cottage industry. An isolated location translates to few other earned income opportunities, to supplement the subsistence lifestyle.

Entrance into the tour occurs by mini-vans only. A series of stops include storytelling in a traditional longhouse (Beaver Clan House) and youth dancing to demonstrate ongoing cultural learning. A glimpse of authentic totem pole carving at the Village Carving Center, while passing on a nearby path, is minimally invasive to ongoing carving work. These well-planned interpretive experiences lend perception of traditional views and cultural retention efforts. At the final stage of the visitor education experience, a lengthy stop at the Native Faces Store—an art gallery selling community-made traditional arts—leads to extensive purchases of handmade traditional arts and souvenirs.

Largely tapping the cruise ship industry in this remote corner of Alaska with no highway access—tourism occurs in a highly managed setting. Success factors include limiting access to the Native community while providing a well-designed interpretive experience and generating local, traditionally based employment through the store. Highly managed access is a key factor to minimal community impacts.

(www.capefoxtours.com/saxman.html)

FURTHER READING

Edgell, David. *Managing Sustainable Tourism*. New York: Routledge, 2006.
   A framework for tourism development addresses ecological, cultural, economic and local sustainability—in relation to heritage, cultural, rural, and nature tourism. An emphasis on strategies and managing tourism gives practical sustainable guidelines. Case studies from Ecuador, Panama, Canada, the Virgin Islands and U.S. destinations illustrate the concepts.

Honey, Martha. *Ecotourism and Sustainable Development.* Washington, DC: Island Press, 2008.

>Ecotourism demands a holistic approach to travel. This text explains the evolution of tourism, gives an overview of how the tourism industry functions, and explains the context for the world travel industry going green, with international examples and a framework for sustainability.

Mowforth, Martin and Ian Munt. *Tourism and Sustainability: Development and New Tourism in Third World.* London, UK: Routledge, 2003.

>The concepts of sustainability, globalization, and development, in relation to their application to contemporary tourism, are critically examined. Topics on tourists, their relationships to new social movements, tour operators, tourist destinations, and policies adopted by national governments question current directions in growth.

Sharpley, Richard. *Tourism Development and the Environment: Beyond Sustainability?* London, UK: Earthscan. 2009.

>Challenging the sustainable tourism development paradigm, topics propose alternative approaches to tourism development which retain environmental sustainability as a prerequisite of tourism development.

Swarbrooke, John. *Sustainable Tourism Management.* New York: CABI Publishing. 1998.

>A critical view of current thinking in the sustainable tourism field, the discussion presents a range of key issues, with numerous examples of sustainable tourism management practice from around the world.

CONCLUSION

Resilience is present when a community can develop its capabilities, recover from stresses and shocks, and not compromise its values. The goal of sustainability is the ability to meet the needs of the present without compromising the ability of future generations ... to meet their own needs.
(The Brundtland Report)[1]

Resilience, or the capacity to adapt to changing conditions, is central to sustainability. Belief that a community is able to continue to draw upon existing strengths—cultural, economic, and its relationship in the natural environment—connects the past and present to the future in a cyclical perspective.

In a world of uncertainty, enhancing adaptation and resilience is a shift in the focus of sustainability. This perspective shifts away from the prior emphasis on maintaining a constant condition. Sustainability requires the long-term protection and maintenance of cultural expression tied to values and natural systems. Culture guides actions, and is therefore the cornerstone of economic and ecological sustainability.

Cultural tourism often offers only history and a brief glimpse of tradition. However, an authentic experience based on connection between cultures, yet not revealing culturally private information, is possible with community-designed cultural tourism. Sometimes a tourism experience changes perception, brings understanding to a viewpoint, or even profoundly changes one's life. How values and a different way of viewing the world are expressed informs visitors. Showing both tradition and change yields the more accurate representation.

Communities embracing place-based practices are more prepared for adaptation to shifting circumstances in the natural world and are keenly aware of long-held traditions. Resilience in planning comes from identifying multiple possible scenarios, lending the flexibility to adjust to changing conditions. This is necessary for projects and entrepreneurial activities to endure over the long-term.

Culture is the cornerstone of sustainability.

To increase sustainability, the process of attracting visitors will need to be carried out in a thoughtful and educational way. The challenge to a community—not knowing exactly which direction the industry is headed—indicates the importance of keeping up to date with visitor desires, community needs, and projections relating to shifting trends.

In summary, strengths are created in the tourism process by:

- Building community consensus and setting priorities;
- Exploring the smaller-scale entrepreneurial alternatives;
- Developing a set of possible scenarios;
- Addressing environmental concerns and anticipating potential loss of land;
- Supporting cultural arts, traditions, and local food supply systems;
- Emphasizing linked networks; and
- Developing collaborative relationships for tourism success.

The process of conscious local action and adaptation to change is an intriguing message to visitors. Tourism that is collaborative, rather than seen as competitive between locally owned businesses, fosters the intriguing and appealing visitor experience.

SUSTAINABILITY IN NATURE

Beyond preventing environmental impacts due to external pressure, sustainable tourism considers the ability for continued cultural practice in local ecosystems—essential for cultural survival. Land stewardship practices, such as tending forest plants, depend upon access and protection of natural and cultural areas. Water, air quality, and diversity of plant life foster biodiversity, one species to another.

Sensitivity to local ecosystems, both in terms of restoration and interpretation, relates to sustainability. Traditional lifestyles reflect the importance of both ecological and cultural restoration, intimately entwined and vital to the health and well-being of communities. This approach requires careful observation of natural cycles, time-tested practical cultural responses, and adaptations.[2,3]

For example, maintaining practice of Indigenous ecology presents a challenge in a post-modern world, given the reality of intrusions. Pueblo scholar Gregory Cajete[4] emphasizes:

Native people throughout the Americas developed environmentally sound ways of living with the land. Traditionally, they deeply understood and venerably practiced the concept of sustainability within a particular environment. This way of sustainable living evolved into numerous ways of maintaining harmony, both at the individual and communal level, is in dynamic balance with the places in which Indian people have lived in North America.

Ceremonial traditions combined with practical ecological knowledge express an orientation to sacred ecology and form the basis for a theology of place.

All Our Relations

Connection in nature is reflected in worldview. For Indigenous cultures, translating basic knowledge of the caring practices regarding people and environment to visitors is complicated by differences in language structure. Worldview differences in concepts of aliveness reach beyond people—extending to plants, rocks, clouds, water, and soil—all part of a universe of sentient beings. The phrase "all my relations" in Native American and First Nation cultures reflects the equal regard of all species, and our intense relationship to them from origin and kinship. Language structure in traditional cultures reflects this aliveness and a process-oriented view toward life, often losing meaning in translation to English.

In Indigenous cultures, time is cyclical rather than linear, and life by the seasons grounds communities to Mother Earth. This cyclical concept of time is important to communicate to other cultures, as the pressing urgency to live in harmony for global sustainability comes to the forefront. When one perceives life by the seasons, an awareness occurs automatically that one exists within the context of nature, is a part of nature, and has the spiritual responsibility of respectful relationship—not only to others, but also to Earth.

> *Differences in worldview underlie entire cultural perspectives critical to orientation in the universe.*

Eco-cultural boundaries are essential to communicate. Where can we visit, where not to visit? How fragile are these local ecosystems? How do we walk, touch lightly and care for Mother Earth? Observe more acutely? How will we be in relationship with Earth and learn the balance of harmony, the lessons of the human animal who must learn to live in nature?

As the future of tourism unfolds and conscious travelers seek a niche in their own ecosystems, rather than dominant roles, appreciation for the opportunity to learn from ecosystem stewardship will increase. Recognizing a shift from knowledge retention as beneficial for a particular group, to the value for all living beings of diverse cultural knowledge, introduces a new level of respect for diversity.

SUSTAINING TRADITION

Culture is never static, but rather ever changing. As the global community expands and interacts, only a few isolated communities are untouched by visitation. Non-participation by a community that attracts the interest of the general public is likely to result in visitors without the fair exchange.

Rapid cultural change tends to cause greater imbalances than smaller, incremental steps of change. The value-based planning processes presented in this book give a framework for evaluating whether to proceed, appropriate directions, and a pace suitable to the community. Occasionally, a community will decide against tourism as a viable option. Such a step, when determined from within, is very significant and should be respected.

Cultural choices are made along the way if a community is proactive. The alternative is to be swept away by mainstream trends, suffering negative impacts. Determining options and choosing alternatives as the basis of a planning process involves assessing existing entrepreneurial strengths, and finding ways to provide ongoing desired support.

Retaining values and underlying principles that support cultural identity may foster resiliency, if rigidity or failure to adapt are avoided. There is a common pattern in tourism of stereotyping cultures, perpetuating a static cultural interpretation and exerting pressure for a society to maintain a particular public presentation. With visitor education, the conscious visitor may perceive the ways in which different cultures manifest resiliency, address conflicting pressures to change, and maintain culture. The visitation experience is then gentler to the community.

Wisdom is the time-tested, culturally accumulated, and shared-value insightfulness maintaining community lifeways over many generations. Knowledge, in contrast, is a specific skill set learned in the immediate time frame. If not embedded in cultural values, continuity of the practice is not likely. Bridging the gap between knowledge and wisdom requires understanding the underlying values of a community and traditional ways of assessing current conditions, making decisions, and involving a whole community for moving forward.

Inherent in spreading the wisdom of what works is cultivating an ability to be keen and open observers, to become aware of our cultural biases and approach livelihood with an ear open to cultural choices. Often, technical assistance strives to import knowledge with a hurried transfer of skills. In these situations, imparting cultural bias is likely to occur.

The alternative for technical assistance is gaining slow and connected rapport with a community and listening to discover internal priorities, as well as cultural ways of moving forward. This process results in the greater likelihood of a sustainable outcome. Respect for internal capacity comes from gaining an understanding of cultural strengths, whether working within one's own culture or working with another. Recognizing the barriers to moving in a desired direction and willingness to persist in finding the resources to maintain a community's basis for thriving, motivates a community toward effective action on the community's terms.

Ultimately, a sense of local hospitality instilled by cultural values—caring for the community, for the environment, and for visitors—fosters the true sense of welcome. Restoring cultural practice increases resilience through community support networks and coping skills. When food, labor, and other resources are regularly shared or otherwise circulated among households or individuals, then these social resources become a viable part of the sustainability of that system. Values then become a "social resource" relating to sustainability during development, for cultural resilience supports individuals as well as social networks.

Zuni tribal member Hayes Lewis explains these interrelationships:

Artisans, craftsmen, farmers and tribal members gain strength from cultural enterprises of a smaller-scale that are linked to spirituality, ecology, culture, and the sacredness of place and space.[5]

Now is the time to either recoil from fear of scarcity and economic downturns, or to recognize global conditions as the indicators of the new path based on diversity in retained knowledge. Cultural worldviews underlie all actions leading to resilience.

Global attention to the need for environmental conservation in this era can lead to reduced waste and the wise use of resources. When planned well, cultural tourism encourages cultural learning, preserves traditional landscapes, and creates local jobs.

The stakes are high for a new cultural tourism. Gaining awareness through travel holds potential for shared planetary solutions. Traveling can be a means of gaining awareness of culturally diverse approaches to environmental stewardship, or cultural styles of relating in a familial way, or cultural solutions to living with fewer resources with joy in everyday life. Examples of communities practicing conscious consumption, or taking only what they need from their environments, teach conservation better than words. The era for recognizing the importance of cultural diversity to a global future is now.

The new tourism paradigm will bring an era of redirection toward small-scale, sustainable efforts. As we learn from cultural traditions practicing harmonious symbiosis in nature for thousands of years—the negative impacts resulting from values of accumulation and consumption become apparent. With the accelerated pace of climate deterioration, we have no time to lose and must act globally from the diverse pool of cultural knowledge, particularly in relation to Mother Earth.

Sustainability, considered at the deepest level, is about cultural survival. We must be mindful with every step. Walking lighter upon the earth happens with a gradual accumulation of small, conscious actions. And not all cultures survive over time. Not all species survive. Cultural resiliency determines our long-term fate, generation to generation.

We are borrowing this earth for a very short time.

Native American saying

FURTHER READING

Cajete, Gregory. *Native Science: Natural Laws of Interdependence.* Santa Fe, NM: Clear Light Publishers, 2000.

The timeless traditions of understanding, experiencing, and feeling in the natural world, form connectedness in the Indigenous view of reality. Art, myth, ceremony, and symbol are explored in relation to the practice of Native science in the physical sphere.

Edwards, Andres. *The Sustainability Revolution: Portrait of a Paradigm Shift.* Gabriola Island, CAN: New Society Publishers, 2005.

Values connected to sustainability form a new paradigm for the recalibration of human intentions to coincide with the way the biophysical world works, through concern for our longevity as a species.

Gunderson, Lance H., Craig R. Allen, and C.S. Holling, editors. *Foundations of Ecological Resilience.* Washington, DC: Island Press, 2010.

This text challenges the misleading equilibrial theories of ecology and economics, addressing new principles of adaptation in conditions of constant change, of nature evolving.

Walker, Brian and David Salt. *Resilience Thinking: Sustaining Ecosystems and People in a Changing World.* Washington, DC: Island Press. 2006.

The concept of resilience as the capacity of a system to absorb disturbance and still retain its basic function and structure, is examined within the context of human behavior—through linked social and ecological systems.

NOTES

Introduction

1. Luo, Yanju and Jinyang Deng. The New Environmental Paradigm and Nature-Based Tourism Motivation. *Journal of Travel Research*, Vol. 46, 2008, pp. 392-402.

2. Guyette, Susan and David White. Reducing the Impacts of Tourism Through Cross-Cultural Planning. *The Culture of Tourism and the Tourism of Culture*, edited by Hal Rothman. Albuquerque, NM: University of New Mexico Press, 2003, pp. 164-184.

3. Commission for Environmental Cooperation. *The Development of Sustainable Tourism in Natural Areas.* Playa del Carmen, MX. 1999.

4. Edgell, David. *Managing Sustainable Tourism.* New York: Routledge, 2006.

5. Shilling, Dan. *Civic Tourism.* Prescott, AZ: Sharlot Hall Museum Press, 2007.

6. Wearing, Stephen, Matthew McDonald and Jess Ponting. Building a Decommodified Research Paradigm in Tourism: The Contribution of NGOs. *Journal of Sustainable Tourism*, Vol. 13, No. 5, 2005, pp. 424-439.

Chapter 1

1. Smith, Valene, editor. *Hosts and Guests: The Anthropology of Tourism.* Philadelphia, PA: University of Pennsylvania Press, 1995.

2. National Geographic Center for Sustainable Destinations, http://travel.nationalgeographic.com/travel/sustainable.

3. Guyette, Susan. *Planning for Balanced Development*. Santa Fe, NM: Clear Light Publishers, 1996.

4. Kraybill, Donald. *The Riddle of Amish Culture.* Baltimore, MD: Johns Hopkins University Press, 2001.

5. Aageson, Tom. Introduction and Common Themes. *Creative Tourism: A Global Conversation,* edited by Rebecca Wurzburger, Tom Aageson, Alex Pattakos and Sabrina Pratt. Santa Fe, NM: Sunstone Press, 2010, pp. 165-170.

6. McKercher, Bob and Hilary du Cros. *Cultural Tourism: The Partnership Between Tourism and Cultural Heritage Management.* New York: Routledge, 2002.

7. Smith, Linda Tuhiwai. *Decolonizing Methodologies: Research and Indigenous Peoples.* New York: Zed Books, Ltd, 1999.

8. Mowforth, Martin and Ian Munt. *Tourism and Sustainability: Development and New Tourism in Third World.* London, UK: Routledge, 2003.
9. McKibben, Bill. *Deep Economy: The Wealth of Communities and the Durable Future.* New York: Henry Holt and Company, 2007.
10. Wilson, Shawn. *Research is Ceremony: Indigenous Research Methods.* Halifax, Nova Scotia, CAN: Fernwood Publishing, 2008.

Chapter 2

1. Gunn, Clare A. with Turgut Var. *Tourism Planning: Basics, Concepts, Cases.* New York: Routledge, 2002.
2. McLaren, Deborah. *Rethinking Tourism and Ecotravel.* West Hartford, CT: Kumarian Press, 2003.
3. Bottril, Christopher and Douglas Pearce. Ecotourism: Towards a Key Elements Approach to Operationalizing the Concept. *Journal of Sustainable Tourism*, Vol. 3, No. 1, 1995, pp. 45-54.
4. Craik, Jennifer. Are There Cultural Limits to Tourism? *Journal of Sustainable Tourism*, Vol. 3, No. 2, 1995, pp. 87-98.

Chapter 3

1. Prewitt, Jana. *Tribal Tourism Toolkit.* National Association of Tribal Historic Preservation Officers, 2002. (www.nathpo.org/Toolkit/NATHPO.pdf)
2. The SWOT originated as a military model and is sometimes criticized as a community planning tool. However, I find the application to be particularly useful in practice for encouraging small communities, through recognition of strengths and building confidence to both protect and proceed.
3. McKercher, Bob and Hilary du Cros. *Cultural Tourism: The Partnership Between Tourism and Cultural Heritage Management.* New York: Routledge, 2002.
4. Adapted from Sargent, Frederic O, Paul Lusk, José A. Rivera and María Varela. *Rural Environmental Planning for Sustainable Communities.* Washington, DC: Island Press, 1991.

Chapter 4

1. Kovach, Margaret. *Indigenous Methodologies: Characteristics, Conversations, and Contexts.* Toronto, CAN: University of Toronto Press, 2009.

2. Elam, Houston G., and Norton Paley. *Marketing for Nonmarketers.* New York: American Management Association, 1992.

Chapter 5

1. Prewitt, Jana. Personal communication, 2004.
2. Li, Xiang and James Petrick. Tourism Marketing in an Era of Paradigm Shift. *Journal of Travel Research.* Vol. 46, No 3, 2008, pp. 235-244.
3. Kaplanidou, Kiki and Christine Vogt. *Destination Branding: Concept and Measurement.* East Lansing, MI: Department of Park, Recreation and Tourism Resources, Michigan State University, 2003.
4. Middleton, Victor. *Marketing in Travel and Tourism.* Amsterdam, NL: Elsevier, 2009.

Chapter 6

1. Cultures with a strong oral tradition may follow a different process. In these instances, community members may remember the detail of a strategy and respond well in talking circles, without a written plan. Discussing the method to be used and meeting frequently will keep community participation at a high level.
2. Tarlow, Peter. *Event Risk Management and Safety.* New York: John Wiley, 2002. (www.tourismandmore.com)

Chapter 7

1. Guyette, Susan. *Planning for Balanced Development.* Santa Fe, NM: Clear Light Publishers, 1996.
2. Cooper, Karen Coody and Nicolasa Sandoval, editors. Starting a Native Museum or Cultural Center. *Living Homes for Cultural Expression: North American Native Perspectives on Creating Community Museums,* edited by Karen Coody Cooper and Nicolasa Sandoval. Washington, DC: Smithsonian Institution, 2006. (www.nmai.si.edu)
3. Chilisa, Bagele. *Indigenous Research Methodologies.* Los Angeles, CA: Sage, 2012.
4. Hill, Richard. Road Map for Native Museum Exhibition Planning. *Living Homes for Cultural Expression: North American Native Perspectives on Creating Community Museums,* edited by Karen Coody Cooper and Nicolasa Sandoval. Washington, DC: Smithsonian Institution, 2006, pp. 17-26. (www.nmai.si.edu)
5. White, David M. Personal communication, 2004.

Chapter 8

1. Patterson, Carol. *The Business of Ecotourism: The Complete Guide for Nature and Culture-based Tourism Operators*. Victoria, BC: Trafford Publishing, 2007.
2. The authenticity debate regarding tourism is extensive and subjective. While several authors have analyzed this debate (see Melanie Smith 2009 for an overview), the focus of the debate revolves around staged events and the experience of the tourist—rather than the perspective of culturally diverse communities hosting the visitors. The viewpoint expressed throughout this book emphasizes community perspectives and efforts to revitalize and retain culture as the focus of authenticity.
3. Trimble, Stephen. *Talking with the Clay: The Art of Pueblo Pottery in the 21st Century*. Santa Fe, NM: School of American Research, 2007.
4. Hollowell-Zimmer, Julie. Intellectual Property Rights: Culture as Commodity. *Cultural Survival Quarterly*, Vol. 24, No. 4, Winter, 2000.
5. Bernstein, Bruce. *Santa Fe Indian Market*. Santa Fe, NM: Museum of New Mexico Press, 2012.

Chapter 10

1. Edwards, Andres. *The Sustainability Revolution: Portrait of a Paradigm Shift*. Gabriola Island, CAN: New Society Publishers, 2005.
2. World Tourism Organization. *What Tourism Managers Need to Know: A Practical Guide to the Development and Use of Indicators of Sustainable Tourism*. Madrid, ES: World Tourism Organization, 1996.
3. Nelson, Melissa, editor. *Original Instructions: Indigenous Teachings for a Sustainable Future*. Rochester, VT: Bear & Company, 2008.
4. Swarbrooke, John. *The Development and Management of Visitor Attractions*. Boston, MA: Elsevier, 2002.

Conclusion

1. Brundtland Commission. *The Brundtland Report*. World Commission on Environment and Development (WCED). Oxford, UK: Oxford University Press, 1987.
2. Martinez, Dennis, Enrique Salmon, and Melissa K. Nelson. Restoring Indigenous History and Culture to Nature. *Original Instructions: Indigenous Teachings for a Sustainable Future*, edited by Melissa Nelson. Rochester, NY: Bear & Company, 2008.

3. Farrel, Bryan and Louise Twining-Ward. Seven Steps Towards Sustainability: Tourism in the Content of New Knowledge. *Journal of Sustainable Tourism*, Vol. 13, No. 2, 2005, pp. 109-122.
4. Cajete, Gregory. *A People's Ecology: Explorations in Sustainable Living.* Santa Fe, NM: Clear Light Publishers, 1999.
5. Lewis, Hayes. Creative Tourism in Indian Country: More than Beads, Feathers, and Casinos. *Creative Tourism: A Global Conversation,* edited by Rebecca Wurzburger, Tom Aageson, Alex Pattakos and Sabrina Pratt. Santa Fe, NM: Sunstone Press, 2010, pp. 183-196.

SELECTED BIBLIOGRAPHY

Aageson, Tom. Introduction and Common Themes. *Creative Tourism: A Global Conversation,* edited by Rebecca Wurzburger, Tom Aageson, Alex Pattakos and Sabrina Pratt. Santa Fe, NM: Sunstone Press, 2010, pp. 165-170.

Bagele, Chilisa. *Indigenous Research Methodologies.* Los Angeles, CA: Sage, 2012.

Basso, Keith. *Wisdom Sits in Places.* Albuquerque, NM: University of New Mexico Press, 1996.

Berke, Philip and Maria Manta Conroy. Are We Planning for Sustainable Development? *American Planning Association Journal,* Vol. 66, No. 1, Winter 2000, pp. 21-33.

Bernstein, Joanne Scheff. *Arts Marketing Insights.* San Francisco, CA: John Wiley, 2007.

Blamey, Russel. Ecotourism: The Search for an Operational Definition. *Journal of Sustainable Tourism,* Vol. 5, No. 2, 1997, pp. 109-130.

Bosselman, Fred P., Craig A. Peterson and Claire McCarthy. *Managing Tourism Growth: Issues and Applications.* Washington, DC: Island Press, 1999.

Bottril, Christopher and Douglas Pearce. Ecotourism: Towards a Key Elements Approach to Operationalizing the Concept. *Journal of Sustainable Tourism,* Vol. 3, No. 1, 1995, pp. 45-54.

Bowles, Elinor. *Cultural Centers of Color.* Washington, DC: National Endowment for the Arts, 1993.

Bramwell, Bill, Ian Henry, Guy Jackson and Jan van der Straaten. A Framework for Understanding Sustainable Tourism Management. *Sustainable Tourism Management Principles and Practice,* edited by Bill Bramwell, Ian Henry, Guy Jackson, Ana Goytia Prat, Greg Richards and Jan van der Straaten. NL: Tillburg University Press, 1998, pp. 23-72.

Brundtland Commission. *The Brundtland Report. World Commission on Environment and Development (WCED).* Oxford, UK: Oxford University Press, 1987.

Bruner, Edward M. *Culture on Tour: Ethnographies of Travel.* Chicago, IL: The University of Chicago Press, 2005.

Burns, Peter M. *An Introduction to Tourism and Anthropology.* New York: Routledge, 1999.

Cajete, Gregory. *A People's Ecology: Explorations in Sustainable Living.* Santa Fe, NM: Clear Light Publishers, 1999.

Cajete, Gregory. *Native Science: Natural Laws of Interdependence.* Santa Fe, NM: Clear Light Publishers, 2000.

Howard, Kathleen and Diana Pardue. *Inventing the Southwest: The Fred Harvey Company and Native American Art.* Phoenix, AZ: The Heard Museum, 1996.

Indian Arts and Crafts Board. *Forming an Arts and Crafts Cooperative.* n.d. (www.culturalentrepreneur.org or www.iacb.doi.gov).

Indian Arts and Crafts Board. *Introduction to Intellectual Property: for American Indian and Alaskan Native Artists, 2010.* (www.doi.gov/iacb).

Inskeep, Edward. *Tourism Planning: An Integrated and Sustainable Development Approach.* New York: Van Nostrand Reinhold, 1991.

International Council of Museums. *Marketing the Arts.* Paris, FR: ICOM, UNESCO, 1992.

Kaplanidou, Kiki and Christine Vogt. *Destination Branding: Concept and Measurement,* Department of Park, Recreation and Tourism Resources. East Lansing, MI: Michigan State University, 2003.

Karp, Ivan and Steven D. Lavine, eds. *Exhibiting Cultures: The Poetics and Politics of Museum Display.* Washington, D.C.: Smithsonian Institution, 1991.

Kotler, Philip, Donald H. Haider and Irving Rein. *Marketing Places.* New York: The Free Press, 1993.

Kotler, Philip, John Bowen and James C. Makens. *Marketing for Hospitality and Tourism.* Upper Saddle River, NJ: Pearson Education, Prentice Hall, 2009.

Kovach, Margaret. *Indigenous Methodologies: Characteristics, Conversations, and Contexts.* Toronto, CAN: University of Toronto Press, 2009.

Kraybill, Donald. *The Riddle of Amish Culture.* Baltimore, MD: Johns Hopkins University Press, 2001.

Luo, Yanju and Jinyang Deng. The New Environmental Paradigm and Nature-Based Tourism Motivation. *Journal of Travel Research,* Vol. 46, 2008, pp. 392-402.

Lanfant, Marie-Francoise, John B. Allcock and Edward M. Bruner, editors. *International Tourism: Identity and Change.* London, UK: Sage Publications Ltd, 1995.

Lewis, Hayes. Creative Tourism in Indian Country: More than Beads, Feathers, and Casinos. *Creative Tourism: A Global Conversation,* edited by Rebecca Wurzburger, Tom Aageson, Alex Pattakos and Sabrina Pratt. Santa Fe, NM: Sunstone Press, 2010, pp. 183-196.

Li, Xiang and James Petrick. Tourism Marketing in an Era of Paradigm Shift. *Journal of Travel Research.* Vol. 46, No. 3, 2008, pp. 235-244.

Loeffler, Jack. Water Heist in the Plains of San Augustín – Part II. *Green Fire Times*. Santa Fe, NM: Vol. 3, No. 11, 2010, pp. 25-27. (www.greenfiretimes.com)

Martinez, Dennis, Enrique Salmon and Melissa K. Nelson. Restoring Indigenous History and Culture to Nature. *Original Instructions: Indigenous Teachings for a Sustainable Future*, edited by Melissa Nelson. Rochester, VT: Bear & Company, 2008, pp. 88-115.

Mason, Peter. *Tourism Impacts, Planning and Management*. Oxford, UK: Elsevier, 2008.

MacConnell, Dean. *The Tourist: A New Theory of the Leisure Class*. Berkeley, CA: University of California Press, 1999.

Mauger, Jeffrey and Janine Bowechop. Tribal Collections Management at the Makah Cultural and Research Center. *Living Homes for Cultural Expression: North American Native Perspectives on Creating Community Museums*. Edited by Karen Coody Cooper and Nicolasa Sandoval. Washington, DC: Smithsonian Institution, 2006, pp. 57-64. (www.nmai.si.ed)

McCabe, J. Terrence. Toward an Anthropological Understanding of Sustainability: A Preface. *Human Organization*. Vol. 62, No. 2, 2003, pp. 93-99.

McDonough, William and Michael Braungart. *Cradle to Cradle: Remaking the Way We Make Things*. New York: North Point Press, 2002.

McKercher, Bob and Hilary du Cros. *Cultural Tourism: The Partnership Between Tourism and Cultural Heritage Management*. New York: Routledge, 2002.

McKibben, Bill. *Deep Economy: The Wealth of Communities and the Durable Future*. New York: Henry Holt and Company, 2007.

McLaren, Deborah. *Rethinking Tourism and Ecotravel*. West Hartford, CT: Kumarian Press, 2003.

Meguid, Ossama A.W. Abdel. Community-Based Ecotourism: Concept, Characteristics and Directions. *Creative Tourism: A Global Conversation*, edited by Rebecca Wurzburger, Tom Aageson, Alex Pattakos and Sabrina Pratt. Santa Fe, NM: Sunstone Press, 2010, pp. 128-137.

Middleton, Victor. *Marketing in Travel and Tourism*. Amsterdam, NL: Elsevier, 2009.

Mill, Robert Christie and Alastair M. Morrison. *The Tourism System*. Dubuque, IA: Kendall Hunt, 2009.

MindTools. *Entrepreneurial Skills: The Skills You Need to Build a Great Business*, 2012. (www.mindtools.com)

Mitchell, G.E., *How to Start a Tour Guiding Business*. Charleston, SC: Gem Group Ltd., 2005.

Morrison, Alastair. *Hospitality and Travel Marketing.* Delmar, AU: Thomson Learning, 2009.

Mowforth, Martin and Ian Munt. *Tourism and Sustainability: Development and New Tourism in Third World.* London, UK: Routledge, 2003.

National Geographic Center for Sustainable Destinations, http://travel.nationalgeographic.com/travel/sustainable.

Nelson, Melissa, editor. *Original Instructions: Indigenous Teachings for a Sustainable Future.* Rochester, VT: Bear & Company, 2008.

Northwest Area Foundation. *Native Entrepreneurship: Challenges and Opportunities for Rural Communities.* Washington, DC: Corporation for Enterprise Development, 2004.

Nykiel, Ronald and Elizabeth Jascolt. *Marketing Your City U.S.A.: A Guide to Developing a Strategic Tourism Marketing Plan.* New York: The Haworth Hospitality Press, 2006.

O'Reilly, Daragh and Finola Kerrigan. *Marketing the Arts.* London, UK: Routledge, 2010.

Orr, David W. *The Sustainability Revolution: Portrait of a Paradigm Shift.* Gabriola Island, CA: New Society Publishers, 2005.

Patterson, Carol. *The Business of Ecotourism: The Complete Guide for Nature and Culture-based Tourism Operators.* Victoria, BC: Trafford Publishing, 2007.

Prewitt, Jana. *Tribal Tourism Toolkit.* National Association of Tribal Historic Preservation Officers, 2002. (www.nathpo.org/Toolkit/NATHPO.pdf)

Prugh, Thomas, Robert Costanza and Herman Daly. *The Local Politics of Global Sustainability.* Washington, D.C.: Island Press, 2000.

Richards, Greg, editor. *Cultural Tourism: Global and Local Perspectives.* New York: Routledge, 2007.

Rojek, Chris and John Urry, editors. *Touring Cultures: Transformations of Travel and Theory.* London: Routledge, 1997.

Rossouw, Dirk, Jo Zeelie, Darelle Groenewald, and Andreas de Beer. *Entrepreneurial Skills.* Johannesburg, ZA: Double Storey Books, 2009.

Sargent, Frederic O, Paul Lusk, José A. Rivera, and María Varela. *Rural Environmental Planning for Sustainable Communities.* Washington, D.C.: Island Press, 1991.

Sharpley, Richard. *Tourism Development and the Environment: Beyond Sustainability?* London, UK: Earthscan, 2009.

Shilling, Dan. *Civic Tourism.* Prescott, AZ: Sharlot Hall Museum Press, 2007.

Smith, Linda Tuhiwai. *Decolonizing Methodologies: Research and Indigenous Peoples.* New York: Zed Books, Ltd, 1999.

Smith, Melanie. *Issues in Cultural Tourism Studies.* London, UK: Routledge, 2009.

Smith, Valene, editor. *Hosts and Guests: The Anthropology of Tourism.* Philadelphia, PA: University of Pennsylvania Press, 1995.

Spenceley, Anna. *Responsible Tourism: Critical Issues for Conservation and Development.* London, UK: Earthscan, 2008.

Swarbrooke, John. *The Development and Management of Visitor Attractions.* Boston, MA: Elsevier, 2002.

Swarbrooke, John. *Sustainable Tourism Management.* New York: CABI Publishing, 1998.

Sweeney, Susan. *101 Ways to Promote Your Tourism Business Website.* Gulf Breeze, FL: Maximum Press, 2008.

Tarlow, Peter. *Event Risk Management and Safety.* New York: John Wiley, 2002.

Theobald, William F. *Global Tourism.* Boston, MA: Elsevier, 2005.

Tilden, Freeman. *Interpreting Our Heritage.* Chapel Hill, NC: University of North Carolina Press, 1977.

Trimble, Stephen. *Talking with the Clay: The Art of Pueblo Pottery in the 21st Century.* Santa Fe, NM: School of American Research, 2007.

Tourism Policy Council. *Tourism: Putting the Pieces Together.* Washington, DC: The Tourism Policy Council, 1994.

Tyler, Duncan and Mark Dangerfield. Ecosystem Tourism: A Resource Based Philosophy for Tourism. *Journal of Sustainable Tourism*, Vol. 7, No. 2, 1999, pp. 146-158.

Urry, John. *The Tourist Gaze.* London, U.K.: Sage Publications, 1994.

U.S. Department of Commerce. *Rural Tourism Handbook.* Washington, DC: United States Travel and Tourism Administration, 1994.

Van der Ryn, Sim and Peter Calthorpe. *Sustainable Communities: A New Design Synthesis for Cities, Suburbs and Towns.* San Francisco, CA: Sierra Club Books, 1991.

Van Otten, Alan A. and George A. *Tourism and Gaming on American Indian Lands.* New York: Cognizant Communication Corporation, 1998.

Walker, Brian and David Salt. *Resilience Thinking: Sustaining Ecosystems and People in a Changing World.* Washington, DC: Island Press, 2006.

Wearing, Stephen, Matthew McDonald and Jess Ponting. Building a Decommodified Research Paradigm in Tourism: The Contribution of NGOs. *Journal of Sustainable Tourism,* Vol. 13, No. 5, 2005, pp. 424-439.

Weaver, David. *Sustainable Tourism.* Burlington, VT: Elsevier, 2006.

Whelan, Tensie, editor. *Nature Tourism: Managing for the Environment.* Washington, DC: Island Press, 1991.

Wilson, Shawn. *Research is Ceremony: Indigenous Research Methods.* Halifax, Nova Scotia, CAN: Fernwood Publishing, 2008.

World Tourism Organization. *National and Regional Tourism Planning.* New York: Routledge, 1994.

World Tourism Organization. *What Tourism Managers Need to Know: A Practical Guide to the Development and Use of Indicators of Sustainable Tourism.* Madrid, ES: World Tourism Organization, 1996.

World Tourism Organization. *Guide for Local Authorities on Developing Sustainable Tourism.* Madrid, ES: World Tourism Organization, 1998.

Wurzburger, Rebecca, Tom Aageson, Alex Pattakos and Sabrina Pratt, editors. *Creative Tourism: A Global Conversation.* Santa Fe, NM: Sunstone Press, 2010.

APPENDIX A
TOURISM AND SUSTAINABILITY ORGANIZATIONS ONLINE

TOURISM

American Indian Alaskan Native Tourism Association
www.aianta.org

American Society of Travel Agents
www.astanet.com

Canadian Tourism Commission
www.canadatourism.org

Conservation International
www.ecotour.org

Cultural Heritage Tourism
www.culturalheritagetourism.org

Cultural and Heritage Tourism Alliance
www.chtalliance.com

Destination Marketing Association International
www.destinationmarketing.org

European Travel Commission
www.visiteurope.org

Green Tourism Association
www.greentourism.on.ca

Green Travel
www.green-travel.com

Heritage Tourism (National Trust for Historic Preservation)
www.preservationnation.org

Hospitality Net
www.hospitalitynet.org

International Association of Amusement Parks & Attractions
www.iaapa.org

International Center for Research and Study on Tourism
www.ciret-tourism.com

International Centre for Responsible Tourism
www.cfrt.org.uk

International Ecotourism Society
www.ecotourism.org

International Travel Statistics
www.bts.gov

Office of Travel and Tourism Industries (OTTI)
www.tinet.ita.doc.gov

National Geographic Sustainable Tourism Center
www.nationalgeographic.com/travel/sustainable

National Park Service Public Use Statistics
www.nps.gov

National Tour Association (NTA)
www.ntaonline.com

National Trust for Historic Preservation
www.nationaltrust.org

Nature Conservancy Ecotourism Programme
www.nature.org/aboutus/travel/ecotourism

Organization for Economic Cooperation & Development
www.oecd.org

Pacific Asia Travel Association
www.pata.org

Recreation Vehicle Industry Association
www.rvia.org

Sustainable Travel International
www.sustainabletravelinternational.org

Tourism Concern (UK)
www.tourismconcern.org.uk

Travel and Tourism Research Association (TTRA)
www.ttra.com

Travel Industry Association of America
www.tia.org

United States U.S. Tour Operators Association
www.ustoa.com

Western States Tourism Policy Council
www.wstpc.org

World Indigenous Tourism Alliance
www.winta.org

World Tourism Organization
www.unwto.org

World Travel and Tourism Council
www.wttc.org

SUSTAINABILITY

Bioneers
www.bioneers.org

Builders Without Borders
www.builderswithoutborders.org

Building Green, Inc.
www.buildinggreen.com

Business for Social Responsibility
www.bsr.org

Business Action for Sustainable Development
basd.free.fr

The Citizens Network for Sustainable Development
www.citnet.org

Coalition for Environmentally Responsible Economies
www.ceres.org

Conservation Economy.net
www.conservationeconomy.net

Cradle2Cradle
www.cradle2cradle.org

Cultural Survival
www.culturalsurvival.org

Earth Policy Institute
www.earth-policy.org

EcoSTEPS
www.ecosteps.com

Fair Trade in Tourism Network
www.globalhand.org

Friends of the Earth International
www.foei.org

Global Center for Cultural Entrepreneurship
www.culturalentrepreneur.org

GreenBiz.com
http://greenbiz.com

Green Globe
www.greenglobe21.com

International Environmental Film and Video Festival
www.planetinfocus.org

International Forum on Globalization
www.ifg.org

International Institute for Sustainable Development
www.iisd.ca

International Society for Ecological Economics
www.ecoeco.org

International Union for Conservation of Nature and Natural Resources
www.iucn.org

ManyOne Networks
www.manyone.net

National Strategies for Sustainable Development
www.nssd.net

Natural Capitalism Solutions
www.natcapsolutions.org

Organic Consumers Association
www.organicconsumers.org

Pew Center on Global Climate Change
www.pewclimate.org

Planet Ark
www.planetark.org

Planetwork
www.planetwork.net

Survival International
www.survivalinternational.org

SustainAbility
www.sustainability.com

SustainableBusiness.com
www.sustainablebusiness.com

Sustainable Communities Network
www.sustainable.org

Sustainability Institute
www.donellameadows.org

United Nations Environment Network
www.unep.org

United Nations Educational, Scientific and Cultural Organisation (UNESCO)
www.unesco.org

World Development Movement
www.wdm.org.uk

World Green Building Council
www.worldgbc.org

World Land Trust
www.worldlandtrust.org

The World Café
www.theworldcafe.com

Worldwatch Institute
www.worldwatch.org

World wide Fund for Nature
www.wwf.org.uk

TRANSPORTATION

Air Transport Association of America
www.airlines.org

Air Transport World (ATW)
www.atwonline.com

American Automobile Association
www.aaa.com

American Bus Association
www.buses.org

American Hotel and Lodging Association
www.ahla.com

American Society of Travel Agents
www.astanet.com

Association of Retail Travel Agents
www.artaonline.com

Cruise Lines International Association
www.cruising.org

International Air Transport Association
www.iata.org

International Airlines Travel Agency Network
www.arccorp.com

International Ecotourism Society
www.ecotourism.org

International Hotel and Restaurant Association
www.ih-ra.com

National Restaurant Association (NRA)
www.restaurant.org

Recreation Vehicle Industry Association
www.rvia.org

United Motorcoach Association
www.uma.org

APPENDIX B
TOURISM TRADE SHOWS

INTERNATIONAL

GBTA-Global Business Travel Association (Boston)
   www.gbta.org

Go Global Expo (Montreal)
   www.letsgoglobal.ca

International Tourism & Travel Show (Montreal)
   www.salontourismevoyages.com

ITB (Berlin)
   www.itb-berlin.de

ITE-International Travel Expo (Hong Kong)
   www.itehk.com

JATA-Japan Association Travel Agents (Japan)
   www.jata-net.or.jp

Pow Wow (United States)
   www.tia.org

World Travel Market (London)
   www.wtmlondon.com

APPENDIX C
BASIC TOURISM CONCEPTS

Amenity: A business or service adding comfort to the journey, such as lodging, restaurants, gasoline and repair service stations, grocery stores, and provisions for other basic needs.

Business incubator: A start-up facility, usually featuring small spaces, joint access to office equipment, business coaching assistance, and a reduced rent for two or three years, until a business is viable on its own.

Competition: Seeing other businesses as competing against each other for a limited pool of dollars.

Cooperation: Seeing other businesses as part of a larger network, all working together to capture a larger percentage of tourist dollars.

Cross-marketing: Marketing several businesses at once in a way that creates synergy between the businesses.

Cultural tourists: Travelers seeking to understand other cultures by observing customs or lifeways, or purchasing items representative of that culture.

Customer service: Providing pleasant interactions and basic services to visitors.

Customer satisfaction: The level of customer approval of services, determined by obtaining customer feedback.

Destination: An area attracting non-local visitors or more recently, the larger-scale concept of "destination resort," with the intention of focusing all expenditures in one business location.

Development: Bias in the assumption of growth as the primary economic intention. The term "sustainable development" implies culturally appropriate form, scale, and timing.

Economic multiplier: The number of times a dollar recirculates in a local economy, therefore preventing economic leakages.

Ecotourists: Travelers seeking a nature-based experience.

Geotourists: A new concept with overlap between cultural tourists, ecotourists, and heritage tourists, connoting concern for local people and their environments.

Heritage tourists: Visitors interested in local history, museums and historic places.

Itinerary: A linkage of possible stops on a trip, in the form of a printed brochure or part of a visitor guide; travel times, information on where to obtain food, service and lodging, and maps are included in an itinerary to guide the visitor on a journey.

Managed tourism: Development that defines allowed areas of visitation, prohibited areas, provides a balance of activities, protects culture and educates visitors about people, places, and access.

Market niche: An opportunity for an unfilled business type or product line or service.

Market segment: A part of the total possible market, with a particular set of characteristics, such as historic travelers or ecotourists.

Multiple income streams: Earning a living through several different types of income or jobs.

Appendix C   351

Person-trips:	An indicator of tourism volume used in the tourism industry; the number of one-way trips between two points, at least 50 miles away from home.
Point-of-origin:	Place where the visitor lives or starts the trip, useful to know for marketing purposes.
Product development:	Matching the existing skills (or desired skills) in a community with ideas for products that are in demand by visitors to a specific area.
Promotion:	Media distribution on activities and services, given free-of-charge to the potential visitor and visitors on their journey.
Quality control:	Making certain that the quality or uniformity of quality of items sold stays at a high level, sometimes referred to as TQM or Total Quality Management.
Recreational tourists:	Travelers focused on hiking, fishing, hunting, boating, sports, birding, and other outdoor activities.
Regional approach:	Including both urban and rural areas, and linking them together in a larger geographical area.
Souvenir line:	A lower-end line (in price, not necessarily in quality) purchased to remember the trip or to give away to friends and family; souvenirs are generally defined as costing $25 or less.
Sustainable tourism:	A managed approach taking into account the preservation of local resources, cultures and long-term self-sufficiency.
Tourism draw:	A pull of visitors created to a tourism offering, through targeted marketing efforts.
Tourism market:	The potential people who could be attracted to a specific area as tourists.

Tourism trade show: A large, international forum where travel agents, tour companies, and other tourism market representatives meet with local providers of tour and tourism experiences, to book tours or learn about visitation opportunities available in geographical regions.

Value chain: Products pass through all activities of a chain in order, and at each activity the product gains some value. The chain of activities gives the products more added value than the sum of the independent activities' values.

Visitor education: Providing information to the potential or actual visitor, on local peoples, history, cultural values, foods, etiquette for behavior, the local environment, and other topics of local interest, for the purpose of enhancing the visitor's learning experience, while reducing impacts on the local community.

Visitor etiquette: Guidelines developed by a community to describe culturally appropriate or respectful behavior according to the viewpoints of a particular community.

Visitor guide: A publication, usually printed in color, with maps, a calendar of events, itineraries, articles on local activities, places, cultures and arts, as well as advertisements showing visitors shops, lodging and eating places. Guides are promotional and given free-of-charge.

Visitor survey: A survey distributed to a sample group of visitors to determine information such as: where they are from, the activities they desire, type of lodging they prefer, how long they plan to stay, items they would like to purchase, and the dollar amount they intend to spend.

INDEX

A

Acoma Pueblo, 289
Acculturation and enculturation, 31
Arts, cultural, 212-213, 243-244, 311
Arts database, 214-216
Assessment, managed tourism, 300-301
Attractions, tourism, 83
Authentic experience, 24
Authenticity issues, 132, 240-244

B

Bias:
    cultural, 5
    in surveys, 105
    tourism industry, 10
Branding, 146-150
Break-even point, 251
Bridging cultures, 25
Brochures, 153
Budget, marketing, 159-160
Budget, tourism program, 187-188
Business:
    formation, 263-264
    plan, 266-284
    plan outline, 267-268
    plan, mini, 248-253
    style and culture, 261-263

C

Capacity-building, 70, 171-172, 179
Change and culture, 26
Collections, museum, 201
Common tourism mistakes, 313
Community:
    concerns, 72-78
    esteem, 71
    focus, 13
    involvement, 108
    meetings, 73-78
Competition, analysis of, 278
Competition and cooperation, 39
Conscious travel, 2
Consensus, 75
Cross-marketing, 145
Cultural:
    bias, 27-29
    centers, 196, 205-206
    choices, 13
    fit, 50, 247, 256, 263
    heritage management, 96
    interpretation, 209-210
    learning, 201-204
    privacy, 17
    retention, 19
    revitalization, 200-201
    survival, 49, 167, 169, 198, 226-227, 324
    systems, 16
    tourism, definition, 3
    values, 18-21
Culture, communicating, 207-208
Customer service, 246-247, 301-303

D

Database, employment skills, 230-233
Draft plan review, 191-192

E

Economic development, 57
Economic multipliers, 58, 60, 73
Ecotourism, 15, 294, 308, 312, 322

Employment:
  cultural survival, 226-227
  primary, 227
  quality of, 228
  secondary, 227
Entrepreneurial:
  failure, factors, 255-256
  niches, 58
  success, factors, 254-255
Entrepreneurs, cultural, 238-239
Environmental impact studies, 72, 95, 177
Equity in tourism, 5
Evaluation:
  criteria, 311-313
  formative, 310
  summative, 310

F

Feedback:
  community, 304-305
  loop, 52
Focus groups, 74
Form, scale and timing, 21-24
Funding:
  museum, 219-221
  tourism, 189-190

G

Ganados del Valle, 97
Gap analysis, 124
Geotourism, 15
Goals, tourism, 171-175
Greeting traditions, 208-209
Guarani Paraty, Brazil, 222

H

Huichol Center, 257

I

Income, gross and net, 251
Income streams, multiple, 227, 261
Indigenous, definition, 18
Indigenous methodology, 31-33 103, 210, 243, 321
Information, tourism, 84
Intangible culture, 16, 129, 169, 177, 184, 310
Integrating culture, 10, 38, 68, 102, 132, 166, 196, 226, 260, 292
Intergenerational involvement, 78
International Folk Art Market, 162
Internet marketing, 150
Interpretive centers, 196
Itineraries, 55

K

Key issues, 81-82, 166-167

L

Land use planning, 72
Length of stay, 40-41
Linking, power of, 53
Listening skills, 69, 73-75
Living museums, 200-202
Loans, 264

M

Makah Nation, 63
Managed tourism program, 297-299
Market:
  data, interpretation, 139-140
  data, sources, 136-137
  research, 132-136
  segmentation, 138-139
  strategy, 142-145

Marketing:
  distribution, 155
  integrated, 150
  options, 151-154
Markets, tourism, 138-139
Mentoring programs, 239-240
Museum:
  support, 219-221
  virtual, 216-218
  definition, 196
  redirecting, 204

N

Negative impacts, reducing, 50, 304
Networks, small-scale, 39-41
Northern Indian Pueblos, 193

O

Objectives, tourism, 171, 174-175
Organizing for tourism, 62

P

Paradigm, cultural tourism, 3, 324
Participation techniques, 76-77, 79
Photographs, culturally-appropriate, 159
Plan outline:
  tourism, 80
  museum, 197-198
Planning as a process, 69-72
Planning processes, 20, 48, 53, 85, 92, 133, 149, 168, 172, 173, 177, 203, 208, 213, 228, 265, 304, 309
Poeh Cultural Center and Museum, 222
Pricing, entrepreneurial, 247-248
Primary data, 108
Process, the planning, 69-70
Product development, 229, 231-236

Pro-forma operating statements, 280-283
Positive benefits, increasing, 304
Project:
  description, 179-180
  design, 176-179
Promotion, 45, 84, 151-154

Q

Qualitative and quantitative approaches, 16, 102-103, 311-313
Qualitative methods, 73, 77, 101-102, 177, 309, 311-313
Quantitative methods, 9, 77, 103, 105, 309, 310-313

R

Redirecting tourism, 313-316
Regional concept, 39, 48
Resilience, cultural, 319, 324
Resource inventory, 83-85
Respectful visitation, 26

S

Safety issues, 180-181
Santa Fe Indian Market, 245
Saxman Native Village Tour, 317
SCOT analysis, 88-89
Secondary data, 109
Selling arts, 244-245
Services, tourism, 83
Skills inventory, 90
Small-economy scale, 32
Stakeholder, 69, 77
Stories, 209, 217
Success factors, 33
Supply chains, 135
Survey:
  community, 104-108

interpretation, 121-124
methods, 110-118
sample size, 120
visitor, 108-128
visitor satisfaction, 307-308
Sustainable development, 63
Sustainability: 6, 16, 94, 160, 291, 309-314
assessment, 300
nature, 320
factors, 292-293
increasing, 295-297
wisdom, 323
Sustainable Travel International, 34
Sustaining tradition, 24, 200-206

T

Talking circles, 73
Technical assistance, 226-227, 231-234, 246, 261-264
Timelines, 181-186
Tour enterprise, 284-287
Tourism:
attractions, 42-52
cooperation, 46
draw, 38, 41, 142
industry, 10, 12
options, 14-16
partner, 47-49
policy, 168-170
protocols, 169
sectors, 45
service system, 42, 82-88
services, 43
trade shows, 160
terminology, 27
types of, 15
vision, 91-93
Traditional:
definition, 18
values, 19

Training:
artist, 238-239
entrepreneurial, 236-240
food service, 239
survey methods, 118-119
tour guide, 239
Transportation, 43, 84

V

Vacation concept, 54
Value-based planning, 18, 93
Value chains, 59
Values, integrating, 19
Vending, 248
Visitor:
education, 3, 196, 206-207
etiquette, 43, 169
guides, 154
satisfaction, evaluating, 305-308
survey, 108-128

W

Websites, tourism, 155-158
WTO indicators, 294

ACKNOWLEDGMENTS

For a book to reflect wisdom beyond knowledge, many experienced teachers contribute along the way. I am grateful to the dozens of Indigenous, Hispanic, and culturally diverse communities who invited me to work with them during the past three decades. Through this involvement, I have come to understand the similarities and differences across communities struggling for cultural survival and the urgency to find solutions for earned livelihood.

Gratitude is expressed to my mentors and colleagues, who helped me "bring this work along." Governor Walter Dasheno (Santa Clara Pueblo) provided guidance in my first job as a tourism director 25 years ago. Seth Roffman, editor of the *Green Fire Times* offers sage insight on sustainability and continually connects me with inspiring community success stories. Anne Hillerman, through her organization WordHarvest, provided me with training as an author and encouragement through many years.

My gratitude is extended to Sonia Tamez, fellow consultant in Native cultural issues, for invaluable insight on the progression of my ideas, coaching, and extraordinary encouragement of this work. Feedback from Brian Mullis, Beth Beloff, and Tom Aageson fine-tuned the sustainable tourism approach. Craig Conley is thanked for the interchanges on sustainability and resilience.

The assistance of Joan Chernock once again helped transform a pile of notes and recordings into the first draft of the book. Robert Jordan continues his friendship, supportive to my writing process. Final stages were assisted by the expertise of Ann Lowe, Robby Bates, Peggy Pfeiffer, and Valerilynne Hendrick.

Contributors to the field of Indigenous methodology encouraged my persistence over the years. Thanks to Charlotte Heth, for paving the way and nurturing so many of us. Gregory Cajete, Linda Tuhiwai Smith, Margaret Kovach, Shawn Wilson, and Bagele Chilisa inspire by challenging mainstream research methods.

Support from friends and family foster every book. My late husband David M. White encouraged my continued writing and shared my passion for projects supporting cultural retention efforts in communities. Many thanks to Earl James for continued support, nudging me to extend beyond my perceived limits. I would also like to thank family members Pat Phillips, Mona St. Jean, Albertine Phillips, and Esther Bell, as well as friends Erica Elliott and Karen Edwards for their inspiration. George Mandel, Diana Lightmoon, and Connie McGhee offered extraordinary support throughout the writing process.

Organizations are important contributors to the skills, persistence, and assistance necessary for getting books out—and into the world. I would like to particularly thank Pacific Northwest Writers, the New Mexico Book Co-op, and the New Mexico Book Association for their invaluable training and encouragement.

The utmost gratitude is expressed to Susan Waterman for her insightful editing, her attention to detail, and for helping me bring this book to the finish line.

ABOUT THE AUTHOR

Susan Guyette, Ph.D. (Métis heritage—Micmac and Acadian French) has 25 years of direct experience working with Indigenous and rural communities in cultural tourism, as well as cultural centers and museums and culturally-based economic development.

Her skill in culturally-based planning techniques for Indigenous methodology is carried further in this text, building upon her prior books—*Planning for Balanced Development: A Guide for Rural and Native American Communities*, and several texts for American Indian Studies—*Issues for the Future of American Indian Studies* and *Community-Based Research: A Handbook for Native Americans*. She is also the co-author of the award winning book on environmental issues, Zen *Birding: Connect in Nature* and a newspaper columnist, writing "Everyday Green" for the *Green Fire Times*.

Her work is continued through Santa Fe Planning & Research in New Mexico (USA). Encouraging cultural renewal programs is her passion. www.susanguyette.com

Made in the USA
Lexington, KY
19 April 2014